THE NEW
SKEPTICISM

THE NEW SKEPTICISM

INQUIRY AND RELIABLE KNOWLEDGE

PAUL KURTZ

PROMETHEUS BOOKS
BUFFALO, NEW YORK

Published 1992 by Prometheus Books

96 95 94 93 92   5 4 3 2 1

Library of Congress Cataloging-in-Publication Data

Kurtz, Paul, 1925–
    The new skepticism : inquiry and reliable knowledge / by Paul Kurtz.
        p.   cm.
    Includes bibliographical references.
    ISBN 0-87975-766-3
    1. Skepticism. I. Title.
B837.K87   1992
149′.73—dc20   92-28358
                                                                    CIP

Printed in the United States of America on acid-free paper.

Contents

CONTENTS

Introduction

The Range of Skeptical Inquiry

Skepticism, like all things, is good if used in moderation. It is essential for the healthy mind; but if taken to excess, it can lead to overweening doubt. Skepticism, if properly understood, is not a metaphysical picture of the unknowability of "ultimate reality"; it does not lead to an inevitable epistemological impasse; it need not culminate in existential despair or nihilism. Rather it should be considered as an essential methodological rule guiding us to examine critically all claims to knowledge and affirmations of value. Without it, we are apt to slip into complacent self-deception and dogmatism; with it, if prudently used, we can effectively advance the frontiers of inquiry and knowledge, and also apply it to practical life, ethics, and politics.

Briefly stated, a skeptic is one who is willing to question any claim to truth, asking for clarity in definition, consistency in logic, and adequacy of evidence. The use of skepticism is thus an essential part of objective scientific inquiry and the search for reliable knowledge.

The sciences have exerted a powerful impact on the modern world. Impressive advances have been achieved in the natural, biological, and behavioral sciences. The applications of science to society have wrought profound changes in human culture.

Technology has provided humankind with expansive Promethean powers over nature. These powers have been forged for the betterment of the human condition, though unbridled they pose dangers to our planetary habitat.

A paradox confronts humankind: the ancient systems of religious superstitions exist side by side with the most sophisticated forms of scientific knowledge. Paranormal beliefs and cults of unreason tempt humans with promises of mystic enlightenment and salvation. Why do occult belief systems persist in human culture in spite of effective critiques by skeptics that provide evidence to the contrary? Why, when prophecies fail, does conviction often intensify?

For many, science is equated with technology. For others, it is a new form of magic, and scientists are viewed as shamans capable of wondrous feats. Some religionists maintain that the scientific view of nature has no validity, but merely expresses another "faith commitment." Some post-modernist critics rail against "modernity," proclaiming that the Enlightenment, which recognized the power of science to improve the human condition, has ended. Unfortunately, it is not widely understood that science is primarily a method of inquiry. Nor is there an appreciation of the essential role that skepticism plays in scientific endeavors. All too rarely is there an attempt to acknowledge the deeper implications of science for expanding our understanding of the universe and the place of the human species in the scheme of things.

Interestingly, science fiction has assumed a dramatic role in the modern imagination, for it gives free play to creative fancy. It nourishes quasi-religious probings of the realms of universes still unknown. It heightens romantic speculations about still undisclosed possibilities. Thus, for many there has been a blurring of the distinction between the scientific outlook and poetic metaphor.

Modern science has made an extraordinarily positive contribution to human civilization. Yet primitive religious and paranormal systems of belief retain their power over the lives of human beings. Indeed, even the most bizarre myths are still accepted as gospel truth by large sectors of humankind. And for every ancient set of dogmas that is weakened, a new paranormal cult is spawned to take its place.

To illustrate the constantly intriguing power of the myths of transcendence: In the late nineteenth and early twentieth centuries spiritualism emerged as a movement to beguile the imagination. The Fox sisters, D. D. Home, Eusapia Palladino, Margery Crandon, and other mediums, claimed that they could communicate with discarnate entities, and there were reports that unexpected occult manifestations occurred in their presence. Spiritualists were able to levitate chairs and tables; ectoplasm would emerge; objects would suddenly materialize or dematerialize; or the medium in a trance state would render messages from "the other side." Interestingly, this spiritualistic faith was accepted not only by the general public but also by some of the best scientific minds of the day, who attested to the authenticity of the phenomena. It has since been demonstrated that such reports were unreliable and that a more likely explanation of the alleged psychical phenomena is a combination of human gullibility and deception. The fact that an authority may be qualified in one field does not necessarily mean that he or she will exercise critical intelligence in others; and in some domains the scientist may be as credulous as the ordinary person.

One can ask whether the level of human gullibility is constant, although often taking on new forms. In the early twentieth century Sir Arthur Conan Doyle, who had an abiding fascination with psychical research, was taken in by the many eyewitness reports of wee fairies and elves found throughout Great Britain. Indeed, actual photographs of the so-called Cottingley fairies were proffered to prove the reality of the phenomena, although careful analysis subsequently demonstrated that the photos were faked. Today we have reports of alien space creatures landing on our planet in "flying saucers" and engaging in biogenetic and sexual experimentation on selected subjects. Some abductees deliver messages they claim to have received from their semi-divine space brothers.[1] These reports are not unlike ancient accounts of visitations by angels in the Old and New Testaments and the Koran. In reading the

---

1. See Whitley Strieber, *Communion* (New York: Wm. Morrow, 1987), and *Transformation* (New York: Wm. Morrow, 1988); Budd Hopkins, *Intruders* (New York: Random House, 1986).

Bible one encounters numerous tales of faith-healing performed by Jesus and others, of exorcising demons, and of restoring life or limb. Today, faith healers likewise claim to be able to heal the sick and downtrodden and herald their "miracles" as evidence of God's intervention. Millions of people are willing to abandon the proved methods of medical science in their hunger for miraculous cures. They flock to Lourdes, Fatima, and Medjugorje, or seek out fundamentalist preachers, mullahs, or gurus in quest of the Holy Grail.

The ancient belief in reincarnation has become popular in the West and has been reinforced by "past-life hypnotic regression." These regressions allegedly can transport a person back to previous lives and in other cases even project a person ahead to future lives. Some claim that they were ancient rulers or slaves, soldiers or prostitutes. Others even recall their past lives as eagles or turtles.[2]

How does one account for the pervasiveness of such beliefs in human culture? How explain the survival of the orthodox systems of religion—Christianity, Judaism, Islam, Hinduism—which have thrived in spite of devastating intellectual critiques and massive social changes, even when transplanted from Europe or Asia to North or South America? Faith in a supernatural deity or deities is no doubt the strongest mythic system that persists in human culture. Efforts to suppress it, as was the case in the Soviet Union and other Marxist countries, usually fail. How account for the endurance of religiosity throughout the ages? There are at least three possible explanations.

First is the possibility that there is indeed a transcendental realm over and beyond the limits of the world encountered by observation and reason. Perhaps gods, spirits, or discarnate beings exist, and perhaps there is an unknown divine universe still to be discovered. Perhaps there are hidden spiritual or paranormal realities of which we are unaware, although some indications of them may have leaked from another reality into our own, or may have been revealed from On High to chosen messengers or the especially gifted. Perhaps there are aliens from other galaxies who

---

2. Frederick Lenz, *Lifetimes: True Accounts of Reincarnation* (Indianapolis: Bobbs-Merrill, 1979).

communicate with us, and perhaps some people have been appointed to receive these messages. If this were true, it might account for the repeated claims of anomalous experiences and of miraculous occurrences. The classical religions differ markedly in content and ostensible legitimacy—Judaism rejects Christianity, Christianity rejects Islam, Hinduism rejects Mormonism, and they all in turn reject each other. Yet in spite of this, they share a common core of beliefs that posit a hidden and unseen realm of spiritual being.

The only objective posture for the skeptic to take is to examine the evidence for such claims and to analyze the arguments adduced to support them. Most skeptics who have investigated the claims of transcendental realities remain doubtful of their veracity, but they usually do not have sufficient opportunity to present their negative findings.

There is, thus, a second possible explanation for the persistence of these beliefs, namely, that humankind has not been sufficiently exposed to the arguments critical of the claims of divinity, the occult, or the paranormal. *If* believers were adequately apprised of the lack of evidence, so the argument runs, they would be disabused of these false mythologies. Here the explanation for the persistence of systems of false belief is a cognitive deficit. According to this line of reasoning, it is simply a question of the believers' mistaken information and faulty logic, with the concomitant expectation that if they were exposed to a critical analysis of such claims they would be convinced of their invalidity. One might hope that this were true, but perhaps the rationalist is too sanguine about the power of reason in human life.

Philosophers have consistently defended the quest for truth and have pointed out the advantages of the rational life. Yet Plato complained that the Athenians killed Socrates because of his search for rational definitions and his subversion of the unexamined sacred cows of society. It was the athletes, poets, and military heroes who were heralded by the Athenians, not its philosophers, who were generally suspect. Yet a former carpenter, whom people thought to be the son of God, has been worshipped for two thousand years. And the founder of Islam—a man who most likely suffered epileptic episodes that were interpreted as revelations received from

Allah—is revered as a divine prophet.

Criticism of mythic systems all too often falls on deaf ears, and dissenters have frequently been burned at the stake or condemned as naysayers. Is humanity congenitally unreceptive to rational criticism of its revered beliefs? Is the laying out of the pros and cons not sufficient to diminish false systems of belief? Religion has been submitted to intense scrutiny for ages, yet it has survived the critique of logicians and empiricists. The philosopher Sidney Hook, as he lay on his deathbed, said, "The truth, the truth is all that really matters." To philosophers, yes, but what of other men and women?

There is thus a third intriguing explanation for the persistence of religious and paranormal belief systems: There are profound noncognitive psychological processes at work within the human species that feed supernatural illusions and paranormal belief systems. The hypothesis that I have introduced is that there is an enduring "transcendental temptation" that entrances people to crave, to search for, and ultimately to believe in the reality of mysterious realms still unknown,[3] and that it is this leap of faith and the accompanying psychological rationalizations that sustain such beliefs and entice individuals to abandon rationality in favor of the consolation they provide. There are powerful noncognitive urges within the human psychological makeup that make illusions and fantasies seem true, or at least that incline us to accept them.

An interesting illustration of this may be seen in the endurance of astrology, an ancient belief system that has survived for more than four thousand years and continues to be strong, even though there is no data to support its claims and considerable evidence to the contrary. Astrologers have built no churches, and thus there has been no entrenched ecclesiastical hierarchy to block inquiry. Astrology has been discredited ever since the beginnings of modern astronomy, but it still thrives. Unlike theological beliefs, astrology can be used as a test case. If the critical scientific data were widely disseminated, would belief in astrology disappear? Large sectors of the public today continue to accept its claims in spite of the

---

3. Paul Kurtz, *The Transcendental Temptation: A Critique of Religion and the Paranormal* (Buffalo, N.Y.: Prometheus Books, 1986).

availability of such scientific refutations. Is the fact that the public has not been sufficiently exposed to the negative results of tests by astronomers and other researchers an explanation for the persistence of the belief in astrology?[4] I submit that, however flawed its empirical data may be, astrology remains popular because it resonates a responsive chord within the believer; for it postulates that the astrological sign under which an individual is born and the position of the heavenly bodies at the time of birth determine or influence his or her personality and future destiny. Although a significant number of people might respond favorably to the scientific studies that demonstrate that astrological readings have no basis in fact, large sectors of the public apparently cling to their willful conviction that astrology works, and no amount of contradictory evidence seems to move them.

Contrary to what was the case in the past, when astrologers were able to influence monarchs and emperors, astrology today has no vested political power, although it does have economic support. Indeed, despite their being barely on the fringe of public respectability, the selling of astrological services sustains tens of thousands of astrologers. But of larger dimension is the fact that a huge astrological industry has grown up worldwide, and the marketing of books, magazines, newspaper columns, and other paraphernalia seems to have attracted a receptive public. Does this explain its persistence?

Perhaps one of our first two possible explanations for the enduring popularity of mythic belief systems may apply here. First, astrology may be true. Perhaps the heavenly bodies do play a role in determining personality traits, even physical characteristics and one's propensities for disease. Astrology is an ancient art allegedly based on thousands of years of observation of human behavior correlated with the movement of the heavenly bodies. In order to appraise astrology's validity, further detailed and careful scientific investigations would have to be undertaken.[5] Or, second,

---

4. For a good critical discussion, see Philip Ianna and Roger Culver, *Astrology: True or False?* (Buffalo, N.Y.: Prometheus Books, 1988).

5. Michel Gauquelin, a French researcher, maintained that he had found some empirical correlations between planetary positions and personality traits.

perhaps the reason this belief persists is that people are uninformed. This explanation holds that it is primarily a cognitive problem, a lack of information, and that if people were properly informed they would abandon their misconceptions.[6]

Similar considerations apply of course to religious claims. Religions are so prominent and powerful in human culture that it would seem in the last analysis that they have seized upon enduring truths about the human condition and ultimate reality. Or perhaps the skeptic is correct when he says that they are more likely fictitious tales invented by the creative human imagination in order to soothe existential *angst*. This implies that there is a constant need for the critical, cognitive examination of religious claims.[7]

But a more entangling list of questions emerge. How far should skeptical inquiries be extended? It is one thing to concentrate on the paranormal or even on religious questions, but what about politics and ideology? Why single out paranormalists or theologians for critical scrutiny? What about social and political programs of action and unexamined ideological convictions? Are these amenable to rational support or should we end up extremely skeptical or totally cynical of the pretentious claims of leading political thinkers? Is not Marxism a pseudoscience? What about libertarian economics? Is there any objective way to resolve disagreements in ideology, which are held with intense fervor by equally sincere and persistent advocates? Many of these ideological positions presuppose ethical assumptions. Partisans hold different ideals about the nature of the just society or the good life. Can one be objective in ethics? How deal with questions of abortion, euthanasia, or the meaning of life? Are these amenable to rational criticism and guidance? Surely there is a historical skeptical tradition in ethics. If one is skeptical in metaphysics and religion, why not in politics, ethics, and other normative fields?

His work had not been sufficiently replicated to confirm his interesting hypothesis, and skeptics were dubious though interested in his thesis. But even if Gauquelin turned out to be correct (which is doubtful) this would in no way validate classical or popular astrology. Indeed, Gauquelin was himself a critic of horoscopes and sun sign astrology, for which he found no empirical evidence.

6. See Appendix I.
7. See Appendix II.

Indeed, what about knowledge itself? It is one thing to defend a program of scientific inquiry, but we know that established scientific disciplines are often rife with controversy, that well-established theories sometimes have to be modified in the light of new discoveries, and that science is not immune to fraud and deceit. Should we adopt the posture of the classical skeptics and argue that all knowledge is specious—including all the tested hypotheses of the natural, biological, and social sciences? Should we go further and say that therefore no knowledge is possible? Some skeptics have been highly critical of the theories advanced on the frontiers of astronomy and physics. They consider some of the theories highly speculative. Yet because of the great advances in technological applications of the natural sciences, these are often considered to be immune from criticism. The fields of medicine and psychiatry should likewise be open to scrutiny. What constitutes a cure and/or proper treatment is also often highly disputable. Indeed, similar considerations apply to virtually every field of human inquiry, such as psychology, where the schools of psychotherapies contend, and the social sciences, where similar levels of controversy are found.

If one is going to be fair, why not apply skeptical methods to *all* areas of human knowledge? Why limit it selectively to only a few? Many skeptics have argued that it is impossible to ever gain knowledge and that we can *never* penetrate the veil of ignorance to say what is real. For them *all* knowledge is unreliable. Are we led to that pessimistic conclusion? Is there not always the danger lurking in the background that skepticism in the last analysis is negative, even nihilistic, and as such is alien to the practical needs and interests of life? Is skepticism by its very nature destructive? Does it have anything positive to say about life? Does it have any normative implications? What is the relationship of skepticism to the way of life we adopt? Can it lead to a meaningful *eupraxophy,* that is, to a well-grounded cosmic outlook and practical wisdom in conduct? Or will it inhibit us from ever gaining reliable knowledge about the universe, or from developing some ethical wisdom in life?

Part One

Skepticism in Perspective

Chapter 1

Three Kinds of Skepticism

Skepticism has deep roots in the philosophical tradition. The term derives from the Greek word *skeptikos,* which means "to consider, examine." It is akin to the Greek *skepsis,* which means "inquiry" and "doubt."

Skepticism provides powerful tools of criticism in philosophy, religion, morality, politics, and society. It is thought to be exceedingly difficult to apply it to ordinary life or to live consistently with its principles. For human beings seek certitudes to guide them, and the skeptical mode is often viewed with alarm by those who hunger for faith and conviction. Skepticism is the intractable foe of pretentious belief systems. When people demand definite answers to their queries, skepticism always seems to give them further questions to ponder. Yet in a profound sense, skepticism is an essential ingredient of all reflective conduct and an enduring characteristic of the educated mind. Still, skeptics are considered dangerous because they question the reigning orthodoxies, the shibboleths and hosannas of any age. Although the skeptical attitude is an indelible part of reflective inquiry, can a person get beyond the skeptical orientation to develop positive directions and commitments in belief and behavior, and will skepticism enable one to do so?

Skeptics always bid those overwhelmed by Absolute Truth or Special Virtue to pause. They ask, "What do you *mean?*"— seeking clarification and definition—and "*Why* do you believe what you do?"—demanding reasons, evidence, justification, or proof. Like natives of Missouri, they say, "Show me." All too often probing skeptics discover that the unquestioned beliefs and many cherished values of the day rest on quixotic sands and that, by digging at their tottering foundations, they may hasten their collapse. Skeptics are able to detect contradictions within belief systems; they discover hypocrisies, double standards, disparities between what people profess and what they actually do; they point to the paucity of evidence for most of humankind's revered belief systems.

Skeptics are viewed as dissenters, heretics, radicals, subversive rogues, or worse, and they are bitterly castigated by the entrenched establishments who fear them. Revolutionary reformers are also wont to turn their wrath on skeptical doubters who question their passionate commitment to ill-conceived programs of social reconstruction. Skeptics wish to examine all sides of a question; and for every argument in favor of a thesis, they usually can find one or more arguments opposed to it. Extreme skepticism cannot consistently serve our practical interests, for insofar as it sires doubt, it inhibits actions. All parties to a controversy may revile skeptics because they usually resist being swept away by the dominant fervor of the day.

Nevertheless, skepticism is *essential* to the quest for knowledge; for it is in the seedbed of puzzlement that genuine inquiry takes root. Without skepticism, we may remain mired in unexamined belief systems that are accepted as sacrosanct yet have no factual basis in reality. With it, we allow for some free play for the generation of new ideas and the growth of knowledge. Although the skeptical outlook may not be sufficient unto itself for any philosophy of the practical life, it provides a necessary condition for the reflective approach to life. Must skepticism leave us floundering in a quagmire of indecision? Or does it permit us to go further, and to discover some probabilities by which we can live? Will it allow us to achieve reliable knowledge? Or must all new discoveries in turn give way to the probing criticisms of the skeptic's scalpel? The answer to these questions depends in part on what one means by skepticism, for there are various kinds that can be distinguished.

It is well that we begin our analysis of skepticism by providing a preliminary working classification of three kinds of skepticism that have appeared historically and still exist in the present day. The following description is only a tentative starting point. We will need to refine and elaborate on these various forms of skepticism throughout our inquiry.

Nihilism

Total Negative Skepticism

The first kind of skepticism that may be identified is nihilism. Its most extreme form is total negative skepticism. Here I am referring to skepticism as a complete rejection of all claims to truth or value. This kind of skepticism is mired in unlimited doubt, from which it never emerges. Knowledge is not possible, total skeptics aver. There is no certainty, no reliable basis for convictions, no truth at all. All that we encounter are appearances, impressions, sensations; and we have no guarantee that these correspond to anything in external reality. Indeed, we have no assurance that we are properly describing external objects "in themselves." Our senses, which lie at the heart of our experiential world, may deceive us. Our sense organs act as visors, shielding and limiting our perceptions, which vary from individual to individual and from species to species. Similar pitfalls await those who seek to root knowledge in the cognitive intuitions or deductive inferences of mathematics or logic, claim total skeptics. Meanings are irreducibly subjective and untranslatable into intersubjective or objective referents. Purely formal conceptual systems tell us more about the language we are using than about the nature of ultimate reality itself. In any case, human beings are prone to err. For every proof in favor of a thesis, one may pose a counter-proof. Like the web that is spun by a spider, the entire structure may collapse when we disturb the glue that holds the threads together.

Not only is epistemic certainty impossible, maintain total skeptics, the very criteria by which we judge whether something is true or false are questionable. Knowledge is based upon the methods by which we evaluate claims to truth—whether empirical or rational. But these are simply assumed, they insist, and cannot be used to validate themselves without begging the question. Thus we can never get beyond the first stage of inquiry. Total skeptics end up in utter subjectivity, solipsists imprisoned in their own worlds, confused about the nature of knowledge. This is the total skeptics' approach to science, philosophy, and religion.

Nihilistic skepticism has also been used in ethics with devastating results. Here the total skeptic is a complete relativist, subjectivist, and emotivist. What is "good" or "bad," "right" or "wrong," varies among individuals and societies. There are no discernible normative standards other than taste and feeling, and there is no basis for objective moral judgment. We cannot discern principles that are universal or obligatory for morality. Complete cultural relativity is the only option for this kind of skepticism. Principles of justice are simply related to power or the social contract; there are no normative standards common to all social systems. In the face of moral controversy, total skeptics may become extreme doubters; all standards are equally untenable. They may thus become conservative traditionalists. If there are no reliable guides to moral conduct, then the only recourse is to follow custom. Ours is not to reason why, ours is but to do or die, for there *are* no reasons. Or total skeptics may become cynical amoralists for whom "anything goes." Who is to say that one thing is better or worse than anything else? they ask, for if there are no standards of justice discoverable in the nature of things, political morality in the last analysis is a question of force, custom, or passion, not of reason or of evidence.

This kind of total skepticism is self-contradictory; for in affirming that no knowledge is possible, these skeptics have already made an assertion. In denying that we can know reality, they often presuppose a phenomenalistic or subjectivistic metaphysics in which sense impressions or ideas are the constitutive blocks out of which our knowledge of the world, however fragmented, is constructed. In asserting that there are no normative standards of ethics and politics, total skeptics sometimes advise us either to be tolerant of individual idiosyncrasies and respect cultural relativity, or to be courageous and follow our own quest to satisfy ambition or appetite. But this imperceptibly masks underlying value judgments that skeptics cherish. This kind of skepticism may be labeled "dogmatism"; for in resolutely rejecting the very possibility of knowledge or value, such skeptics are themselves introducing their own questionable assertions.

Neutral Skepticism

One form of nihilistic skepticism that seeks to avoid dogmatism does so by assuming a completely neutral stance. Here skeptics will neither affirm nor deny anything. They are unwilling to utter any pronouncements, such as, that sense perception or formal reasoning is unreliable. They reject any type of skepticism that masks a theory of knowledge or reality in epistemology, metaphysics, ethics, and politics. Neutralists claim to have no such theory. They simply make personal statements and do not ask anyone to accept or reject or be convinced or persuaded by their arguments. These are merely their own private expressions they are uttering, and they are not generalizable to others. For every argument in favor of a thesis, they can discover a counterargument. The only option for neutral skeptics is thus to suspend judgment entirely. Here agnosticism rules the roost. They are unable in epistemology to discover any criteria of knowledge; in metaphysics, a theory of reality; in religion, a basis for belief or disbelief in God; in ethics and politics, any standards of virtue, value, or social justice.

The ancient pre-Socratic Greek philosopher Cratylus (fifth–fourth century B.C.E.) was overwhelmed by the fact that everything is changing, including our own phenomenological worlds of experience; and he therefore concluded that it is impossible to communicate knowledge or to fully understand anyone. According to legend, Cratylus refused to discuss anything with anyone and, since it was pointless to reply, only wiggled his finger when asked a question. The neutral state of suspension of belief, now known as Pyrrhonism, was defended by Pyrrho of Elis and had a great impact on the subsequent development of skepticism. It applied primarily to philosophical and metaphysical questions, where one is uncertain about what is ultimately true about reality, but it put aside questions of ordinary life, where convention and custom prevail. This form of skepticism also degenerates into nihilism, for in denying any form of knowledge it can lead to despair.

25

Mitigated Skepticism

There is a fundamental difficulty with the forms of skepticism outlined above, for they are contrary to the demands of life. We need to function in the world—whatever its ultimate reality—and we need to develop some beliefs by which we may live and act. Perhaps our beliefs rest ultimately upon probabilities; nevertheless we need to develop knowledge as a pragmatic requirement of living and acting in the world. A second form of skepticism was called *mitigated skepticism* by David Hume, the great eighteenth-century Scottish philosopher. It is a position that was also defended by the Greek philosopher Carneades of the second century B.C.E. Mitigated skeptics have confronted the black hole of nothingness and are skeptical about the ultimate reliability of knowledge claims. They are convinced that the foundations of knowledge and value are ephemeral and that it is impossible to establish ultimate truths about reality with any certainty. Nonetheless, we are forced by the exigencies of practical life to develop viable generalizations and to make choices, even though we can give no ultimate justification for them. One cannot find any secure basis for causal inferences about nature, other than the fact that there are regularities encountered within experience, on the basis of which we make predictions that the future will be like the past. But we have no ultimate foundation for this postulate of induction. Similarly, one cannot deduce what *ought* to be the case from what is. Morality is contingent on the sentiments of men and women who agree to abide by social convention in order to satisfy their multifarious desires as best they can.

Mitigated skepticism is not total, but only partial and limited, forced upon us by the exigencies of living. It would be total if we were to follow philosophy to the end of the trail, to irremediable indecision and doubt. Fortunately, we take detours in life, and thus we live and act *as if* we had knowledge. Our generalizations are based upon experience and practice, and the inferences that we make on the basis of habit and custom serve as our guide.

Unbelief

The term *skepticism* has sometimes been used as synonymous with *unbelief* or *disbelief* in any domain of knowledge. Actually there are two aspects to this—one is the *reflective* conviction that certain claims are unfounded or untrue, and hence not believable, and this seems a reasonable posture to take; the other is the negative a priori rejection of a belief without a careful examination of the grounds for that belief. Critics call this latter form of skepticism "dogmatism." The word *unbelief* in both of these senses is usually taken to apply to religion, theology, the paranormal, and the occult.

In religion the unbeliever is usually an atheist—not simply a neutral agnostic—for this kind of skepticism rejects the claims of theists. The atheist denies the basic premises of theism: that God exists, that there is some ultimate purpose to the universe, that men and women have immortal souls, or that they can be saved by divine grace.

Reflective unbelievers find the language of transcendence basically unintelligible, even meaningless, and that is why they say they are skeptics. Or, more pointedly, if they have examined the arguments adduced historically to prove the existence of God, they find them invalid, hence unconvincing. They find the so-called appeals to experience unwarranted: neither mysticism nor the appeal to miracles or revelation establishes the existence of transcendental realities. Moreover, they maintain that morality is possible without a belief in God. Unbelievers are critics of supernaturalistic claims, which they consider superstition. Indeed, they consider the God hypothesis to be without merit, a fanciful creation of human imagination that does not deserve careful examination by emancipated men and women. Many classical atheists (Baron d'Holbach, Diderot, Marx, Engels) fit into this category, for they were materialists first, and their religious skepticism and unbelief followed from their materialistic metaphysics. Such skeptics are dogmatic only if their unbelief is a form of doctrinaire faith and not based on rational grounds.

In the paranormal field, unbelievers similarly deny the reality of psi phenomena. They maintain that ESP, clairvoyance, precognition, psychokinesis, and the existence of discarnate souls are without sufficient evidence and contrary to our knowledge of how the material universe operates. Some skeptics deny paranormal phenomena on a priori grounds, i.e., they are to be rejected because they violate well-established physical laws. They can be considered dogmatists only if they refuse to examine the evidence brought by the proponents of the paranormal, or if they consider the level of science to have been reached at any one day to be its final formulation. Insofar as this kind of unbelief masks a closed mind, it is an illegitimate form of skepticism. If those who say that they are skeptics simply mean that they deny the existence of the paranormal realm, they are aparanormalists. The question to be asked of them always is, *Why?* For much as the believers can be judged to hold certain convictions on the basis of inadequate evidence or faith, so the dogmatic unbelievers may reject such new claims because these violate their own preconceptions about the universe. This latter kind of skepticism has many faults and is in my judgment illegitimate. These skeptics are no longer open-minded inquirers, but debunkers. They are convinced that they have the Non-Truth, which they affirm resolutely, and in doing so they may slam shut the door to further discoveries.

Skeptical Inquiry

There is yet a third kind of skepticism, which differs from the kinds of skepticism encountered above. Indeed, it is a strong critic of nihilism, total and neutral; mitigated skepticism; and dogmatic unbelief—though it has learned something from each of them. This kind of skepticism I shall label "skeptical inquiry," with inquiry rather than doubt as the motivation. I call it the *new skepticism,* although it has emerged in the contemporary world as an outgrowth of pragmatism. A key difference between this and earlier forms of skepticism is that it is *positive* and *constructive*. It involves the transformation of the negative critical analysis of the claims to knowledge into a positive contribution to the growth and development of skeptical inquiry. It is basically a form of *methodological* skepticism, for here skepticism is an essential phase of the process of inquiry; but it does not and need not lead to unbelief, despair, or hopelessness. This skepticism is not total, but is limited to the context under inquiry. Hence we may call it *selective* or *contextual* skepticism, for one need not doubt everything at the same time, but only certain questions in the limited context of investigation. It is not neutral, because it believes that we do develop knowledge about the world. Accordingly, not only is human knowledge possible, but it can be found to be reliable; and we can in the normative realm act on the best evidence and reasons available. Knowledge is not simply limited to the descriptive or the formal sciences, but is discoverable in the normative fields of ethics and politics. Although this is a modified form of skepticism, it goes far beyond the mitigated skepticism of Hume; for it does not face an abyss of ultimate uncertainty, but is impressed by the ability of the human mind to understand and control nature.

The new skepticism is not dogmatic, for it holds that we should never by a priori rejection close the door to any kind of responsible investigation. Thus it is skeptical of dogmatic or narrow-minded atheism and aparanormalism. Nonetheless, it is willing to assert reflective *unbelief* about some claims that it finds lack adequate justification. It is willing to assert that some claims are unproved, improbable, or false.

Skepticism, as a method of doubt that demands evidence and reasons for hypotheses, is essential to the process of scientific research, philosophical dialogue, and critical intelligence. It is also vital in ordinary life, where the demands of common sense are always a challenge to us to develop and act upon the most reliable hypotheses and beliefs available. It is the foe of absolute certainty and dogmatic finality. It appreciates the snares and pitfalls of all kinds of human knowledge and the importance of the principles of fallibilism and probabilism in regard to the degrees of certainty of our knowledge. This differs sharply with the skepticisms of old, and it can contribute substantially to the advancement of human knowledge and the moral progress of humankind. It has important implications for our knowledge of the universe and our moral and social life. Skepticism in this sense provides a positive and constructive *eupraxophy* that can assist us in interpreting the cosmos in which we live and in achieving some wisdom in conduct.

The new skepticism is more in tune with the demands of

everyday knowledge than with speculative philosophy. Men and women may ponder the following questions: "What is the meaning of life?" "Why am I here?" "How shall I face death?" "What is the nature of reality?" "Can life be good?" "What is the just society?" And they may not be satisfied with the skepticisms of the past that refuse to deal with their existential quest. Extreme skepticism for them offers no help or guidance. They cannot wait for a response. The pace of life places urgent demands upon them. "What are the causes of this disease?" "Can it be cured?" "Which of the laws of physics and principles of engineering must I follow if I am going to build an airplane or a bridge to get where I wish to go?" "How can I best maximize the crop yield and increase the food supply?" "How shall I educate my children?" "What kind of society should we wish to live in?" These are practical questions that the sciences and arts help them to resolve with greater or lesser degrees of reliability. It is clear to ordinary men and women, if not skeptical philosophers, that we *do* have considerable knowledge and that there *are* practical guides in many fields of endeavor.

Skeptics have had all too little to say about the evident achievements of constructive skeptical inquiry. And derisive skeptical jabs hurled from the wings of the theater of life are not always appreciated, especially if they inhibit life from proceeding without interruption. Skeptical doubt is thus only part of the kaleidoscopic picture of the human drama. Skepticism, however, needs to be supplemented. What else do we need to fill in if we are to live and function effectually in the world? The earlier forms of skepticism do not always allow us to do so. We need to get beyond the excessive skeptical frame of mind. How? The soup of skeptical doubt is generally too thin for those who hunger for a feast or seek the delights of a banquet, or extol reverie and mystery. Yet some mitigated and probabilistic forms of skepticism can play a constructive role in human endeavor. To forever float in a sea of indecisive doubt is to be out of touch with experience as we attempt to cope with the problems encountered in living. To live entirely *without* some honest doubt, however, is to live in folly and play the part of the fool.

Chapter 2

A Historical Overview

Since this study is intended as a systematic examination of skepticism, it is necessary to distinguish in greater detail the new skepticism, *skeptical inquiry,* from other forms that have appeared historically. It is difficult to compress the entire history of skepticism into one chapter. Thus the following historical overview is not intended as an exhaustive survey, but will focus only on those aspects of skepticism that are relevant to my main thesis.

Ancient Skepticism

Historically, skepticism designated a school of philosophy that flourished for more than five centuries in ancient Greece and Rome. Early skepticism developed into two schools of thought. The first was inspired by Pyrrho of Elis (c. 360–270 B.C.E.) and became known as Pyrrhonism, and the second developed in Plato's Academy, culminating in the skepticism of Carneades (c. 213–128 B.C.E.). The word *skeptic* was used to refer to those who cultivated doubt and the suspension of judgment. Skeptical philosophy thrived in Rome, where it was expounded by Cicero (106–43 B.C.E.), who studied in Athens at the Academy, and by Sextus Empiricus (3rd century C.E.), from whose name the term *empiricism* was derived. Skepticism was attacked by St. Augustine in the fifth century, and it was virtually eclipsed during the Dark Ages, when faith reigned supreme. Skepticism reappeared during the Renaissance, when the ancient texts of the skeptics, notably Cicero and Sextus, were rediscovered. It thus played a major role in the development of the modern outlook, particularly in philosophy and science, and in the writings of Bayle, Bacon, Montaigne, Descartes, Hume, the French Encyclopedists, and Kant. Skepticism is vital to the contemporary world of science and is essential to its methodology. Skeptical critiques have been offered by many influential thinkers—Marx, Freud, Nietzsche, Sartre, Heidegger, Russell, Wittgenstein, Dewey—to shake the foundations of modern civilization.

The Sophists

Skepticism, like most professed philosophical schools, had its roots in classical Greek civilization. The first skeptics were not so named, however. They were the sophists, i.e., itinerant teachers who traveled between the various city-states of the ancient Hellenic world in the fifth century B.C.E., claiming to teach the skills of practical success. They were skeptical in their outlook because they observed the great variety of moral customs and political practices that existed among the Greeks; and they were relativists because they could find no basis in nature for morality. Good and bad, right and wrong, were based on social conventions; and those who wished to forge ahead in life should recognize this fact and use it to their advantage. These sophists often expressed the most extreme form of total negative skepticism, verging on absolute nihilism. They represent the first type of skepticism described in Chapter 1.

Our knowledge of the sophists is best encountered in the Platonic dialogues, for Plato was a critic of their point of view and sought to ground the knowledge of the Good in ultimate reality, as discovered by reason. The term *sophist* has since come to refer to one who uses fallacious reasoning and engages in unfair disputations for gain. In its original sense it was an honorable term, referring to a wise or learned person. Socrates himself was considered a sophist, in the sense that he used the art of logic to persuade the young men of Athens to seek a life of virtue based upon rational inquiry. He constantly engaged in debate with

Gorgias, Thrasymachus, Prodicus, Hippias, Polus, and other sophists.

No doubt the greatest and most eminent sophist was Protagoras (c. 485–410 B.C.E.), to whom Plato attributed the statement "Man is the measure of all things." Plato sought to challenge the relativity of all knowledge and value. Protagoras had offered a basic epistemological principle, found in both humanism and skepticism, namely, that it is difficult to find absolute standards of truth or value in the nature of things, but that such principles are relative to individuals and societies. Protagoras was skeptical about theology, metaphysics, and the sciences. He identified knowledge with sense perceptions, which were based on the flux encountered in all things. Our conception of "reality" thus may be said to be subjective, because it varies from individual to individual. Each person's perceptions are true for him alone. "About the gods," he said, "I can know nothing, neither that they exist or do not exist—because of the obscurity of the subject and the briefness of human life."

Gorgias (c. 483–376 B.C.E.) also denied the existence of an objective reality, which he attempted to disprove by a series of disjunctive propositions.[1] He argued, for example, that existence must be either something or nothing or both together; and if something, it must be either finite or infinite or both, and either one or many or both, but we could not say which. Even if we granted that the world existed independently of us, he said, it could not be depicted; for thoughts do not reflect facts and there is no criterion for distinguishing true from false ideas. Even if we conceded that there is knowledge, he added, "we could not communicate it to another person, because our sense impressions and consciousness differ." Many of these views reflected the position later adopted by skeptics.

Plato differed fundamentally with the thesis that there is no objective reality, that it could not be known, or that knowledge of it could not be communicated. He postulated a realm of eternal essences over and beyond the world of appearances, which he

---

1. See A. W. Benn, vol. 1, *The Greek Philosophers* (London, 1882), p. 426.

held we can discover through reason. In one sense Plato's greatest dialogue, *The Republic,* was written to respond to and refute the skeptics, such as Thrasymachus and others, who maintained that there is no such thing as justice, that it is simply "the interest of the stronger" or the expression of social conventions, and that a man of power and ambition ought to recognize that and forge ahead. Plato insisted that the ideas of justice and of the good were eternal, and he set down a standard by which we could judge states and individuals. Plato was here dealing with various forms of skepticism, especially total negative and dogmatic skepticism—in ethics, politics, epistemology, and metaphysics. Some commentators have found in Socrates a seminal source for the philosophy of skepticism; i.e., in the statement Socrates made that no man was wiser than he because he knew how ignorant he was and how much he did not know. All those about him in Athens, he said—poets, statesmen, artisans, and others—claimed to have the truth; but he found how little they actually knew, and he recognized the difficulty in discovering truth.

In many of the dialogues Socrates ends up uncertain as to the outcome. What is "piety"? he asks in the *Euthyphro,* submitting the concept to detailed analysis. He rejects the conventional definitions of piety as proposed by Euthyphro, but does not offer a final definition. Similarly, for the concept of "truth" in the *Theatetus,* which Plato finds to be an exceedingly complex idea. We know what truth is not, says Socrates, but we cannot say for certain what it is. Thus Socrates is open-minded, interested in the process of dialectical argument and logical analysis. Here he is not an absolutist, but an inquirer after definition and classification. Although later neo-Platonists converted the "theory of ideas" of Plato into a realm of eternal essences, they have overlooked the dialogues themselves, which present men arguing and examining a wide range of ideas as part of a process of ongoing inquiry. It is thus difficult to narrowly construe Plato simply as an absolutist; for he was well aware of the arguments for skepticism, which were skillfully presented throughout his dialogues.

A similar case can be made for Aristotle, who is usually not considered a skeptic. Indeed, he was a critic of extreme skepticism. Although Aristotle never denies the possibility of scientific knowledge, practical or philosophical wisdom, and although he thinks that nature is intelligible, still his writings reflect a keen inquiring mind. He is always examining questions with probing analysis, rejecting those explanations that appear to him to be specious; and he is rarely absolutistic in his formulations. It may surprise some to say that Aristotle represented one form of skepticism, at least on the far end of the scale. For he was not dogmatic and he sought to base his knowledge claims on empirical observations and deductions; although unlike other skeptics, he claimed to have metaphysical knowledge. The process of dialectical inquiry displayed in Aristotle's works nonetheless represent the application of skeptical methods in analyzing and evaluating ideas.

There were two explicit forms of philosophical skepticism that developed in the ancient world; and these schools have had a major impact on the course of the movement: (1) Pyrrhonism, a school of skepticism that took its name from Pyrrho of Elis (c. 360–270 B.C.E.) and exerted considerable influence on the Roman world; and (2) Academic Skepticism, as it emerged in the later Academy of Plato.

Pyrrhonism

There are no extant writings of Pyrrho, and therefore what we know of him is only secondhand. What is unique about him is that he tried to develop a eupraxophy (or at least an encapsulated form of it), that is, a theory of practical conduct based upon his skeptical philosophical outlook. Although he avoided stating a theory of reality, he presupposed some epistemological principles; these, he said, were at best only personal, not objective. Nonetheless, the kind of skepticism that Pyrrho lived was intended to enable him to achieve a state of *ataraxia*, or unperturbedness. Skepticism competed with Epicureanism and Stoicism, particularly in the Roman world, for the minds and hearts of educated men and women; it was offered as a way of life enabling one to achieve peace of mind from worries and cares. It is interesting to note that classical skepticism did not narrowly express a theory of knowledge, but had a broader concern for achieving a way of life. Pyrrhonism, as it was called, took the form of universal agnosticism and the suspension of belief.

According to Diogenes Laertius, writing in the third century, Pyrrho attempted to lead a life consistent with this doctrine, "going out of his way for nothing, taking no precaution, but facing all risks as they came, whether carts, precipices, dogs, or what not and generally leaving nothing to the arbitrament of the senses."[2] He was kept out of harm by his friends, who customarily followed him. According to Laertius, Pyrrho rejected any ethical theory, denying that anything was honorable or dishonorable, just or unjust. There is "nothing really existent but customs and conventions to govern human conduct." Aenesidemus (first century B.C.E.) maintained that Pyrrho's suspension of judgment applied to philosophy and questions of truth but that he did not lack foresight or sound common sense in everyday affairs. His ultimate quest was moral, for the suspension of judgment was supposed to have positive results in the individual skeptic's life. Yet Laertius describes Pyrrho's behavior as follows: "When his fellow passengers on board a ship were all unnerved by a storm, he kept calm and confident, pointing to a little pig on the ship that went on eating and telling them that such was the unperturbed state in which the wise man should keep going himself."[3]

The historian Edward Zeller sums up Pyrrho's philosophy in three statements: "We can know nothing as to the nature of things. Hence the right attitude towards them is to withhold judgment. The necessary result of suspending judgement is imperturbability."[4] Pyrrho's student Timon (c. 320–230 B.C.E.) carried his ideas further. But the philosophical conceptualization of skepticism was due primarily to Aenesidemus. He attacked both the dogmatic philosophers, who claimed that they had discovered truths, and the Academic skeptics.

The most complete explication of Pyrrhonism may be attributed to Sextus Empiricus, who lived in the third century, five

---

2. Diogenes Laertius, *Lives of Eminent Philosophers,* vol. 2 (London, New York: William Heinemann, 1925). See also Benn, op. cit., p. 475.

3. Benn, p. 481.

4. Edward Zeller, *The Stoics, Epicureans, and Skeptics* (London: Longmans, Green, 1880), p. 527.

centuries after Pyrrho. Whether Sextus was entirely accurate in his account of Pyrrho's views is unclear. In any case, his writings are the only major source that we have of Pyrrhonism. And so we will turn directly to his *Outlines of Pyrrhonism,* a book that has had a considerable influence on the history of philosophy.[5] Indeed, it was the rediscovery of this text during the European Renaissance in the fifteenth and sixteenth centuries that led to the resurgence of skepticism in the modern world. Sextus states that there are three kinds of philosophy: (1) Dogmatists (Aristotle, Epicurus, the Stoics), (2) Academics (such as represented by Carneades), and (3) Skeptics (Pyrrhonists). Skeptics differ from others, he maintained, in that "[we] do not make any positive assertions that anything we say is wholly as we affirm it to be. We merely report accurately on each thing as our impressions of it are at the moment."[6] The Pyrrhonists were both philosophers and medical empiricists. They questioned whether illnesses and diseases had causes, and the denial of this, and they also disputed knowledge claims in logic, mathematics, physics, astrology, and other fields.

Sextus characterized his skepticism as follows: It is *zetetic* (i.e., it is searching and examining); it is also *ephectic* (i.e., it involves the suspension of judgment); and it is *aporetic* (i.e., it involves a state of doubting). This form of skepticism is unable to offer final assent or denial and therefore it is not equivalent to a simple negation. Nor does it simply involve unbelief or the rejection of beliefs.

The problem we encounter, says Sextus, is that for every appearance or judgment, we can find a contrary appearance or judgment. By appearance, he means the object of sense perception. By contrary judgments, he means that we find arguments that are "conflicting" and that each has some equality and force. The only sensible posture to take as a result of this is the suspension

---

5. Sextus Empiricus, *Outlines of Pyrrhonism* (Buffalo, N.Y.: Prometheus Books, 1990).

6. Philip P. Hallie, ed., *Skepticism, Man and God: Selections from the Major Writing of Sextus Empiricus* (Middleton, Conn.: Wesleyan University Press, 1964), p. 41.

of judgment, which means "the cessation of thought processes," in which we neither affirm nor deny anything.

The purpose of this form of skepticism is to achieve a state of "mental tranquility," or "undisturbed calm." Thus Pyrrhonistic skepticism does not have a narrow intellectual interest but a moral purpose, for it is interested in the implications of suspension of judgment in the life of the individual. Indeed, Sextus maintains that "skepticism has its conception and cause . . . in the hope of finding mental tranquility."[7] Men of noble natures, he says, are disturbed at the irregularities encountered and puzzled as to what to believe. They thus investigate the truth and falsity of things so that they might achieve "tranquility." And this can occur only when we cease to dogmatize.

When he uses the word *dogma,* Sextus tells us, he is not referring to ordinary feelings that derive from everyday sense impressions. "Dogma" applies to "nonevident things which form the object of scientific research."[8] The dogmatist, he says, accepts the real existence of objects independent of himself. For example, he might claim that these objects are objects of sense or thought or are real in themselves, and so on. The skeptic neither affirms nor denies this. He is not denying the possibility of knowledge, but he makes no epistemological or metaphysical claims at all. The skeptic is only recording his personal feelings about such matters and is not going beyond that. He thus does not have a philosophical system of beliefs, although he does have a discipline that, in accordance with appearance, "follows a certain line of reasoning, that line of reasoning indicating how it is possible to seem to live rightly."[9]

Sextus says that skeptics do not deny appearances. They say only that they do not wish to interpret what these appearances are. While living undogmatically, he says, we pay due heed to the appearances and observe the requirements of daily living. Indeed, the skeptic is guided by nature; the compulsion of feelings; the traditions, laws, and customs of society; and by the arts. In

---

7. Ibid., p. 35.
8. Ibid., p. 36.
9. Ibid., p. 37.

essence, if skeptics can find no truth in philosophy or science, they can at least follow their commonsense inclinations and their feelings and be guided by the conventions of society. David Hume, who was influenced by Sextus, seemed to echo similar sentiments in the eighteenth century.

How do skeptics achieve this suspension of judgment? As a general rule, by putting things in opposition to what is claimed by others; according to Sextus, "We oppose appearances to appearances, thoughts to thoughts, or appearances to thoughts."[10] Sextus outlines ten modes, arguments, or forms by which suspension is to be attained. They all point to the great relativity, variety, and subjectivity of perceptions and thoughts and the difficulty of finding some underlying epistemological criteria that will tell us which are true and which are false: (1) The first mode is about differences in animals, i.e., the same object does not produce the same impressions in different animals, and the impressions vary from species to species. (2) Similarly there are differences in perception between human beings, contingent upon our different figures, constitutions, and peculiarities. (3) There are differences due to the construction of our unique sense organs. (4) There is also some relativity in the circumstances in which we find ourselves, which necessarily color our view of the world. (5) Similarly for the positions, distances, and places of those involved. (6) Also by the different mixtures that result. (7) Similarly, by the quantities and the compoundings of the individual objects. (8) There is thus some relativity of claims. (9) Our perceptions and thoughts are also relative to the frequency or rarity of occurrences. (10) Last, the variety of ethical standards, institutions, customs, laws, mythical beliefs, and dogmas influence our perceptions and judgments.

These modes apply either to the subject who is judging or the objects that are being judged, or a combination of these. Sextus later observes that there are unresolved disagreements and opinions between judges and that any proofs offered can go on ad infinitum. People differ in their assumptions, which they accept without proof; and they are prone to argue in a circle, thus begging the question.

---

10. Ibid., p. 43.

As a result of these snares, the skeptic prefers to cultivate a suspension of judgment. But Sextus warns that, unlike the dogmatists, he is *not* offering a philosophical theory, but only saying "as it appears to us," or in first person language, "as it appears to me."

What should be clear about this is that Pyrrhonist skeptics are not denying or refuting the claims of others. They are not, for example, denying the existence of God or the gods. They are only saying that they neither believe nor disbelieve. They use the expression "I suspend judgment," instead of saying "I cannot say which of the objects presented I ought to believe and which I ought to disbelieve."[11] In regard to credibility and incredibility, the objects appear equal. "We make no positive claims as to whether they are equal," but we merely state what our impressions of them are at the time they come to our notice.[12] Sextus terms this process "suspension" because of the equal validity of the objects of investigation and because he can neither confirm nor deny anything in regard to them. Thus Pyrrhonistic skepticism is *neutral* in its approach. The skeptic determines nothing about such questions, for "all things appear to him to be undetermined." Similarly the skeptic reports his own state of mind, that such things are "nonapprehensible to him." He is not affirming as a universal theory that for every argument in favor of a thesis there is a counterargument. Rather, he modifies this to mean that for every argument that has been put forth by those who seek to accept a point dogmatically, it appears to the skeptic that upon examination there is another argument that can be found opposed to it. Skeptics insist that they are not dogmatists, but are simply describing a human state of mind as it appears to them. Thus skepticism is simply offered as a kind of therapy by freeing us from dogmatism and enabling us to be indifferent to its lures and traps.

I will offer criticisms of this form of skepticism in later sections of this book, but some general observations are relevant here. First, I think that this rather excessive form of complete neutral skepticism is impossible to live by. Skeptics admit that in ordinary life we

---

11. Ibid., p. 82.
12. Ibid.

need to make choices; indeed, they argue that to be unperturbed we should follow the existent customs that prevail. Thus no sharp dividing line can be drawn between the beliefs of common ordinary life and more complex scientific theories or philosophical conceptions. Second, writing in the second and third centuries C.E., the skeptics were troubled by the widespread disagreements that prevailed among philosophical and scientific schools. Many of these disagreements no doubt persist today, but the difference is that we now have a considerable body of scientific knowledge and learning that has been tested by evidence, logical coherence, and predictive powers—knowledge that may be said to be reliable. Thus to insist that there is no objective basis for any knowledge, that all claims to truth rest on similar grounds of equality, and that our only recourse is to suspend judgment, simply does not accord with human experience. Third, neutralist skeptics are asserting a sweeping form of universal dogmatism—by denying that they can discover knowledge and by claiming that they are not making a general philosophical statement, but only a personal one. Their masking of a universal claim is totally disingenuous. The skeptic doth protest too much, methinks, about the unbelievability of knowledge.

Lurking in the background is a set of questionable philosophical assumptions about the nature of reality and the human perceiver. How and in what sense this is the case, I will analyze later. Let me say, however, that these caveats do not deny that *some* suspension of judgment in some situations is a necessary ingredient of skeptical inquiry in the quest for reliable knowledge. But this is a selective suspension in limited contexts of inquiry and it is not universalizable. What I am denying is the principle of complete suspension of doubt and the lapse into neutral know-nothingism as a viable posture. Interestingly, at the time of the rediscovery of Pyrrhonistic skepticism, it had a profound and salutary effect on modern philosophy. Also it is interesting to note that Christianity was able to make vast inroads in a Roman world filled with skeptical doubt. If the philosopher says that nothing is true or false and that there are no reliable standards of judging, then why not accept Christian revelation and why not revert to faith and custom as the sources of inspiration? Thus, the reaction

41

to neutral skepticism can lead to the most extreme forms of dogmatism. This kind of purist skepticism is ultimately self-defeating.

Academic Skepticism

Let us now turn our attention to a form of skepticism that I think is more reliable than Pyrrhonism, and which Sextus unfairly identified as "dogmatic." It is the kind of skepticism that emerged in Plato's school and was espoused by his successors at the Academy in the third century B.C.E. As we have seen, Plato was a philosophical genius who could be interpreted in many ways, as both a skeptic and an absolutist. His great *Dialogues* were excursions in philosophical inquiry in which a wide range of viewpoints were expressed. As I said, Plato often ended his dialogues with no fixed certainties. Yet he is best known for his "theory of ideas," the postulation of a realm of eternal essences and the division of the universe into "appearances" and "reality"; he thought the latter could be known by a dialectical process of rational intuition. Arcesilaus (315–240 B.C.E.) doubted these metaphysical and epistemological doctrines. Similarly, a century later, Carneades, who many consider the greatest of Academic skeptics, rejected Plato's epistemology and metaphysics. Unfortunately, we do not possess any of the writings of Carneades or of other Academic skeptics, and what we know about their doctrines is derived from the Roman author and statesman Cicero, who studied at the Academy; Diogenes Laertius, who wrote about the lives of philosophers; Sextus Empiricus; and Saint Augustine (354–430 C.E.), who sharply attacked the skeptics from the standpoint of Christian faith.[13]

It is well to point out again that "skepticism," as originally derived from *skeptikos,* had nothing to do with doubt, but with inquiry; it meant "to consider" or "to examine." It was only later that the word was connected to doubt and that a historical school was defined. The Academic skeptics, as they were later called, may not have known much about Pyrrho's theories and were simply continuing the tradition of doubt found in Socrates. It is difficult

---

13. Cicero, *De Academica and De Natura Deorum;* Diogenes Laertius, *The Lives and Opinions of the Philosophers;* St. Augustine, *Contra Academicus.*

to resolve these historical questions because of the lack of original sources.

The Academic skeptics offered a sustained critical attack upon the metaphysical doctrines that prevailed, notably Platonism and Stoicism. These doctrines denied that skepticism meant utter doubt, indifference, and paralysis, and concentrated on dealing with experience and applying certain rules to ordinary life. According to Cicero, Arcesilaus was the first to use the word *epochē* for the suspension of judgment in philosophical arguments. the Academic skeptics wished to deny the Stoic claim that there were certain perceptions that were self-evidently true. Arcesilaus introduced a doctrine of the *eulogon,* i.e., the probable or reasonable, which gives us some basis on which to act and make practical judgments, even though it may not be conclusive and may not tell us about the inner nature of things. Although we may suspend our judgment about metaphysical questions, we do not undermine practical reason and thus can achieve a life of happiness. Thus skepticism was not unlike the two other predominant philosophical schools of the day, Epicureanism and Stoicism, which also attempted to provide a guide to living, or eupraxophy.

The views of Carneades especially bear close attention, for he expressed a more positive and constructive form of skepticism not unlike the kinds of skeptical focus of modern-day pragmatism and positivism. Carneades did not entirely reject the possibility of knowledge; he thought we could discover probabilities by which we could live. Nor did he advise a neutralist state of suspension of judgment of all things. Thus his skepticism was similar to the *mitigated* form as later espoused by David Hume. Nonetheless, he was skeptical concerning the foundations of knowledge. Carneades did not think that we had ultimate knowledge about the nature of things but that, although nothing is certain, some things are more probable than others.

Carneades, like the Pyrrhonists, was impressed by contradictory arguments that could be offered to philosophical claims. The following story dramatizes the role of the skeptic historically and of the fate that skepticism—even of the mitigated kind—often suffered. In 156 B.C.E., the Athenians had made an unprovoked raid on the town of Oropus, and they were fined 500 talents by

Rome as retribution. In order to see whether the sentence could be remitted the Athenians sent three philosophers as special ambassadors to Rome, including a Stoic, a Peripatetic (Aristotelian), and Carneades, representing Academic skepticism. In the course of negotiations, the philosophers gave public lectures. Those of Carneades caused a sensation. On two successive days he gave lectures on the nature of justice. The first lecture eulogized what had been said about justice and virtue by Plato and Aristotle. In the second, however, he upset all of the conclusions that he had drawn the day before. He attempted to show that there is no such thing as an immutable rule of justice and that the greatest and most powerful states, such as Rome, had prospered by violating the rights of their neighbors. Moreover, from the standpoint of the individual, one's self-interest may at times override considerations of virtue. In this display of virtuosity, Carneades was simply demonstrating that, for every argument in favor of a thesis, it was possible to balance it with a contradictory argument. He was attempting to point out the inconsistencies, vanity, and easy dogmatizing about one's positions to which human beings are prone. But this skeptical tactic was viewed with disfavor by the Romans, who shortly thereafter were persuaded by Cato to pass a law against philosophy. The satirical arguments presented by skeptical philosophers no doubt were viewed by the leaders of Rome as an attack on its public policies and dangerous to its integrity.

Sextus's account of Academic skepticism is instructive. According to him there were three Academies, the first being that of Plato and his followers in his own day. The second was that of the Middle Academy, which was led by Arcesilaus and his student Polemo. The third was called the New Academy, which was led by Carneades and Clitomachus. Some, he says, add a fourth, of Philo and Charmides, and a fifth, of Antiochus. Sextus points out that some of the Platonic Dialogues evinced skeptical attitudes, especially the *Meno* and *Euthyphro,* where Socrates is engaged in a dialectical process of inquiry and is uncertain about finding any definite answers. Thus one cannot simply accuse Plato of being a dogmatist.

Concerning the skeptics of the New Academy, Sextus says that they are distinguishable from the Pyrrhonists because they are willing to make definite and positive assertions, such as "All things are inapprehensible," whereas his own group simply follows ordinary usage undogmatically and makes no claims. We assert, he says, that sense impressions, insofar as their essences are concerned, are equal in regard to their credibility "where they assert that some are probable and others improbable."[14] They further distinguish degrees of probability, saying that some are probable only, others are probable and tested, and still others are "probable, tested, and irreversible." He gives an illustration of a man entering a dark room and seeing a rope lying coiled up. His first impression, simply improbable, is that it is a snake. But after careful investigation, he finds that it does not move and is probably a rope. He remembers that snakes are sometimes congealed by cold in the winter. So he touches the coil with a stick and satisfies himself that the appearance does not represent a snake.

According to the account of Carneades's views, the Stoic epistemological theory was mistaken. The mind does not receive *phantasiai* (representations or appearances of which it could be certain), as the Stoic believes, for the subjective element is actively involved in perceiving and knowing. Carneades could not find an epistemological criterion for distinguishing between our subjective experiences and our actions, and so we cannot say anything firmly about the reality behind the appearances but must suspend judgment about the ultimate basis of our knowledge. In response to a challenge from a Stoic, Carneades formulated the doctrine of the *pithanon,* or the probable.

Carneades is thus describing how prudent men and women are guided in life. There are three degrees of probability: The first stage is simple perception (as seeing the coiled object); the second stage occurs when our first impressions are confirmed by similar perceptions received under attendant circumstances; and the third degree of probability occurs when we test our impressions by further examination. The probability is increased as the perceptions received are confirmed by investigating the conditions under which they occur. Here Carneades is using a form of inductive inference by relating his present impressions to past experiences and testing

---

14. Hallie, op. cit. p. 94.

them carefully. The empirical probabilism of Carneades is very important, for it is similar in part to the third type of skepticism that I have enunciated in Chapter 1 (although I would go beyond it); and it points to a constructive role for the skeptical inquirer.

There is a fundamental difference between Pyrrhonism and probabilism. The contrast between these two forms of skepticism can perhaps best be seen by reference to the different views of religion and belief in the gods. Sextus makes it clear that the Pyrrhonists "conform to the ordinary view, in that we affirm undogmatically the existence of gods, reverence gods, and affirm that they are possessed of foreknowledge."[15] He criticizes the dogmatic philosophers who claim to have knowledge of "divine things." He points out the diverse and contradictory conceptions that men and women have had of the gods, and he believes that the efforts to prove their existence are invalid. By the same token, he thinks that any efforts to disprove the existence of the gods are fallacious, especially when contrasted with arguments on the opposite side. Since one cannot resolve the dilemma of the existence or nonexistence of the gods, Sextus declares for the neutral, disinterested state, i.e., the suspension of belief. His moral quandary is resolved by reverting to his ancestral customs. He therefore declares that the "gods do exist," and he avers that he "performs everything that conduces to their worship and veneration."[16]

Carneades, on the other hand, is a strong critic of belief in the gods, or at least he is skeptical of their foundations, and we have no record that he professed piety. A good deal of our knowledge about Carneades is provided by Cicero. Cicero studied Stoicism, Epicureanism, and Skepticism and was familiar with the disputes of these schools about the nature of the gods and whether or not they exert any governance and control over the universe and the affairs of mortals. Cicero sought to defend the Stoic view of a divine universe, but he tells us that Carneades criticized the philosophical arguments used to support such a view and to show their contradictory nature.[17] Carneades, for example, denied the

---

15. Ibid., p. 175.

16. Ibid., p. 188.

17. In *On the Nature of the Gods,* Cicero has Cotta argue the views of Carneades.

Stoic claim that there was a social consensus that everyone believed in God; and he argued that even if belief in the gods was universal, one surely should not appeal to views of the foolish and unthinking masses to establish the case, for this does not make it true. Carneades also attacked the use of the teleological and design arguments to prove the existence of God, saying that one could give a natural explanation for the processes we view in nature without attributing these to the purposes of a personal God. In any case, he maintained that the idea of God was embroiled in contradictions. If God is infinite, he is also limited; if perfect, he cannot at the same time be virtuous. As a critic of the alleged rational and providential order of the universe of the Stoics, Carneades found disorder and imperfection in nature. Thus the problem of evil wreaks havoc with the Stoic conception of God. Incidentally, Carneades was also a strong critic of belief in divination, oracles, and prophecies—paranormal events that were widely believed in at that time in the Roman world. Although Carneades was able to argue both sides of the question and to develop the suspension of judgment (*epochē*), and although he was a strong agnostic and cynic about the prevailing Stoic views of God, it was likely that he was also an *unbeliever* about such matters and hence did not simply revert to custom or avow his belief in conventional religion as Sextus did.

According to Cicero, Carneades did not formulate his arguments for the purpose of destroying belief in the gods, but in order to show how insubstantial the arguments were. He did not simply repeat the arguments of the Stoics, but showed their contradictory nature and sought to induce the suspension of doubt. He thus stands midway between the atheist and theist. Sextus rejected the doctrines of probability and reasonableness produced by the Academic Skeptic. He also rejected Carneades's degrees of probability, for he thought that they might be dogmatic. Yet both the Pyrrhonist and Academic schools of skepticism shared a practical concern: They were the opponents of metaphysical dogmatism and certainty, which can lead to undue fanaticism. They both attempted to deal with experience in order to find some direction for the good life. Neither school ended up with schizophrenic indecision, nor with overwhelming doubt. As eupraxophers, they both had a practical goal: to provide some moral direction for a meaningful life.

One further point needs to be made. There has been some dispute by scholars as to the real meaning of Carneades's position. Some said that Carneades himself lacked any positive beliefs and that his main focus was on *epochē*—suspension of belief, and that this is indicated by the fact that he was generally able to argue both sides of a question. Clitomachus, head of the Academy after Carneades, said that he was never able to find out what Carneades himself actually believed, and he revered him as a champion of *epochē*. Some have thus said that Carneades did not put forward the *pithanon* theory as one to which he was committed, but simply used it as a dialectical device in order to respond to the Stoics. If so, Carneades's point of view would have been essentially negative. No doubt Carneades was gifted at arguing on both sides of the question; for example, he argued that there was a criterion of the "convincing impressions," but he also argued that there was not. Under this interpretation, Carneades did not commit himself to a positive doctrine, but only used the *pithanon* to corner the Stoics. What he *actually* believed is therefore sometimes difficult to say. The later followers of Carneades in the Academy, such as Philo, Clitomachus's successor, and Metrodorus, argued to the contrary, that Carneades did indeed believe in the *pithanon*, and they themselves supported a form of *mitigated skepticism*. In any case, whether or not Carneades himself actually believed in the *pithanon*, within the later Academy it was appealed to as a positive form of skepticism. These skeptics held that we should "calculate well," use "a balance sheet" of facts, and follow a prudential course in life. In so doing they were advocating an eminently positive purpose for skepticism.

As we have seen, Sextus Empiricus considered this move to be dogmatic; for him the suspension of belief was the only sensible approach that skeptics could take. It is unfortunate that during the modern period the Pyrrhonism of Sextus rather than the positive *pithanon* of Carneades was taken to be the primary representative of classical skepticism. For it was the complete suspension of belief and the cultivation of complete doubt that began to have a major effect upon the development of modern thought. Yet there are actually two kinds of skepticism here: on the one hand, skepticism as the suspension of belief or doubt, and on the other, skepticism as a positive methodological principle of inquiry. In this latter form of skepticism there is open-mindedness, a questioning of absolute or self-evident premises; it is sometimes noncommittal in its pursuit of truth, yet it never denies totally the possibility of achieving reliable knowledge.

Postscript on Saint Augustine's Contra Academicus

St. Augustine in a sense marks the end of the influence of skepticism in the Roman world. He is a transitional figure, for with him Christianity began to emerge as an influence in the Roman empire, and the Christian faith came to dominate by overwhelming the schools of philosophy that prevailed in the pagan world. Philosophical inquiry was replaced by absolute certainty based on religious faith. Augustine recounts his own personal odyssey from skepticism to conviction. He tells us that as a young man he became acquainted with the skepticism of the Academy and was intrigued by its philosophical arguments. He felt, however, that skepticism was insufficient for his hungry soul; skepticism had threatened to undermine his interests and energy. Moreover, Augustine was interested in finding the truth, not simply in seeking it or in suspending judgment. In his *Contra Academicus* he makes his break with the philosophy of skepticism on philosophical grounds, by first arguing that we could know certain truths: in logic, through the laws of contradiction, the excluded middle, and identity. These are immediately evident and universal truths of validity. They are not subject to time and are beyond change. Similarly, he finds fixed truths in ethics and aesthetics. In the final analysis, Augustine postulates a Platonic realm of ideal essences, all unified under the authorship of God. Augustine is a skillful dialectician. He anticipates the famous *cogito, ergo sum* of Descartes, arguing that even to doubt everything entails at least the certainty that doubt is going on, which cannot itself be doubted without contradiction.

Augustine's philosophy expresses a new intellectual and ethical mood. He does not find happiness in the quest for truth or by means of a process of inquiry. The life of reason is not enough.

The state of doubt is unsatisfactory to him. To say that we can live by probabilities is not attractive either. Augustine wishes indubitable certainties. This depends on a kind of a priori Platonic intuitionism. But reason in this sense is still insufficient for him, and it must be supplemented by faith and the authority of revelation. Reason is unable to solve the deepest mysteries of life, he says. Man needs divine fulfillment by faith. Only by submission to divine authority and accepting Christ's revelations can one hope to transcend the doubts of skeptical philosophy.

It goes without saying that the skeptic is extremely critical of Augustine's appeal to faith. Skepticism raises doubt about the reliability of revelation. It finds no ultimate justification for grounding the truths of logic in absolute intuitions. It does not believe that the standards of ethics or of aesthetics are universal. It questions the postulation of a realm of essences based upon God.

Modern Skepticism

With the eclipse of pagan philosophy and letters, and submission to the authority imposed by the church, learning declined. It took a long time for European civilization to be freed from domination by Christian doctrine. Europe was reawakened from its dogmatic slumber in the thirteenth and fourteenth centuries, and the Renaissance occurred in part because of the rediscovery of the classical texts of Greece and Rome. This revival of humanistic studies was accompanied by the secularization of society and the eventual emergence of modern science.

Among the great classics that were read in the late Renaissance and early modern period were those by two skeptical authors: Cicero and Sextus Empiricus, with the lion's share of the attention being devoted to the latter. Diogenes Laertius's *Life of Pyrrho* was also of some influence. The Greek text of the *Outlines of Pyrrhonism* was first brought to western Europe from the Byzantine world in the fifteenth century. It was translated into Latin in 1562, and into other languages somewhat later. By the seventeenth century skepticism began to exert a major impact on modern thought. It was unfortunate that the kind of skepticism that

50

appeared at that time was identified with the cultivation of a state of universal doubt and that skepticism was therefore viewed by many as excessively negative rather than as a constructive feature of inquiry.

Negative Skepticism and Fideism

The skepticism that first began to prevail was that of Pyrrhonism, i.e., the complete doubt about the possibility of knowledge, the belief that both the senses and reason fail to provide us with any degree of certainty and that the only thing we are left with is total doubt. Pyrrho said that since he did not know whether or not the world existed, he relied on the customs and religion of his day. One of the surprising by-products of the impact of skepticism was the growth of fideism in the early modern period; for if both natural reason and sense experience were unreliable guides to ultimate truth, many skeptics concluded that only religious faith could satisfy our quest.

During the Reformation, when Protestantism waged a war against the Roman Catholic church, questions concerning the nature of truth became central to the controversy. Was truth a matter for the church to determine or could one return to the Bible, read the Scriptures, and judge for oneself? The humanist scholar Erasmus (1466–1536) advocated the skeptical suspension of judgment in his criticisms of scholastic philosophy, but he defended Christian faith. Martin Luther lashed out at Erasmus, maintaining that a true Christian could not be a skeptic: "Sanctus Spiritus non est scepticus." Although he deferred to individuals to read the Bible for themselves, he insisted that revelation contained Absolute Truths. Many Catholics became skeptics in philosophy and science. Rejecting the Protestant appeal to inner conscience, they nonetheless defended the traditions and the faith of the Mother Church. Thus in the early modern period skepticism was not used as a weapon to discredit religious belief, but rather as a tool of natural knowledge and philosophy. It was only later that skepticism became avowedly anti-religious and was identified with unbelief and atheism.

One of the first major figures to take an interest in skepticism was Gianfrancesco Pico della Mirandola (1469–1533). Like Erasmus he used skepticism against Aristotle and on behalf of Christianity. The only reliable truth to be found, he said, was in the Scriptures. Similarly Gentian Hervet, an influential member of the church, attempted to use Sextus to refute Calvinism. Human reason was frail, he maintained, and the claims of Calvin pretentious.

Two influential authors who gave impetus to skepticism were Francisco Sanchez (1550–1623) and the French essayist Michel de Montaigne (1533–1592). Sanchez adopted the classical skeptical critiques against dogmatic Aristotelian science and reverted to faith, although he did suggest that there was another constructive or mitigated form of skepticism that was available. Montaigne had a strong influence on the growth of skepticism. Suffering from a *crise pyrrhonienne,* Montaigne doubted the very possibility of knowledge, for both sense experience and reason were deceptive and unable to comprehend reality. Only by the suspension of belief and accepting God's revelation, he suggested, could we find a way out of the impasse.

Other skeptical authors seemed to follow a similar path—for example, Bayle, Berkeley, Pascal, and, later, Kierkegaard. One question that can be raised is whether these skeptical writers were truthful in their reversion to religiosity, or whether given the intolerant temper of the times, they felt unable to come out of the closet to reveal their true skeptical doubts about religion itself. Religion was a prominent part of the socio-cultural landscape, and it was dangerous for a man to profess atheism or agnosticism. A person wears many masks in life; perhaps it was not possible to remove the mask hiding religious unbelief without placing one's reputation and livelihood in serious jeopardy.

The French philosopher and critic Pierre Bayle (1647–1706) at the end of the seventeenth century expressed the most thoroughgoing skepticism of the time. His *Dictionnaire Historique et Critique* presented scathing indictments of a wide range of theories. He delighted in challenging his readers by demonstrating time and again that holes could be found in virtually all theories and that they contained many contradictions. He also turned his attention to religious systems and found them riddled with absurdities. For example, he poked fun at the moral integrity of David of the

Old Testament. Atheists, he said, could be more moral than Christians; religion was not necessarily a basis for ethical conduct. His writings led his critics to conclude that he was an atheist, which Bayle denied. Bayle stated throughout that he was a Christian and a Calvinist, and he remained a member of the Reformed Church in the Netherlands where he lived. After refuting theory after theory—using skepticism as his demolishing tool—he appealed to faith as the only source of truth. Whether he was indeed a believer, or only feared to reveal his irreligion, is difficult to say. In any case, he had a major impact on the Enlightenment and the turning of skepticism to unbelief and irreligion.

Unlimited or total doubt—the heritage of Pyrrho and Sextus—had a powerful impact on the modern world. It led some authors to conclude that since there is no reliable criterion of knowledge, the only prudent course is to follow the customs and religions of the day, and thus paradoxically skepticism was used to defend the faith.

Other skeptics came to draw contrary conclusions about fideism itself. If all knowledge was specious, so were religious claims to truth and revelation, including those in the Bible. The inevitable implication of this line of reasoning was the emergence in the eighteenth and nineteenth centuries of total religious unbelief and atheism.

But we are running ahead of our story, for skepticism did not emerge in a vacuum, but was impelled by many social forces.

The Birth of Modern Science

In addition to the Renaissance and the Protestant Reformation, there were other influences at work. Men and women were breaking out of Europe and voyaging to all corners of the globe, bringing back tales of strange lands and peoples; and these stories were unsettling not only to the established religions but to cultural and ethnic chauvinisms. At the same time there was an impressive attempt to forge a new science of nature. Questioning the revered truths of scholastic philosophy and theology and turning to the book of nature itself, a new natural science emerged. The growth of modern science in the sixteenth and seventeenth centuries thus played an especially powerful role in encouraging skepticism. But there were problems, for if the skeptics deny that knowledge is possible, how explain the experiments of Galileo and the impressive theories of Copernicus, Kepler, and Newton in astronomy and physics, all of which seem to have been confirmed by mathematics, observation, and experiment? Elegant physical theories emerged that seemed to move knowledge beyond indecision and doubt. Were these contrary to what the skeptics denied: that there were criteria for truth, which would enable us to comprehend how nature operated? Could we discover the causes at work? The entire development of modern philosophy can be interpreted as an effort to resolve two basic problems posed by the new science and skepticism: First, the nature of knowledge: What is truth? and What are the most reliable methods of discovering and testing it? Second, the nature of reality: What was knowledge about? What was ultimate reality? What was the extent and limit of knowledge?

Cartesian Doubt

A key figure exemplifying the impact of both skepticism and the new science on human knowledge was René Descartes (1596–1650). His work illustrates the profound influence that skeptical thought was having on the modern world, though he attempted to find an answer to the skeptics and to refute them. Descartes's autobiographical account of his personal search for secure foundations for knowledge in his *Discourse on Method* and *Meditations* tells us that his quest began when he found himself in a quagmire of doubt. As a young man, Descartes had the advantage of the best scholastic education; but he soon began to doubt the received doctrines, for he found that the best authorities often disagreed about fundamental questions. He was also struck by the fact that customs varied from nation to nation and that what was considered good or bad, right or wrong, in one country was often denied in the next. Moreover, he was disturbed by the fact that perceptions often deceive us, that what appears true to the unaided senses under one set of conditions can be distorted under other conditions. He was unable to find certain and indubitable truths upon which he could base his assurance, except in mathematics and geometry, where he thought the authorities did not disagree but found unanimity. But he decided to defer his quest for certainty until later in life, when he would be older and would have had more experience.

At last, after several years, Descartes resumed his search. Alone in a room in winter quarters in Germany, he resolved to begin anew and to see whether he could reconstruct the various elements of his systems of beliefs and find secure foundations for them. It is here that Descartes's famous method of unlimited doubt— Cartesian doubt, as it is called—comes into full play, and in three stages. First, he remarks how the senses are apt to deceive us and are thus unreliable as a basis of truth. Next, in a second wave of doubt, he asks how he can know that he is not now dreaming. How can he distinguish his dreams from reality? And third, in a move into another state of complete doubt, he introduces his *malin genie* argument. How do I know that some evil demon is not deceiving me, and that everything that I have believed in or held sacred may not be true?

"I will suppose," he says, ". . . that some malignant demon, who is at once exceedingly potent and deceitful, has employed all of his artifices to deceive me; I will suppose that the sky, the air, the earth, colors, figures, sounds, and all external things are nothing better than illusions or dreams. . . ." He then goes on to complete his state of psychological puzzlement. "I will consider myself as without hands, eyes, flesh, blood, or any of the senses, and falsely believing that I am possessed of these." Descartes then adds that he will "continue resolutely fixed in this belief" and shall do what is within his power, viz., by "suspending my judgment" and guarding against "giving my assent to what is false."[18]

Here the influence of Pyrrhonism has reached its apogee and nothing is presupposed about any claims to truth. Descartes has reached a state of indecision, unable to distinguish reality from chimera, truth from falsity, dreams from mad illusions. Where do we go from here? Is there any way out of the morass? Yes, he believes that there is a way out, and that is by using the methods employed so successfully in mathematics, geometry, and logic to

---

18. René Descartes, *Meditations on First Philosophy,* Meditation I.

establish truth claims; that is, he will see if he can discover one idea that is so clear and so distinct that he cannot doubt its veracity. And he settles on a rock that he thinks is solid, a *cogito:* I cannot deny that I am doubting. But doubting is a form of thinking. Even to doubt that I doubt is to affirm it. Therefore I know that I exist, at least as a thinking being. *Cogito, ergo sum*—I think, therefore I am.

This famous argument of Descartes's can be interpreted as an attempt to refute skepticism, for it is precisely in the state of total doubt that Descartes finds a glimmer of truth. And he believes that once he has established such a universal principle he can go on to see if there are any other clear and distinct ideas that are self-evidently and intuitively true, and any deductive theorems that can be inferred from them.

Several questions can be raised about Descartes's entire procedure. First, did he accurately report his own private soliloquies; was his state of doubt genuine or only feigned? An extreme form of psychological skepticism is akin to a schizophrenic state of doubt. Second, was he able, by using the rationalistic a-priori method of intuition, and deductive inferences from his intuitions, to escape from his state of doubt? Did he truly discover a brilliant intuition of truth that we cannot doubt? Had Descartes really resolved the question of the criterion of truth, so essential in philosophy, science, and religion? Serious doubts have been raised about both questions by his critics, who not only did not believe that Descartes truly was in a suspended state of animation, but also doubted that by using his method of pure cogito he was able to prove his own existence. There are those who deny that Descartes was never a skeptic. His main concern was to *respond* to skepticism, says philosopher Bernard Williams, not to defend it.[19]

Skeptics have in turn responded critically to Descartes's arguments. Descartes's entire exegesis is based on circular reasoning; for he has presupposed his method of proof. One may ask, How do we really know that reason is reliable? If the senses deceive

---

19. Bernard Williams, "Descartes's Use of Skepticism," in *The Skeptical Tradition,* ed. by Myles Burnyeat (Berkeley, Calif.: University of California Press, 1983).

us, why not cognition also? Why should the laws of contradiction be held valid for everyone? Why not imagine that we are deceived about them as well? Why can't there be alternative geometries? Empiricists have asked of the rationalist: How can we move from a valid argument based upon formal truths to empirical claims without some observations to provide experiential content to the concepts? Descartes denied that the senses were reliable; only understanding can get us to the external world. But there are flaws in his proof. In any case, Descartes did not completely doubt everything; for he presupposed the language in which he wrote and he assumed his methodological criteria. Moreover, he confessed that he never carried doubt to practical everyday life, so that the existence of the external world was never really in question.[20]

The point I wish to emphasize is that Cartesian doubt—whether genuine or feigned—is among the purest expressions we have of total negative and nihilistic doubt, at least as a methodological postulate if nothing else. And it is this kind of doubt that so exercised the modern imagination. Is there any way to refute total skepticism? Can we ever transcend the state of utter denial of all claims, premises, and presuppositions? The course of modern philosophy, from Locke, Berkeley, and Hume to Kant, in one sense is fixated on the Pyrrhonist challenge. Is there any way out of the egocentric predicament? Even if one establishes the existence of the ego, mind, self, soul, consciousness, can one ever say that it is more than a bundle of ideas, and/or can one affirm that one has a corporeal body? Descartes is unable to bridge the mind/body dualism between ideas and external bodies. He attempts to do so by first demonstrating that God exists, by a questionable resort to the cosmological and ontological arguments; and he then rationalizes that since a good deity would not knowingly deceive his creatures, we may deduce that we have a body. This adroit argument does not follow, and it is only an ad hoc artifice introduced by Descartes literally to save his skin, but it still is not convincing to the probing darts of the skeptics.

---

20. Descartes, *Meditations*, VII, 16. There are two interpretations of Descartes: that he took extreme skepticism to the end of the road, and that he also refuted it.

What remained of Descartes's systematic efforts to lay solid foundations for knowledge was even more doubt. What emerged for so many was a heroic glorification of the Cartesian method of doubting, and the development of the full implications of his method for all areas of knowledge. Yet in spite of himself, Descartes had a point. "Look," you say, "you cannot overcome your doubt." "I say that there are some truths that we cannot doubt," he plaintively asserts. But some of the truths that he accepted, such as the existence of God, could be doubted, and Descartes's efforts to reestablish theology on new grounds were specious.

Mitigated Skepticism

There is yet another form of skepticism that emerged in the modern period, not unlike the kind of skepticism that flourished in the New Academy under Carneades. For if we could not affirm with certainty any kind of universal proposition, as Descartes had attempted to do, we nonetheless do have a kind of probabilistic knowledge about the world that we accept and on the basis of which we live and act. In 1628 Descartes had heard a famous chemist, Chandoux, deliver a lecture in Paris to the effect that if we could not say anything about what our impressions were about, at the very least we could find probability regularities between them on the basis of which we could develop scientific knowledge. This, as we have seen, Descartes sought to disprove, though without success. But other philosophers in the early seventeenth century attempted to work out constructive forms of mitigated skepticism as a compromise between absolutist dogmatism, on the one hand, and total skepticism, on the other. This line of argument culminated in the work of David Hume, the most renowned skeptic of modern philosophy. Mitigated skepticism was an effort to overcome the utter nihilistic implications of Pyrrhonism.

Marin Mersenne (1588–1648) was a devout Catholic who defended the faith, but he was also interested in supporting the new science that was then emerging. Simply stated, he held that even if skepticism could not be refuted, we still are able to develop a kind of knowledge that is essential if we are to realize our purposes in the world. Here Mersenne is not talking about the ultimate nature of things, but the hypotheses and predictions that we can make about "the connection of events and the future course of experience."[21] He concedes that there are some things that transcend our ability to know, i.e., the real nature of things. Nonetheless we have a good deal of knowledge about the world of appearances.

Pierre Gassendi (1592–1655) also advocated a "constructive skepticism." He presented an atomic theory as the best explanation of the world of appearances. Although the things in themselves are shielded from our knowledge, we can develop a science of nature by observing our senses and carefully interpreting them. We can correct any errors in sense perception by careful reasoning.[22]

Gassendi was a particularly sharp critic of Descartes. He was doubtful that we could attain true knowledge solely by reference to "clear and distinct ideas in our understanding." We may be prone to error, and what seems clear and distinct at one time may not be at another.[23] Gassendi would rather have us consult experience—something that Descartes rejected—as a better guide to knowledge. Like other empiricists, Gassendi sought to separate science from metaphysics. Science provided hypothetical systems about appearances and practical guides to conduct, not ultimate accounts of reality.

Humean Skepticism

David Hume (1711–1776) is no doubt the greatest and most influential skeptical philosopher of the modern world, though it is not at all clear whether he continued to hold a Pyrrhonistic view of knowledge as well as a mitigated form of skepticism. His views have been interpreted as following from the theories of his predecessors, notably Locke and Berkeley. One of the basic puzzles of modern philosophy was the attempt to square Newtonian materialistic and mechanistic science with commonsense experience. A central problem concerns the nature and limits of knowledge. What do we know when we know? The starting point of this

---

21. See Henry Popkin, *The History of Skepticism from Erasmus to Descartes,* rev. ed. (Netherlands: Van Gorum and Co., 1960), p. 1

22. Ibid., p. 145.

23. Ibid., p. 147.

analysis for both rationalists and empiricists were "ideas," "impressions," or "perceptions" in someone's mind.

John Locke (1632–1704), like Descartes, raised the question of the relationship of ideas to external bodies, of perception to material things. A popular distinction made in modern science was that between primary and secondary qualities. For Locke, the primary qualities or properties of an object were the real physical properties, independent of us, such as its shape, size, extension, and mass. The secondary properties, such as taste, color, and sound, are somewhat subjective inasmuch as they depend on a perceiver for their being. Locke never doubted that there were real objects that primary or objective properties described, but he thought that the underlying atomic structure of such objects was unobservable. Thus substance was basically unknowable. He ended up with a qualified form of skepticism.

George Berkeley (1685–1753), a Bishop of the Anglican Church in Ireland, considered himself a foe of atheism and materialism. He reduced all properties to secondary qualities, for he maintained that they were dependent upon the perceptions in some mind for their being. We could not know material substances. All that we know are ideas or perceptions imprinted on our senses. And these are caused by God, who serves as the epistemological guarantor of the universe. This was hardly a solution to the problem of knowledge. But what then was reality and what caused our perceptions?

Hume was heir to this impasse. He begins with his familiar distinction between impressions and ideas. By the term "impressions," he means all of our more "lively perceptions, when we hear or see or feel or love or hate or desire or will." By "ideas" or thoughts he refers to the "less lively perceptions when we reflect upon our impressions."[24] All of our ideas and thoughts are copies of our impressions. Hume goes on to say that the creative power of the mind is nothing more than the ability to associate ideas— to compound, transfer, augment, or diminish the data provided to us by sense impressions. The key point is Hume's use of the empiricist criterion to critique metaphysical abstraction. In order

---

24. David Hume, *An Enquiry Concerning Human Understanding* (Buffalo, N.Y.: Prometheus Books, 1988), Section II.

to find out what terms mean, we should always ask, "From what impression is that supposed idea derived?"

Hume applied his skeptical doubts to the operations of the understanding. He divides all objects of human reason into (1) relations of ideas and (2) matters of fact. The first applies to the formal sciences (geometry, algebra, and arithmetic), which are affirmed intuitively or demonstratively. The truths of these assumptions are dependent upon the operations of thought and have no relation to what exists in the universe. Questions concerning matters of fact, however, do not depend upon the principle of contradiction, but upon the present testimony of our senses and the recorded memory of past events. Using this criterion, Hume rejects the Lockean distinction between primary and secondary qualities. Our knowledge of solidity and extension, like taste and smell, is dependent on the lively impressions we receive. The unknowable substance that Locke postulated is an abstraction for which we have no evidence, says Hume in *A Treatise of Human Nature*.[25] Thus we can find no direct evidence of "corporeal" matter. But he also attacked Berkeley's postulation of mind, agency, soul, or God, the immaterial substance used to hold up the world. All evaporate under Hume's skeptical probes.

In the youthful *Treatise,* Hume is led to a kind of Pyrrhonistic skepticism of an extreme sort. The world seems to evaporate into bundles of impressions, for he could find no rhyme or reason for substance or structure. Here Hume is mired in theoretical skepticism of the negative or totalistic sort. He tells us that when he follows philosophical arguments to their end, he cannot dispel the clouds of skeptical doubt or "philosophical melancholy and delirium." Yet he says he finds himself "absolutely and necessarily determined to live, and talk, and act like other people in the common affairs of life . . . [and] I am ready to throw all my books and papers into the fire, and resolve never more to renounce the pleasures of life for the sake of reasoning and philosophy."[26] This leads him to a form of mitigated skepticism, for we have to live and act and there are other sources of knowledge within us that go

---

25. David Hume, *A Treatise of Human Nature,* ed. by L. A. Selby-Bigge.
26. Ibid., p. 269.

beyond pure reason. Thus mitigated skepticism is found in both his earlier *Treatise* and his later, more mature work, *An Enquiry Concerning Human Understanding.* Here Hume acknowledges that we do have knowledge, on the basis of which we live and act in the world. All of our reasons about matters of fact, he says, are grounded in our ideas of resemblance, contingency, and cause and effect.

Of special significance is Hume's view of causality. How do we arrive at causal knowledge? Hume asks. It is not by a priori reasoning, he says, for there is no logical or necessary relation between cause and effect, but only by what we discover in our experience, where we find objects that are constantly conjoined in time and contiguous in space. We can observe no real causes or hidden powers. All that we can say is that on the basis of past experience we come to expect that certain effects will most likely occur in the future as in the past: "I have found," says Hume, "that such an object has always been attended with such an effect." And he says, "I foresee, that other objects, which are, in appearance, similar, will be attended with similar effects."[27] This is based on custom and habit, where we expect that like causes will lead to like effects. But we do not observe the hidden real causes at work—these are unknown to us—allowing his skepticism to remain. Moreover, he is well aware that "the problem of induction" has not been resolved. For all inferences from experience presuppose that "the future will resemble the past and that similar powers will be conjoined with similar sensible qualities."[28] But we cannot prove the assumption itself. In the face of these skeptical doubts, we are able to function only because of instinct, custom, and habit, on the basis of which we draw causal inferences.

In what sense is Hume a skeptic? In the concluding section of the *Enquiry,* he sums up his views. Here he criticizes Pyrrhonistic skepticism. The chief and most confounding objection to it, he says, is ". . . that no durable good can ever result from it; while it remains in its full force and vigor . . . A Pyrrhonist cannot expect, that his philosophy will have any constant influence in the

---

27. *Enquiry,* op. cit., p. 36.
28. Ibid., p. 39.

mind . . . or . . . that its influence would be beneficial to society."
On the contrary, he states, ". . . that all human life must perish,
were his principles universally and steadily to prevail."[29] He
recognizes that we are faced with a quandary. For "nothing can
ever be present to the mind but an image or perception, and the
senses are only the inlets, through which these images are conveyed,
without being able to produce any immediate intercourse between
the mind and the object."[30] Moreover, we can never know matter
in itself, "for if you bereave it of all its intelligible qualities, you
annihilate it and are left with an inexplicable something, as the
cause of our perception."[31]

The only solution for Hume is mitigated or Academic skepticism. We are able to free ourselves from Pyrrhonistic doubt by
the power of "natural instinct." This species of moderate skepticism
is very reasonable—at its best it allows us to preserve a proper
impartiality in our projects and to avoid prejudices. It is this kind
of skepticism that Hume applies with devastating effect upon
theology. In his posthumous *Dialogues on Natural Religion,* it
enables him to question cosmological and teleological arguments,
and also the argument from miracles. He uses this to destroy rational
or natural theology.

But Hume is not a total skeptic, for if we cannot make absolutely certain statements about matters of fact, we nonetheless can
make judgments that have degrees of probability because they are
based on observation of matters of fact. This kind of moderate
skepticism he considered therapeutic. It is not based on abstract
reason. Hume said, "When we run over libraries, persuaded of
these principles, what havoc must we make? If we take in our
hand any volume of divinity school metaphysics, for instance let
us ask, Does it contain any abstract reasoning concerning quan-
tity or number? No. Does it contain any experimental reasoning
concerning matters of fact or existence? No. Commit it then to
the flames: for it can contain nothing but sophistry and illusion."[32]

---

29. Ibid., p. 144.
30. Ibid., p. 137.
31. Ibid., p. 140.
32. Ibid., p. 149.

Latter-day Skepticism

The impact of skepticism on modern and post-modern thought continues unabated. Indeed, almost no thinker worthy of the name can do philosophy without attempting to respond to or drawing upon the skeptical tradition.

For example, Kant's mature philosophical work was developed in an effort to reply to Hume's skepticism. Although Kant (1724–1804) believed that he could provide solid foundations for our knowledge of the world, and he did so in terms of his critical philosophy, he never entirely abandoned skepticism, particularly about that which transcends phenomena and lies in the noumenal realm. Thus Kant maintained that we can say nothing about pure or ideal concepts if they have no perceptual content. Accordingly, he concluded that, although our scientific knowledge about the world or common sense is secure, speculative knowledge about the noumenal world cannot be obtained.

Various movements in the modern world have drawn heavily on one aspect or another of skepticism. French Enlightenment philosophers—Voltaire, Diderot, d'Alembert, von Humboldt, et al.—believed in the ideals of reason and science. Although quite independent of classical nihilism or mitigated skepticism, they were debunkers, selectively submitting the claims of religion and theology to scrutiny, and indicting them for hypocrisy.

The Romantic protest expressed a form of skepticism, for it objected to what it considered the inordinate emphasis on reason and science, and it sought to leave room for other passionate and intuitive aspects of human experience. Many other skeptical thinkers, such as Marx, Engels, Nietzsche, and Freud, applied their critiques to classical philosophy, ethics, and politics, debunking the view that man was a rational animal. This tended to undermine confidence in the unexamined assumptions of Western culture. Similarly, Mill and Russell, for the empiricist tradition, drew extensively on skepticism. The logical positivists were extremely skeptical of metaphysical speculation. They attempted to develop a criterion of meaning by which they sought to exclude metaphysical and emotive language from consideration. Anything that was either not tautologically true or that violated the principle of verifiability fell within this domain. Wittgenstein rejected his earlier effort to formulate a logically elegant language of reality, and he dealt with language in its functional contexts. Other analytic philosophers used linguistic analysis to clarify muddles and puzzles. Existentialists also indicted classical essentialist philosophy, particularly the effort to apply abstract reason to existence. In one way or another, Sartre, Camus, and Heidegger question the view that man has a fixed nature or essence, and that we can use language to penetrate the veil and mystery of existence. Neither science nor technology can put us close to Being, said Heidegger.

Recent post-modernist French philosophers have developed their own form of skepticism. Although generally not considered part of the classical skepticial movement, they share in a radical critique of science and the possibility of objective knowledge. Jacques Derrida, Jacques Lacan, Michel Foucault, Jean-François Lyotard, and other philosophers have rejected "modernity"; that is, they are skeptical of the Enlightenment's confidence in human reason and the possibility of human progress. Their skepticism has been extended to humanism (its belief in the autonomy of the individual), to Marxism (its historicism), and to philosophy itself (denying that there are any philosophical truths).

Derrida expresses skepticism about our ability to decipher in any objective way the meanings of signs and signifiers. He uses a procedure called "deconstruction" to unravel the significance of linguistic terms within a text. These are not easily translatable into clear conceptual definitions. We are instead confronted with metaphors, which are irreducible, full of ambiguities, nuances, and ironies. This would seem to undermine any program of logical clarification thought to be necessary for philosophical or scientific truth to advance.

Lyotard believes that science is only one form of knowledge and that we also use parables, myths, and narratives to convey truths. He doesn't think that it is possible to develop unifying narratives. He wishes to avoid any metanarratives of emancipation. The Enlightenment desire to liberate humankind from superstition and myth is a hopeless dream. Instead we are left with the fragmentation of language, of time, technology, the human subject, and society. There is a decline in the earlier liberal optimism of the modern period.

It would be impossible in this brief survey of modern philosophy to do justice to the richness of the skeptical themes running throughout. I wish to focus on only one kind of skepticism in the rest of this chapter, namely, pragmatism, especially since it leads to the third kind of skepticism. This new form of skepticism is selective, constructive, and positive, and it relates doubt to the process of inquiry.

Pragmatism

The American pragmatists drew from the traditions of skepticism, empiricism, and rationalism. They reformulated the role of skepticism in the development of knowledge. They rejected "solipsistic" or "subjectivistic" skepticism, for they maintained that it is based on a false mind/body dualism and on questionable psychological grounds. The concept of "mind," "self," or "the ghost in the machine," is the nexus of the problem. Rather, the pragmatists took Darwin seriously by biologizing thought, consciousness, or awareness, as a function of the organism, not as an inner two-dimensional entity. Using holistic concepts, they argued that the organism behaves as an integrated agent that interacts in the real world. Ideas, impressions, and perceptions are manifestations of behavioral processes. "Mind" emerges over a long period of biological evolution. Language is a form of behavior, playing an instrumental role in social interactions. Human powers and abilities evolved because of their adaptive role in human survival.

Given this background, the function of doubt is equally transformed. It is not a subjective state of an isolated mind immersed in a sea of indecision and abstracted from its environment, but a form of behavior, an organic irritant stimulating deliberative conduct. Similarly, belief spills out into action and is not separate from it; it is transformed into explicit plans of action; and it takes on meaning in fields of dynamic interaction. Of special significance to skepticism is the fact that doubt initiates inquiry and leads to the formation of belief.

Charles Sanders Peirce (1839–1914), the founder of Pragmatism, makes this interpretation clear in his celebrated essay, "The

Fixation of Belief,"[33] "The object of reasoning," he says, "is to find out from the consideration of what we already know, something else which we do not know. . . . Reasoning is good if it be such as to give a true conclusion from true premises." In this process we seek beliefs in order to "guide our desires and shape our actions." There is a difference between the sensation of believing and that of doubting. "Doubt is an uneasy and dissatisfying state from which we struggle to free ourselves and pass into the state of belief." Both doubt and belief thus have positive therapeutic value for us. Indeed, a "real and genuine doubt" is not a feigned doubt, but a precursor to genuine belief. Thus unlike the doubt of a Pyrrhonist or a Cartesian, a skeptical inquirer's doubt is not simply a theoretical state but an actual behavioral expression that he or she seeks to resolve. It is the "irritation of doubt" that stimulates "a struggle to attain a state of belief." This initiates a process of inquiry, the sole aim of which is the attainment of belief and "the settlement of opinion." Accordingly, for Peirce doubting is not a schizophrenic-like state of total indecision, but is continuous with selective and directive forms of behavior. Here, human inquirers seek to achieve a purpose: the overcoming of quandary and confusion by formulating beliefs upon which they may with some confidence act. Peirce makes it clear that he is not talking simply about the internalized beliefs of the private person, but with fixing beliefs in a community of inquirers.

In his essay, Peirce investigates the most effective way of fixing beliefs. There are various methods that have been used: tenacity (where we cling to old habits and beliefs), authority (defined by political or ecclesiastical powers), a-priori methods (based on pure reason or metaphysics). These all fail in the long run, he says. The most effective way of fixing beliefs is "the method of science," i.e., the inductive/deductive method of establishing hypotheses and testing them experimentally. The scientific mode of inquiry and inference in the long run succeeds better than the others because its claims are tested by reference to "some external permanency," i.e., by reference to "real things," independent of any subjective

---

33. Charles Peirce, "The Fixation of Belief," in *Popular Science Monthly,* 1878.

opinion of the human mind. The scientific method is most effective because its hypotheses are verified publicly in their own terms. Where it has been used, a whole body of reliably tested beliefs have been formulated and incorporated into the encyclopedia of human knowledge. Unlike the other methods for establishing truth claims, the methods of scientific inquiry are self-corrective, open to further revision or elaboration in the light of effective inquiry.

Other pragmatists, such as John Dewey (1859–1952) tried to show that the methods of science were not esoteric, available only to specialists, but were commonly present in ordinary modes of thinking. Thinking, says Dewey, is a response to problematic situations. Its purpose is to resolve existential problems. Our ideas function as instruments of behavior, not as representations of reality. Hypotheses introduced in the course of inquiry are judged by their observed consequences. This entails an essential role for doubt, for it is the means by which we pose questions and attempt to answer them. Pragmatism, accordingly, draws upon skepticism, but only in its constructive and positive form. Of special significance is the fact that the pragmatists were critics of the attempt to find absolute truth or absolute certainty.

Peirce clarifies this by his famous principle of fallibilism, which is not a metaphysical doctrine, but a rule of inquiry. The first rule of reason (particularly as applied to philosophy) is, "Do not block the way of inquiry."[34] An unpardonable offense in reasoning is to set up barricades to an advance toward the truth. We should not make "absolute assertions" or maintain that "this, that, and the other can never be known." We should not restrict inquiry by claiming that one element of science is "basic," "ultimate," "independent of aught else," or "utterly inexplicable." Nor should we assert that "this or that law or truth has found its last and perfect formulation." The principle of fallibilism therefore casts out any "absolute certainty, exactitude, and universality."

Peirce applied this principle to revelation. We cannot be absolutely certain that such deliverances are genuinely inspired from

---

34. "Notes on Scientific Philosophy," from *Collected Papers of Charles Sanders Peirce,* vol. 1, ed. by Charles Hartshorne and Paul Weiss (Cambridge: Harvard University Press, 1931).

On High; and even if inspired, we cannot be sure that the claims are true. They may be subject to human distortion and coloring. Moreover, such inspirations are generally so incomprehensible in nature as to suggest that they may not have been accurately apprehended. Peirce similarly doubts the absolute certainty of the axioms of geometry, principles of logic, and the maxims of causality; for the historical claims to inviolable truths were subsequently seen to have been mistaken. The fact that new geometries have been developed to replace classical Euclidean geometry undermined the previously held firm convictions of mathematicians that they had discovered the eternal structure of space. Peirce admits that we cannot deny that two plus two is equal to four, and he does not deny that men can attain sure knowledge of the creation of their own minds. Thus he says that we may have certainty about a statement concerning the system of numbers that is our own creation, but that no formal system is beyond error. He also denies that we can have complete certainty concerning questions of fact, for our observations may be mistaken. The appeals to direct experience cannot escape our doubt, for individuals are often confronted by delusions, hallucinations, and dreams, and we still may question the certainty of what presents itself. Peirce thus concludes that there is no aspect of human knowledge that cannot be questioned or considered to be infallible.

One aspect of pragmatism that bears special attention is its emphasis on *method*. The fundamental historic problem of epistemology—to try to penetrate the veil of perception and plumb the nature of reality—is considered to be illusory. On the contrary, the central issue is to delineate the methodology by which human intelligence and experience can cope with the world. Dewey held that the methods of scientific inquiry are the most reliable strategies for warranting claims to knowledge. These methods are continuous with those used in common everyday life as we attempt to solve problems. It was Dewey's belief that scientific methods could be extended to other areas of human concern, ethics, politics, and religion, all areas where we formulate judgments of practice.

Richard Rorty, in many ways the most influential pragmatist today, agrees with the pragmatistic critique of Philosophy, spelled with a capital *P*. In *Philosophy and the Mirror of Nature*,[35] he attacks the Cartesian-Lockean-Kantian tradition that is followed in epistemology and that seeks to discover a foundation for our knowledge of the external world. Rorty takes the core of pragmatism to be "its attempt to replace the notion of true beliefs as representations of the 'nature of things' and instead to think of them as successful rules of action." He differs, however, with those who emphasize the continuity of methods. He is willing to "recommend an experimental, fallibilistic attitude" toward knowledge, but he says that it is hard to isolate a " 'method' that will embody this attitude."[36] Rorty is thus critical of Dewey, and of Dewey's student Sidney Hook, for attempting to bring the scientific method to bear throughout culture. This he thinks unfortunately smacks of "scientism," a concept also roundly attacked by post-modernist critics.

There are thus two different contemporary conceptions of pragmatism. The first attempts to relate inquiry to the objective and experimental methods of scientific intelligence. The second, defended by Rorty, maintains that this is not possible and that what we need is a holistic, poetic, and metaphorical approach to knowledge. Rorty thus is skeptical, in the final analysis, of the pragmatic attempt to reconstruct knowledge by using the methods of scientific inquiry. He abandons this quest for the insight and vision of the literary approach. He agrees with Dewey and Hook's nonideological liberalism, but he does not think, for example, that we can use experimental methods to justify the liberal democratic way of life. He thus would appear to arrive at a subjectivistic viewpoint not unlike classical skepticism.

Sidney Hook (1902–1989), perhaps better than anyone, defends the objectivist approach to knowledge. Hook described his philosophy as experimental or pragmatic naturalism. He thought that the term *experimental* was appropriate in the sense that it emphasized the fact that ideas must be tested by their experimental

---

35. Richard Rorty, *Philosophy and the Mirror of Nature* (Princeton: Princeton University Press, 1979).

36. Richard Rorty, "Pragmatism Without Method," in Paul Kurtz, ed., *Sidney Hook: Philosopher of Democracy and Humanism* (Buffalo, N.Y.: Prometheus Books, 1983).

consequences. Like Rorty and Dewey, he was critical of "the quest for Being," an effort to penetrate transcendental realism beyond experience. But he cautioned that experimentalism did not imply any kind of universal skepticism. It employed doubt, but only in the contexts of scientific inquiries. Hook believed that we are able to derive reliable knowledge about the world and human affairs. In the broadest sense, pragmatic naturalism for him was a philosophy that "holds that the logic and ethics of scientific method can and should be applied to human affairs."[37] Hook held that one can frame warranted assertions about values as well as facts and that it is possible to gain objective knowledge not only about "the best means available to achieve your ends . . . but also about the best ends in the problematic situation in which the ends are disputed or become objects of conflict."[38] Hook thus believed that there are some criteria of objectivity that can be used in testing all claims to knowledge. "Unless there is some appeal to evidence or argument that has universal validity—call it reason or science or common sense—there is no more ground for accepting these criticisms than for rejecting them."[39] Here Hook, like Dewey, is interpreting "scientific" in a broad, not narrow, sense, as continuous with critical thinking, used in common sense and examplified in the scientific disciplines. Thus for Hook there is a "common pattern of inquiry" that is applicable to all fields of study in which claims to truth about the world are made. This applies to the natural and social sciences, history, politics, and ethics. Hook agreed with Dewey's statement that "scientific" signifies "the existence of systematic methods of inquiry which, when they are brought to bear on a range of facts, enable us to understand them better and to control them more intelligently."[40] This commitment to science as the model is an expression of naturalism, the philosophy that maintains that "all human knowledge is scientific knowledge."[41]

---

37. Sidney Hook, *Pragmatism and the Tragic Sense of Life* (New York: Basic Books, 1974), p. 7.

38. Ibid., p. ix.

39. Ibid.

40. Ibid., p. xii.

41. Sidney Hook, *The Quest for Being and Other Studies in Naturalism* (New York: St. Martin's Press, 1961), p. 216.

This statement is not simply a historical description of what we consider knowledge to be, but a *normative* proposal that the methods of scientific inquiry as broadly conceived serve as an ideal by which we may evaluate claims to knowledge.

Hook does not take scientific method to be a rigorous set of rules or simple recipes to follow; nor is it limited to the hard sciences and alien to common sense; on the contrary, he finds it to be embedded in the ways in which we ordinarily act, reason, and function in practical affairs. This approach is not unsympathetic to Thomas Kuhn's critique of *the* scientific method, for it recognized the impact of cultural and societal influences historically on scientific inquiries. But Hook rejected the epistemological anarchism in the philosophy of science of Paul Feyerabend, because he maintained that there are *some* objective criteria that we use in appraising truth claims and that knowledge is not simply a matter of taste, caprice, or the slave of the intellectual fashions of the day. Hook maintained that "there are working truths on the level of practical living which are everywhere recognized." This conception of rationality is not limited to Western culture, for science simply refines the canons of rationality and intelligibility "involved in the arts and crafts of men."[42] This method of inquiry is not justified deductively, nor is it simply assumed as an article of faith; it is tested comparatively by reference to its achievement earned over a long period of human history and by its effective contributions to the growth of reliable knowledge.

Skeptical Inquiry

The account above is not intended to be an exhaustive review of the history of skepticism, but has been introduced only to pave the way for what I consider to be a new, more meaningful, and justifiable skepticism. Thus, for want of a better name, I have called this "skeptical inquiry." This skepticism is essential in any quest for knowledge or deliberative valuational judgment. But it is limited and focused, selective, and positive, and it is part and parcel of a genuine process of inquiry. This form of modified

42. Ibid., p. 173.

skepticism is formulated in the light of the following considerations:

First, there has already been an enormous advance in the sciences, both theoretically and in technology. This applies to the natural, biological, social, and behavioral sciences. The forms of classical skepticism of the ancient world that reemerged in the early modern period were unaware of the tremendous potential of scientific research. Pyrrhonistic skepticism is today invalidated, because there now exists a considerable body of reliable knowledge. Accordingly, it is meaningless to cast all claims to truth into a state of utter doubt. The same considerations apply to post-modernist subjectivism, or Rorty's pragmatism, which I believe is likewise mistaken.

Second, contrary to skeptical doubts, there are methodological criteria by which we are able to test claims to knowledge: (a) empirical tests based upon observation, (b) logical standards of coherence and consistency, and (c) experimental tests in which ideas are judged by their consequences. All of this is related to the proposition that it is possible to develop and use objective methods of inquiry in order to achieve reliable knowledge.

Third, we can apply skeptical inquiry to many areas. Thorough-going investigations of paranormal claims can only be made by means of careful scientific procedures. Religious claims, using biblical criticism, the sciences of archaeology, linguistics, and history, have today given us a basis for skeptical criticism of the appeals to revelation and theories of special creation.

Fourth, we have long since transcended cultural relativism in values and norms and are beginning to see the emergence of a global society. Thus extreme cultural subjectivity is no longer valid, for there is a basis for transcultural values. There is also a body of tested prima facie ethical principles and rules that may be generalizable to all human communities.

Therefore, the methods of skeptical inquiry can be applied to the political and economic domain in which we frame judgments of practice. Indeed, it is possible to develop a eupraxophy, based on the most reliable knowledge of the day, to provide a generalized interpretation of the cosmos and some conceptions of the good life.

Fifth, doubt plays a vital role in the context of ongoing inquiry.

It is, however, selective, not unlimited, and contextual, not universal. The principle of fallibilism is relevant. We should not make absolute assertions, but be willing to admit that we may be mistaken. Our knowledge is based upon probabilities, which are reliable, not ultimate certainties or finalities.

Sixth, skeptical inquirers should always be open-minded about new possibilities, unexpected departures in thought. They should always be willing to question or overturn even the most well-established principles in the light of further inquiry. The key principle of skeptical inquiry is to seek adequate evidence and reasonable grounds for any claim to truth in any context of inquiry.

Part Two

Inquiry and Objectivity

Chapter 3

Beyond the
Egocentric Predicament

In this chapter I would like to enter into a detailed critique of classical skepticism in its nihilistic and mitigated forms. These theories are basically flawed, I submit, because of their questionable assumptions. The underlying quandary of skeptics, from Pyrrho and Sextus down to Descartes and Hume, is the "egocentric predicament." Because they cannot get outside of the sticky stuff of experience, they claim that we are locked within an inner world of ideas. Although both negative and neutral skeptics claim to offer no metaphysical theory, they actually presuppose a highly elaborate theoretical interpretation of the nature of experience and its relationship to the world. The foes of all idle speculative philosophizing, such skeptics seek to refute abstract metaphysics, but they do so by postulating their own speculative doctrines. The skeptic's desperate conclusion that no knowledge is possible and that ultimate reality is unknowable is itself a product of a process of theoretical reasoning. Complete skepticism, I submit, rests upon a mistake: for the skeptic has psychologized knowledge and reduced the world to subjectivity.

The Pyrrhonists begin their philosophical quest by analyzing knowledge. They ask, What can we say we know about the world? But they begin their quest by assuming their first principle: that the basic building blocks of knowledge are subjective appearances, impressions, images, ideas, sensations, perceptions, or thoughts. It is this initial given that is most questionable. For if I analyze my experiences of everyday life, I am not aware of appearances as flat, two-dimensional entities. Vision is pivotal to the skeptics' interpretation of knowledge, and thus their phenomenological world is based upon appearances; but surely these are not the only kind of reports that we get about the external world. There are sounds and smells, bumps and screeches, a wide range of diverse interactions that we have with the brute world. Thus we do not begin primarily with screenlike, flat phantasms of what's out there. My first intimations of reality confirm that it is a three-dimensional pluralistic world of different objects, people, and events that intrude upon me, my awareness, and my conduct. The stuff of experience is thus not comprised of slabs of appearances.

It is true that I can close my eyes and allow my memory and reverie to take hold. I can dream while awake or asleep and I can imagine or think of things not now present in my phenomenological given. Fantasies can excite and arouse me. But still, one must be impressed by the fact that there are things out there outside my window, or in here in my office, that press upon me and that I cannot avoid. I live in a world that I do not passively apprehend, but encounter in an active mode of response.

The earliest exchange that a baby has with the world is when she feels pangs of hunger and these are relieved by sucking furiously at the nipple of a breast or a bottle. In the beginning is the *act*, not the appearance of a fact; and in the first instance, it is eating and consuming, urinating and defecating. The baby first reacts to the world by grabbing something warm and delicious in her mouth, squeezing hard and sucking the fragrant milk. How satisfying it is. My infant granddaughter, Anne, smells, sees, and hears people and things in and around her crib. She learns early how to touch and feel these strange objects and persons, and in time to grasp and hold onto them. She coos contentedly as she is fondled affectionately. Her diapers are changed and she loves to be bathed in warm water. In time she learns to crawl around in her newly discovered rich world of adventure and delight. She learns to sit up and to stand, to jump out of her crib, to walk, and to run through the room. As Anne is held, she grasps tightly to those of us who provide loving care. She is introduced to new foods—cereals, fruits, vegetables, and meat. The world throughout is permeated with objects and things that she needs to consume or use. She is dressed, but soon learns to dress herself and to put on her shoes. She plays with toys and rocks her doll in a carriage. She learns to ride a tricycle. She falls and bleeds, is bandaged, and is healed. She loves to go for rides in the car. She is tightly strapped in the car seat so as not to get banged or injured. Anne's world is a world of doing and acting, of stimuli and her responses to them. She cries out in distress and her needs are satisfied; but she has to actively engage in a process with what's out there and bring it into her zone of attention and reaction. Her senses are coordinated. If a thing she sees stimulates her she can confirm what it is by squeezing it, putting it in her mouth, or trying to bounce it. There are many ways of affirming what she has encountered. She soon learns what is expected of her by those within her social group: to make her bed and straighten her room, to study her lessons, to learn how to read out loud, perhaps to play the piano or to sing and dance. Her conduct in the world is modified and channeled by those around her.

Language is crucial in the process: for signs, words, and symbols are used to point to objects or to express moods, and when they are combined in sentences they enable her to interpret the world, to order it, and to communicate her thoughts and feelings about it to others. Language takes Anne outside of any solipsistic prison, enabling her to share her world of beliefs, experiences, fears, and joys. Language transports her to an intersubjective community of shared meanings and realities.

What is basic to living and learning how to behave and function in the world is a recognition that one must actively interact or transact (as John Dewey has described it)[1] with the world. There are many modes to describe this dynamic process. It is a world in which a person actively participates: experiences, manipulates objects and makes, consumes, uses, or discards them, engages in

---

1. John Dewey, *Experience and Nature* (Chicago: Open Court, 1925; revised edition, 1929).

conduct, moves about, carries out tasks, enacts, and creates.

The key point that I want to emphasize is the double-barreled inner/outer, subjective/objective character of our experienced world. The mistake of nihilistic and mitigated skeptics is to abstract themselves and their experiences from the world as the first premise. A person does not begin with the "I," "me," "ego," "mind," or "self." Actually the sense of one's own personal identity comes later, as the child matures and becomes aware of himself or herself as a being separate and distinct from others. The life world, then, is multi-polar. It involves objects and persons, activities and processes. It is not a static world of mute essences or abstract appearances, but is a rich world chock full of diversity. In this world there can be little doubt that objects exist; and they are not simply independent of me, for I am dependent upon them. Without this piece of bread, this glass of water, the clothing on my back, or the roof over my head, I could not survive. Thus the philosophical problem of the "existence of the external world" is a hollow problem: for it is the first premise of my life. And it is not a pure postulate of animal faith, as George Santayana thought,[2] but a brute fact of my existing as a living being. It is forced upon me. I invade the world and am invaded by it. For the baby, the mother and father who hold, kiss, rock, bathe, and feed her are essential for her existence. How can one possibly say that realism is an "unproved assumption"? On the contrary, to deny reality flies in the face of everything we know or learn about the world.

Thus, the response to the nihilistic and mitigated skeptics' challenge is that they do not draw upon direct experience, but interpose an abstract postulation based on a speculative psychological construct. "Appearances," "ideas," "phenomena," "sense data" are arrived at after the act, not antecedent to it. The quandary of these skeptics is their inability to break out of their isolated boxes, for they have built their own chambers from which they cannot emerge. Here, the skeptic is like a spider who has woven a fine web and cannot disentangle itself from it. For these skeptics, there is no

---

2. George Santayana, *Skepticism and Animal Faith* (New York: Scribners, 1923).

world beyond or independent of themselves. But the spider weaves her net to catch insects in order to consume them. These skeptics have nets that they apprehend, but never can use. They are like autistic children or schizophrenics, fixated on their own inner soliloquies, unable to fathom or relate to others in the world; they are out of touch with facticity.

The complete or neutral skeptic responds, "Whatever I know must be known to me in terms of internalized ideas or perceptions. How do I know that these correspond to or describe what's out there? Perhaps I have colored my world by my own subjective juices. How can I possibly know what objective reality is separate and distinct from what I have added to the process?" And he or she might further ask, "If activity is our chief means of contact with the outer world, and is not reducible to two-dimensional perceptual reports, then how does the act relate to the fact? Is there not an equivalent *act-centric* predicament; that is, how relate the external world to my sphere of actions?" A fair question that needs careful analysis, for although I think we may safely reject total and neutral skepticism, some residual skepticism may still remain about the nature of the external world beyond our active intercourse with it.

Permit me to establish three salient points in response: First, there is a real world of material objects, events, living things, persons, and processes. Second, I interact with and depend upon this world of objects, events, things, persons, and processes for my survival. Third, these objects, events, things, persons, and processes interact with each other independent of me, and their interactions impinge on my life-world. Volcanoes erupt, birds fly in flocks, other people pursue their separate goals, and planets follow their course around the sun impervious to my cares or concerns.

Thus realism is essential to my mode of acting in the world and is not merely assumed. It is the jumping off point from which all science and philosophy begins. It is not simply presupposed or feigned, but is the necessary material-existential stage upon which I live and function.

This world has at least three components: (1) Myself as a subject and other human subjects within my face-to-face community of interactions. I cannot survive without others. Thus there is an intersubjective community of persons with whom I communicate and am involved. (2) A world of inanimate material objects, and other animate biological systems and beings. (3) Relationships between these and active transactions based on various forms of praxis or conduct.

Now this theory of human experience is a behavioristic theory. For we are behaving beings actively functioning in the world. We do not passively apprehend the world in isolation. I differ with Berkeley when he argued that "to be is to be perceived," and Descartes in his effort to reduce his knowledge of himself to his inner cogito. I say that "to be" is for us to be related in some essential way to a wide range of "behavioral interactions": seeing, eating, micturating, copulating, hearing, moving, using, manipulating, and so on. This doesn't mean that things in the world do not exist separate from my behavioral actions, but only that my actions impinge upon them and are impinged by them.

The Newtonians maintained that there is a real world of physical objects. Material science is only concerned with primary qualities, i.e., those properties of things in the external world that can be measured and weighed. All secondary qualities are dependent upon the perceiver and are beyond scientific understanding. Modern philosophers have puzzled about this distinction. Are primary qualities, the physical objective properties of things, different from or independent of secondary qualities? Are the subjective qualities dependent on some perceiver? Berkeley argued that some perception in a person's experience is necessary for one to know anything about anything.[3] He concluded that all qualities, including primary qualities, were secondary. If perception is a necessary condition for our knowledge of any quality, is it also sufficient? In one sense we can never talk about anything that transcends our perceptions or experiences of it. But Berkeley mistakenly inferred from this that "to be is to be perceived." There is a leap in the argument from a necessary condition to a necessary *and* sufficient condition.

We can turn the tale around. We can maintain that we cannot perceive (as distinct from dream or fantasize in the imagination)

---

3. George Berkeley, *A Treatise Concerning the Principles of Human Knowledge* (1710), and *Three Dialogues Between Hylas and Philonous* (1713).

anything unless it has some real content in the external world; that is, for perceptions to make sense there must be some object of perception that stimulates it. Some objective external thing is a necessary condition for my perception. But I do not conclude by this that to be is to be an objective reality entirely independent of perceptual (inductive) or ideational (deductive), or behavioral ("act-ductive") content. Process is the stuff of our world. But this does not reduce our world to pure acts in isolation, for they involve real objects and events out there *and* our active experiential, interactive contact with them. Activity is at least bipolar. It involves an agent and objective(s). It is actually multi-polar, for it involves many agents in the intersubjective or transsubjective community and many diverse objects in the context of intercourse.

What is really central for the biological organism is the concept of a *field,* a frame of reference, or a context. For we enter into different contextual situations and we transact in different ways and on different levels. The squirrel consumes the acorn, which if it could philosophize, it could never doubt exists. I deal with my cat as I feed her milk. I have intercourse with my sweetheart or wife, and I ride a roller coaster, lecture before a class of students, or lead an army in war. One can build a dam, take a jet to Nairobi or a spaceship to the moon, or view the galaxies through a telescope or a cell through a microscope. These contexts of transaction all have different dimensions. Moreover, we pursue diverse activities for different purposes: love, rivalry, adventure, creativity, excitement, learning, knowledge.

The point is, there is a real world out there, but we interact, modify, or interpret it in different ways in terms of our contexts or fields of behavior. But the world does not evaporate into, nor is it totally assimilated by, a person's action. Reality is not equivalent to activity; activity presupposes a real world independent of oneself. It is that which exists and causally interacts with other things, separate and distinct from an individual. It is that which continues to exist for an intersubjective community of observers, experimenters, and actors independently of oneself. And it is that which endures and functions in some sense independent of my activities. My activities do not consume the field in which I roam or romp, although my activities are the ways that I can discover what is or would be in the field if I were not there. The real is that which exists or would exist if I were not around, but I could say little about it if I did not observe, study, probe, manipulate, or use it.

Classical skepticism was developed before the advent of movies, television, or radio, all of which enable us to understand the difference between a two-dimensional and a three-dimensional world. Moreover, it was developed before the advent of brain surgery and modern neuroscience. We know full well today that psychological functions can be correlated to brain geography and chemistry and that the stimulation of the brain can cause the stimulation of the consciousness. It is highly unlikely that the self exists separately from the brain and nervous system.

The skeptic will no doubt reply that we still have a problem of relating brain function to the external object. We begin with objects in common experience: by analysis we soon learn that the flower in the garden is known by me only by means of a complex process of causality. Light bounces off the flower; the light then strikes my retina and is recorded by my brain. How do I know that the picture of a flower that I have in my brain is equivalent to the actual flower out there? What exactly is the *ding-an-sich* (thing in itself)? asks Kant. How relate the data of phenomena to the hidden noumenal reality? If I ask, Is that a lilac in the garden? I can look at it in the light, whiff its fragrance, stoop down and touch it, pluck it and hold it in my hand, or throw it and allow it to gently waft down in the breeze. I can take it into my laboratory and place it under a microscope and scan its structure. Or I can give it to my cat to suckle on. I have many ways of relating to a lilac. If I am uncertain, I can call my wife to corroborate whether or not there is a lilac in the garden. I can ask a botanist to classify it, or go to the garden shop with my specimen and inquire whether it is a pansy or a lilac. There are a whole series of behavioral interactions that I can engage in with the flower. I water it daily and fertilize it from time to time. I can gather lilacs together and present a bouquet to my wife as a reminder of my love. I may describe, define, classify, or photograph it for a book that I am writing. Or I may simply enjoy its fragrance and beauty on its own terms.

So I may safely conclude that there is a real world, and that it contains lilacs. It is not a vacuous world of appearances, but an objective world containing, at the very least, delicate, fragrant, beautiful lilacs. There is no imponderable subjective/objective dualism that I cannot bridge. I am not locked into my inner self, or ego. My world is not a bundle of sensations unrelated to one another, without rhyme or reason. For I learn very quickly that there are some things that I can and cannot do, and that there are limits imposed upon my actions. I cannot plant lilacs in the winter snow and expect them to sprout. If I plant them in the shady part of my backyard with insufficient sunlight, they will most likely languish and perhaps wither and die. And there are many potential properties that lilacs possess. If I fertilize them often they will bloom gloriously, though they need to be pruned to have the fullest growth. We learn that the world is not only objectively populated by flowers and other things, but that these things have causal relationships, that some things will or will not happen, and that there are certain things that we can and cannot do.

The question emerges, How do I know that what I claim to know about the thing out there is really true? Is my knowledge a real and accurate description, or is it only contrived? This raises the basic question of critical realism, a topic perennially debated in philosophy. Perception is only *one* of the many ways that I can relate to the world of objects. But philosophers have been troubled by the question of whether that which is perceived is the same as that revealed in the act of perception, whether there are limits to what we can perceive, and whether we can know anything beyond the range of our perceptions.

John Locke was a skeptic about the extent of knowledge. He thought that we could not know the "real nature" of an object. Take an orange, for example. What we know about it may be interpreted by our experiential contact with it. We can see, smell, taste, touch, buy, sell, peel, squeeze, mash, cut, play catch with it, or drink its juice. For Locke, the primary qualities of an object were its objective physical properties. Its secondary qualities depended upon us for their content, but these were also caused by the powers that the object had. These presumably were resident in its underlying material substratum. Locke did not think we could know its innermost structure. But he lived before the full application of the microscope and the increase in its magnitude. We know full well that there is a cellular, molecular, atomic, subatomic structure, and that this is physical-chemical. Physicists, chemists, and microbiologists have attempted to unravel the physical-chemical structure of living things. In Locke's day the atomic theory was purely conjectural. In later centuries, as science evolved, the atomic theory was viewed as a theoretical construct that provided some help in explaining and predicting physical processes. This has now been confirmed by laboratory experiments. We can bombard particles, view their effects in the laboratory, and simulate their behavior by means of computer technology.

What does the atomic theory do to our own conception of the world? We observe galaxies and stars, mountains and oceans, plants and animals. Are they real as we view them, or are they really *only* microscopic collocations, swarms or fields of particles and energy? If we had microscopic vision, would the planet Earth and all that is on it reduce simply to microentities with vast amounts of space between them? Should we become reductionists and insist that all that exists are fields of energy, microparticles, and their interactions?

This would be rather paradoxical. For we begin with the world on the macro-level, as we transact with it and as we analyze it in the physical laboratory. Do we end up saying that our theories disconfirm that anything exists on the macro-level? The answer to the reductionist is to say that *things exist on many levels and in many ways* on the micro- and macro-levels. To be is not simply to be an atom or subatomic particle in motion; for there are different ways in which things in nature are organized and function. There are systems of material objects: oceans and planets, birds and feathers, lilacs and plants, vassals and kings, religious and social institutions, human passions and dreams. This is the stuff of which things are made. I am here offering a contextual interpretation of nature. What is real for us—*the properties that we observe—depends on the context of inquiry and the purposes of our transactions with nature.* The physical-chemical-material structure is primary in the sense that the orange would not exist as a thing without it. If we destroy or transform it by making orange juice or orange marmalade and consuming it, it would disappear. But to say that about the orange is not to complete the tale, for it is more than that. It is the product of a living system, an orange tree, and it serves a function. If the seeds of its fruit fall to the ground and one of them takes root in the soil, in time, under proper conditions, it would sprout and become another orange tree. The tree sheds millions of seeds, most of which are wasted. A human male ejaculates billions of sperm, only a few of which in a lifetime may impregnate an egg, develop into a fetus, and eventuate into a human being. So the orange can be viewed from a biological context: it is the ways in which this organic physical-chemical matter can grow, develop, and reproduce itself that tell us something about the tree that we would not know otherwise.

The orange on the tree has any number of accidental properties, not essential to its nature. It can be picked by birds, or consumed by worms, or plucked by humans and given a price, sold to supermarkets, bought by a consumer to be peeled and eaten at some dinner table. The objects in nature are so varied and diverse that I am suggesting a pluralistic approach to understanding what we encounter. But let us return to a central question of classical philosophy. If we focus only on the passively viewed act of perception and not the many other types of interaction, is the orange as perceived exactly the same as it is independent of perception? The naive realist thinks it is. He claims that what we see or what appears to us is as it really is. But this view is difficult to sustain: for it is not the orange per se that enters into our heads, but an image of it. What we see is a product of a process of perceptual involvement. Light photons from the object are recorded on our retina, and information is transmitted to our nervous system and brain. This information is then interpreted in the form of a message that assumes the form of an orange.

But we can ask, Is the photograph of the orange the same as the orange? Of course not. What about a movie rendition? Again, no. The best that we can maintain is a form of *critical realism*; that is, that which is perceived is done so by means of our biological lenses, the focus, interpretations, and classifications that we give. All of our observations and transactions within nature thus depend upon the actors/agents and are not separable from us.

The central question in modern neurophysiology and psychology is thus raised: At what point does the brain become consciousness? In classical terms, What is the relationship between body and mind? Ever since the emergence of experimental psychology in the nineteenth century, scientists had hoped that by understanding the structure of the brain we could understand the higher processes of consciousness, including perception and thought. The brain is such an exceedingly complex neural network that this is still an elusive quest. Sir Charles Sherrington, in his Gifford Lectures, *Man on His Nature*,[4] confessed his inability to explain consciousness. He refers to a star that we perceive, and he traces the energy radiating from it and entering the eye. The light image of a star is found at the bottom of the eye. There is an ensuing photochemical action of the retina, and energy impulses travel across the nerve to the brain, where there are further electrical disturbances. But he says that how the star is perceived by the mind as an end result still remains a mystery.

Consciousness for Sherrington thus remained refractory to critical science and incomprehensible by it. The problem is that although we experience the outside world as a series of sensory objects, what actually is received by our senses is energy vibrations of different frequencies. These radiations trigger perceptual ideas in the brain. Neurophysiologists can study brain waves and electrical patterns. But can they understand, it is asked, how consciousness emerges? Some thinkers have thus postulated the existence of mind as separate from the body and have said that we can never understand consciousness by understanding brain structures and brain chemistry.

There are two separate questions here: first, the methodological question of how to best understand human behavior, including conscious psychological processes; and second, the nature and reality of the subject matter under scrutiny.

In answer to the first question, it may very well be and perhaps is the case that the reductionist model fails, i.e., we cannot hope to develop comprehensive laws on the micro-level to understand what emerges or is found on the macro-level. This seems to me to be an open question. We cannot say antecedent to inquiry

---

4. Sir Charles Sherrington, *Man on His Nature* (London, 1941).

whether this methodological approach will be entirely successful. I think that the best strategy is to utilize a coductive method of inquiry; indeed, that is what we employ. I have introduced the term "coduction" to describe how the behavioral and social sciences now seek to understand human behavior in its various dimensions.[5] There are levels of inquiry; we need to treat the observable data in its own terms. Thus psychology as the science of human behavior may not be reducible in toto to neurophysiology, though neurophysiology will no doubt assist us in understanding the preconditions of behavior. For example, whether we will be able to reduce anthropology or political science or economics to antecedent physical-chemical science on the micro-level seems highly unlikely, though lower-order explanations may indeed be useful. We ought to coduce explanations from a variety of levels, and this means that we should avoid the reductionist fallacy. The reductionist program in the last analysis is an article of faith. The reductionist hopes that it will be eventually fulfilled. Many exciting discoveries have been made in biogenetics that enable us to better understand human behavior. Coduction, however, seems to be a methodologically more convenient strategy, at least at this stage of inquiry, for it allows us to coduce explanations of both a reductionist and holistic type.

The second question should not be confused with the first. The fact that a reductionist scheme has not been as yet fully achieved does not mean that mind or consciousness can exist separate from the body or the brain. Some have made a leap in logic. For example, Arthur Eddington, James Jeans, and other phenomenalists sought to reduce all of reality to the stuff of ideas or mind. I submit the contrary: neural networks and brain mechanisms are real and they provide preconditions for our understanding nature. But the human being is an extremely complex biological organism capable of higher-order processes, although we do not understand fully how these occur.

Our discussion leads us to some skeptical conclusions. What we know is a function of our interactions within nature. What

---

5. See Paul Kurtz, *Decision and the Condition of Man* (Seattle, Wash.: University of Washington Press, 1968; New York: Dell Paperbacks, 1969).

is known is a function of both the agent and that which is known. There is a real world out there, which we may describe, classify, and explain on many levels of analysis and description. But we have no ultimate guarantee that the knower and the known are the same and/or that the known is known entirely independent of the knower. I deny that this reduces us to the total skepticism of the solipsist, who claims that we cannot disentangle ourselves from the egocentric predicament. Yet we are still left with a predicament of sorts: the act-centric predicament, the relationship of our actions to the external world and whether we may say that our description and/or explanations of nature are true. But this raises the further question, What is genuine knowledge and what is it about?

Chapter 4

Reliable Knowledge

Knowledge as True Belief Intersubjectively Corroborated

Is it possible to have reliable knowledge? Or is that which we claim to know reducible simply to illusion and self-deception? When Pyrrhonist skeptics analyze the basis of knowledge, they claim that it dissipates into sheer human presumption. Knowledge is like a house of cards, they say; by disturbing the foundations, the entire edifice topples. All knowledge, they conclude, is uncertain, untrustworthy, vacuous. There are *no* standards for judging truth, they insist; for all criteria collapse into human subjectivity.

Now I submit that although knowledge is relational, it need not be subjective. For there are effective criteria for judging claims to truth, and these are used throughout life. Knowledge is not about a fixed realm of essences; it does not give us ultimate truth; nor can it be understood entirely independent of the processes of investigation and discovery. As we have seen, knowledge is a product of a behavioral process of active inquiry. The verb *know* is more descriptive of the process than the abstract noun *knowledge*. *Knowing* has both a relational function and an objective referent. It is best viewed as a transactional concept. It involves a subject or subjects; that is, to say that we *know* something means un-

91

doubtedly that it is known by some conscious being or beings who are aware of, recognize, record, and respond to things in the world. It makes little sense to talk about knowledge in abstraction from living organisms and the behavioral activities and reactions to the objects and processes encountered within their fields of transaction. The knower is not passive. Knowledge is not simply a description of a picture of reality—though to be effective it must be based on, or at least not be completely out of touch with, the external world. Rather, it is an active affair of doing and exchanging. It is a means by which human beings fulfill their purposes and ends, and it is the most powerful tool of action that humans possess. Knowing thus has an instrumental function in human behavior. It is not simply an internalized state of awareness separate or distinct from its objective reference. Its content includes some indelible reference to that which is known. There are accordingly some objective anchors in the real world. This enables us to distinguish the dreams, fancies, and figments of our imagination from things objectively independent of the knower. It is true that in some sense it is the knower who may entertain dreams or illusions, but these have some causal basis within conscious experience. Although they are subjective psychological constructs, they may seem real within one's fantasies and have a profound effect upon one's outlook. But they are different from objective claims to knowledge that have some external referent.

To say that one has knowledge means that what one knows is true; and truth implies some knowledge about obdurate realities independent of the knower's wishes and desires. A useful distinction thus can be made between belief and knowledge. We may believe something to be true; but our beliefs may be false; and if so, they are not equivalent to knowledge. We may think that we have knowledge, but if our beliefs are false we are laboring under misapprehensions or harboring misconceptions. We may, for example, believe that it is snowing outside, but if it is not, we are mistaken. Only if these beliefs are found to be warranted independent of our beliefs do we possess knowledge. Thus knowledge refers only to those items of a person's or a community's beliefs *that have been found to be justified by adequate grounds*. A true belief is equivalent to knowledge when the claim made on its behalf is supported by evidence and reasons. A belief is any state or habit of mind in which we affirm that something is the case. To believe something is to be convinced or persuaded that it is true. To believe something is to affirm that there is an actual fact to which we can respond. A belief is something upon which we are prepared to act.

There is a difference, however, between believing *that something is the case,* as a descriptive assertion about nature or the world or ourselves, and believing *in something* as a prescriptive commitment to ideals. I may believe that the isles of the Caribbean Sea generally have warm weather and sunshine year-round. Whether this is true or false will depend upon direct visits by myself or others, the testimony of people who live there, or the careful studies of meteorological charts. But this is somewhat different from saying that I believe in free enterprise or socialism, which involves factual but also normative factors. We will defer consideration of belief *in* and concentrate upon belief *that.*

Many people may be convinced of their beliefs, but these beliefs may turn out to be false. I may believe that "Grandma's chicken soup will cure a common cold." Only careful testing will confirm or disconfirm that. If it does turn out to be the case, then I have a piece of information that is a part of the body of knowledge, and I could affirm that I know it for a fact because I can confirm its effectiveness empirically. The distinction between belief and knowledge is essential, for a large part of the body of beliefs that many or most people hold may be nothing more than illusions or fantasies and be simply untrue. Yet people may cling to their beliefs tenaciously, cherish and venerate them, especially in religion and metaphysics, even though they are patently false.

An important distinction must be made between beliefs that are irremediably subjective, inner, and private, and those that a person can communicate to others and thus have some inter-subjective interface. Some of our beliefs may be primarily intro-spective and personal in content and reference, such as those that I have experienced in my life-world that are uniquely my own. Since we live in a common world, however, most of our beliefs concerning objects or events in nature can be intersubjectively corroborated. If I claim that it is humid outside, it may be because I am perspiring. Yet, presumably, once I define the meaning of "humidity" in terms of standard measuring rods, anyone can consult a hygrometer to verify the claim and determine the percent of moisture in the air.

C. S. Peirce properly pointed out that we fix beliefs, at least in science, in a community of inquirers and not in a lone, inner solipsistic self. We share common experiences by means of trans-subjective standards of measurement and we develop independent criteria of verification. We often can get intersubjective agreement because the objective facts under experimental observation enable us to resolve the issue. Whether water boils at 100 degrees Centigrade and freezes at 0 degrees Centigrade can easily be resolved by establishing test conditions for the claim. Anyone who understands what we're talking about can enter into a public process of confirmation.

It is important here to focus on the concept of a *claim*. For in the world of social transactions, individuals often make claims and are asked to justify them. Thus we may assert that something is the case and that it should be acknowledged as true. But is it? Some people may believe that the earth is hollow and that UFOs use caverns in the center of our planet as landing bases. Science-fiction writers may have stimulated their fertile imaginations. Accordingly, a belief should be interpreted in the form of a claim, especially if it is a controversial belief. Here the burden of proof is placed upon the claimant to show why others should accept the belief as true. A key issue concerns the conditions under which we may resolve disagreements. Some claims are so poorly expressed that there may be no identifiable grounds under which we can ever confirm or deny them. If there are no conditions whatsoever by which they can be falsified, these claims are beyond the pale of truth and may be said to be virtually without content. At some point there must be some grounds specifically appealed to by which the claim may be considered to be adequately justified.

Knowledge, at least ideally, is true belief intersubjectively corroborated by reference to objective factors observed, examined, and tested. That an invisible pink rabbit is in constant communication with someone is difficult to deny or affirm, especially where there is elusive evidence, such as anecdotal testimony, adduced to support such a claim. A meaningful knowledge claim may be mistaken; but at least in principle it can be disconfirmed. We believe that something is the case and think that we *know* that it is, and moreover we think we can confirm it; for example, that Mike Tyson was heavy-weight champion, or that Mark Spitz won six Olympic Gold Medals for his swimming performance. Such knowledge claims have both an intersubjective source and an objective referent. What constitutes adequate grounds, evidence, or reasons for accepting a claim that a belief is true?

Firsthand Testimony

There are various conditions under which we say that we know something and that this knowledge is adequate. In its simplest form, when we say we know something, this is usually based on direct testimony as perceived and interpreted in someone's immediate experience. Here I am referring to "knowledge by acquaintance," the "having" of an immediate experience. For example, as I look outside my study, the sun is shining on the leaves, the birds are chirping and fluttering about, crickets are chanting, water drops fall now and then, a gentle breeze is floating in through the screen. The scene I view is not totally incoherent or confused, but has been filtered through my senses, is examined and manipulated by my behavior, and is interpreted by my understanding. I know the immediate world in the present context because of perceptions, conceptions, and behavioral interactions. What we encounter is both given and taken, perceived and used. It is confirmed by active processes of behavioral confrontation.

As a test case, I can hold up my hand and wiggle my fingers under the light from my lamp. They cast a shadow on the desk. All of these items of perception are evident through my senses. The pen grasped in my fingers moves over the white sheet emitting lines of blue ink; words appear in sequences. I rub my forehead, open and close my eyes. I hear children laughing, a dog barking, a car passing in the distance. In this context what I believe to be true describes an immediate world of encountered objects and events. If I am confused or unclear about any phase of the process, I can further corroborate it so as to avoid distortion. Are there really children laughing? I can go to the window and peer out and even call them. Is a dog really barking? Let me look and see; perhaps I can throw him some dog crackers. Did a car pass? If there is time perhaps I can still see it and even run after it. I can turn the light switch off and on to see if the shadows of my hand and fingers are still cast on my desk. I can pound my fist on the desk. Thus I can corroborate what I perceive with my senses with my activities and attempt to replicate the experiences.

How certain am I that the reports I receive are true? A "fact," as I have suggested, is not an isolated phenomenon sensed in abstraction, but is interfused with the acts that I can engage in to corroborate it. A *fact* is thus a *function of an act(s)*. Even in the realm of my immediate context of experience, I can call upon others to confirm what I believe to be present. "Jonathan," I can call to my son, "Who are those children out there laughing?" "Whose dog is barking?" "Is it beginning to rain?" And he might reply, "No, Dad, there are no children laughing or a dog barking. I think you are mistaken. I had the television set on. You must have heard that." Or, "It is not raining outside, Dad. I have the sprinkling system going on the lawn under your window."

Now extreme skeptics raise the question of the accuracy of knowledge, and whether we can be *certain* about anything; they deny that we can achieve certain knowledge; and so they end up in a state of indecision. But this can degenerate into a fetish, especially if pushed to its outer limits. For clearly we may be said to have knowledge in the immediate context of direct factual observation. But I may be mistaken about whether it is raining, the birds are chirping, a dog is barking, or children are playing and laughing outside. Usually I do not need others to corroborate these observed facts or to show whether my beliefs are veridical and present true knowledge. I can usually check for myself, and there are commonsense methods of doing so.

But I may run into problems if I am, for example, near-sighted, or color-blind, or schizophrenic, fearful and anxious, or possessed of a rich creative imagination ready to read into facts or events more than what is present. "Grandpa," asks my granddaughter later that day, "is that a wolf standing outside the window?" "No, darling," I reassure her, "it is a German shepherd from up the street."

For all intents and purposes, human beings are capable of

direct observation and correct interpretation of the world as immediately encountered. Observations are never simply pure or unaided. They are informed by knowledge. Information involves interpretation and naming. Feeling drops of water may be random to my cat, who runs away to seek shelter. They are raindrops to the keener human animal who is capable of more complex interpretations of the world. In principle, I may be mistaken about the immediate knowledge by acquaintance that I may have; therefore such experiences are corrigible. Yet at some point I can accept what is given with some degree of conviction after I have corroborated the facts: whether it is actually raining, my hand is casting a shadow, the birds are chirping, a car has rounded a corner, or children are laughing outside.

I do not see why we need to be mired in a state of suspended judgment about such elementary matters. For by means of a process of justification, I can find grounds to accept what I believe to be true, and I can state that it is known. This is based on the testimony of my own experience (provided I am normal and not psychotic or out of touch with reality). We cannot have absolute certainty about the present moment of observation, for we may be in error; but this does not mean that we may not have high degrees of certainty. G. E. Moore insisted that he was certain about the sense-data reports of his hand, which he was holding up to his face. I think it a mistake to break my hand down into an abstract bundle of "sense-data" reports. Yet I know that I have a hand and I can tell the difference between my elbow and a hole in the ground. To deny that we cannot know either or both is to make a mockery of life, and philosophical skepticism is reduced to playing semantic games.

A question has been raised about the status of our private or personal beliefs. It would surely be a problem here if we were to demand intersubjective behavioral corroboration for all of them. There are some kinds of personal knowledge that a person may wish to shield from others. We all wear masks, so to speak. Our hidden sexual fantasies, the things that turn us on, our love for another person, our ulterior motives, our deepest dreams, fears, and anxieties, these are rooted in a person's private life-world and tied up with past memories and future aspirations. They include our attacks of insomnia, gas pains, embarrassment at giving a public lecture, our first defeat at chess, and other personal adventures and traumas. These may even be deeply lodged in our subconscious. This issue is often debated as a conflict between introspection and behaviorism. The starting point of such knowledge is related to the probings of our interior life-worlds; but all of this, too, is related to what we do and has some connection to our behavioral states. These inner soliloquies have some behavioral correlations, causes and effects: they are not abstract, disembodied experiences, but are fused with our entire life-world of expectations and actions. Granted, they may be difficult to fathom, not only by our friends and colleagues, but even by ourselves, especially if self-deception is at work.

Thus far I have been focusing primarily on our knowledge of the present. But the present moment in one sense is indeed ephemeral, for like a flowing stream it rapidly eludes us. Another enduring feature of my life-world is my memory of the past—immediate, short, or long range—without which the present makes no sense. For I am constantly drawing upon past experiences, which, stored in my memories, are the bases from which I draw generalizations in the present and interpret the future. Some of my firsthand memories may remain intact and fairly accurate. I can recall vividly my first kiss, the great fun that I had during my first skiing adventure, the time I visited the Parthenon in Athens, how nervous I was in teaching my first class, and so on. Unfortunately, memory often fades and is distorted by wishes and desires and is devastated by time. Instant recall may become difficult as I get older. I may forget names and suppress unpleasant events. There may be degrees of certitude about some things in the past. I'm sure that Uncle Harry died in Newark, New Jersey, at age 57. I was there when it happened. I went to his funeral the next day. On the other hand, many events remain buried in my subconscious, and I am often deceived by the things I conveniently choose to forget. My wife seems to remember almost every detail of our life together. She embroiders these details with people, places, and things I have long since forgotten. I only remember the "big events," those that seem significant to me, or so I say. One way to keep our memories accurate is to keep a diary or a journal or notes of conversations and events. These help to corroborate what occurred. Or we can take photographs and collect newspaper stories about some events before they become part of the faded past. But we are all well aware that our memory may deceive us. We romanticize about the past, perhaps highlight the good parts and conveniently forget the bad (or vice versa, depending upon our personalities). Thus we need to be extremely wary about remembering "facts" of years past unless they can be corroborated. Some skepticism is a necessary component here, but it is contextual and not universal. Skeptics are surely mistaken when they deny the accuracy of historical events that have been duly recorded in writings or other notations of the past, such as on tombstones or monuments, for we can check the accuracy of descriptions of past events by careful investigation.

My memory bank of past events also includes the plans, projects, and resolves that I undertook in the past and whether or not I fulfilled them. I resolved to give up smoking, and I did; to stay on a diet, and I did not; to buy a house and repair it, which I did; to fix up a summer place at a lake, which I did not; to write a book and finish it, which I did; to relocate to a warmer climate, which I did not. Thus in the immediate context the present surges forward. There were expectations of future events, which I awaited with delight or foreboding and which I prepared for and made provisions for; other events were totally unexpected and surprising. I made some predictions that came true and others that were falsified by future events. I worked for Adlai Stevenson's election both times he was a presidential candidate. I resolved year-in and year-out to cut down a poplar tree, but never got around to it. I planned to put in a rock garden and I did, with gratification. I helped found a committee to defend academic freedom on campus, and another to defend the rights of a Canadian physician unjustly persecuted, which I did and which gave me immense satisfaction.

Thus awareness of a temporal past, present, and future are forever pressing on my consciousness, and I have knowledge about all three phases. My present observations are usually correct, though at times I have been mistaken; my memory of the past is sometimes accurate and sometimes in error; and my projections and predictions are sometimes right and sometimes wrong. Personal knowledge of this sort involves common sense, critical intelligence, and informed expectations based upon past experience.

We may ask, Are we always correct about our private soliloquies? The answer is yes and no. Sometimes friends and relatives can know us better than we know ourselves. They may have a kind of dispassionate objectivity that we lack about ourselves. Some people may be overly headstrong or eager to rush to hasty conclusions; others may be shy and reticent about themselves, given to self-condemnation; still others may be too pessimistic about their potentialities or overly exuberant about them. And sometimes objective bystanders, by observing our behavior and interpreting our language, can make fairer appraisals of our virtues or excesses than we can ourselves. Thus one goes to a psychiatrist, teacher, lawyer, or counselor for advice about what one should do. Moreover, we may lie to ourselves, and our behavior may better reveal our innermost feelings and wishes. Slips of the tongue or bizarre behavior may contradict our fondest illusions about ourselves. Other people may experience similar fears and delights that they can share with us, and thus help us to better interpret our true feelings and desires. Introspection is thus amenable to some objective interpretation by those about us; it is not closed to scrutiny. However, I will grant that, of all forms of human knowledge, that which is most immune to intersubjective corroboration may be the private idiosyncratic life-world of the individual, in spite of the best efforts of behavioristic interpretation to unravel its meaning.

Thus far I have been dealing primarily with firsthand testimony of one's experienced world as lived. This no doubt is the bedrock of our knowledge as it grows and functions. But our firsthand knowledge is constantly invaded and expanded by others on the intersubjective level. In the first instance, language is a social product. It takes us beyond and outside of our private worlds. We can share our knowledge with other people by a process of communication. Words are cultural vehicles by which two or more persons meet in the common framework of shared meanings. Language is not totally private, as Wittgenstein pointed out; if it were, it would make no sense. It provides a scaffolding from which we are able to peer into common meanings that we share with others and to which we may respond. The deconstructionists' breakdown of language into untranslatable metaphors is contradicted by the fact that we are able to communicate our feelings and thoughts to others. Symbols and signs are the products of culture: they are intersubjective. They enable us to arrive at a kind of knowledge that takes us beyond the limited perspective of our own space-time to secondhand and plural forms of testimony removed from our direct experience, that is, to indirect testimony by others.

Secondhand Testimony

If our knowledge were confined to our own direct fund of experience, past, present, and future, it would be sharply circumscribed and connected only to our own limited space-time biographical slab. Yet we are willing to make assertions about things with which we have not had any direct contact. I knew that Acapulco was a resort city on the Mexican coast, though I had never been there. Friends of ours visited the city for a week and reported on their vacation and the fact that they enjoyed it. Why should I accept what they tell me? Perhaps they exaggerated. Perhaps what they saw was enhanced by their own predilections. I visited the city myself later on and had a similar set of impressions. Both our visits were all too brief. Yet I may be willing to accept another person's testimony because I understand that if I duplicated his or her efforts my experiences might be the same. Thus the underlying premise, which is continually confirmed by my experiences, is that other individuals have experiences that, if I were in the same place, I could more or less replicate. Since I can't be everywhere at the same time, other people become my surrogates. Thus I am willing to defer to the eyewitness accounts of others.

Skeptics might ask, How do you know that what others see is the same as what you see—unless you can be wired into their brains? Perhaps what we experience is different. Yet, as I pointed out, we have common structures of language by means of which we can compare notes. We can and do communicate. We describe what we see, and we use common words. Descriptions of objects can be clarified by means of color words. This object is yellow and that is purple. And we have general conceptual models. We name objects and we teach the names to our children as we point and compare. We make generalizations from experience. We denote and classify; we discern similarities and differences, and we catalogue them. Moreover, we can interact in a common world. We play baseball with our friends, throw and catch the ball. What's "in here" must be correlated with what we experience "out there," or else we could not coordinate our movements and our responses. We are all functioning in related behavioral fields and we presuppose commonalities, shared objects and their properties within the range of our common endeavors.

Secondhand testimony often may be unreliable. Some people are farsighted while others are hard of hearing, so that without glasses or hearing aids they cannot distinguish clearly or distinctly. Still others may be color-blind or tone deaf. Eyewitness testimony may deceive us. Thus one must be very cautious about accepting eyewitness accounts unless they can be corroborated by other witnesses, and even then we need to exercise prudence, for they may all be mistaken. A half-dozen persons at the same accident may give contradictory reports. In the Japanese film *Rashomon,* widely differing accounts were given of the same event by four different observers, just as persons looking at an elephant from different vantage points can result in radically different perceptions.

I have observed that eyewitness observers of alleged paranormal events are often unreliable; their perceptions often depend on what they expect to see. Anecdotal accounts or hearsay testimony are no substitutes for rigorous observations, particularly where novel claims are being made. Numerous accounts have been given about so-called psychics—or magicians posing as psychics—being able to bend keys or spoons with their minds. Did the psychic touch the object beforehand? "No," is a common reply by untrained observers, "I never took my eyes off the object," when they in fact had. And people will evaluate events according to their predispositions, as in UFO-visitation claims. I have questioned those who maintain that they were kidnapped and taken aboard a UFO by extraterrestrial beings who allegedly probed the orifices of their bodies. Perhaps they did. On the other hand, imagination often plays havoc with people, confusing fantasy with reality. Misperceptions, even the wildest of them, are not the exclusive property of the confused or gullible.

Empiricism provides an essential component of any reliable methodology. Empiricists state that we ought to test any claims to knowledge by the eyewitness observations of evidence by ourselves or others. And I concur; for evidence is the bedrock of our knowledge of the world. But one needs constantly to be cautious and to apply methodological skepticism. One must be especially careful of self-deception, i.e., the tendency to read one's wishes into the data under observation. To accept the secondhand testimony of others, we must have reasonable guarantees of the veracity of their judgment, and some assurance that they are not prone to accept things without careful scrutiny and deliberation. We ask whether such observers are easily given to error and whether they are trustworthy and honest. Even the latter can be deceptive and would be no guarantee of the former in regard to observation colored by bias or misconception.

In addition one must guard against deception by others (whether consciously or unconsciously intended), the tendency to distort what they have observed, to embellish an event, to inter-polate a perspective, or to seek to convince others that a claim is true. There clearly have been cases of blatant fraud in religion, economics, and politics, especially where the purveyors are inter-ested primarily in money, power, or fame, and will distort the truth to serve ulterior motives. Some skeptics in appraising para-normal claims say that they will not believe anything that anyone says if it contradicts their own experiences, because many people have a powerful temptation to believe the incredible. This posture may go too far in the direction of caution, and sometimes may become dogmatic. We must be prepared to admit unexpected data and novel discoveries. We cannot close our minds to anomalous events. We surely need to be cautious, and we should try to corroborate the claim of someone who reports a strange event. We can do so by finding other trustworthy witnesses, if they are available, or by uncovering supporting data.

The central question here concerns the kind of testimony that is being reported. If it accords with our experience, we have no problem. If someone reports that there was a cyclone that destroyed

150 buildings, this would be an unusual event, but not so unusual that it is unlike other kinds of disasters that people have experienced and have been recorded in history. Moreover, we can visit the scene of destruction or view a film about it. Here modern technology is a tremendous boon, capable of extending the parameters of observation and enabling us to discover new facts. Voyager II made it possible for us to observe the blue atmosphere of Neptune and the surface of its moon Triton. No one was actually there, yet cameras were able to send back signals, and these were unscrambled and shown on a picture screen. We can thus expand the dimensions of the observed world. Our perceptual knowledge has been extended by the use of microscopes, telescopes, cameras, radar, sonic devices, computer screens, and other technological instruments.

One question that is often raised is whether we ought to accept reports from others that contradict our previously held theories based on past experience. The answer is in the affirmative if the new facts reported are accurate. How else can we widen the horizons of knowledge, unless we are prepared to revise our theories in the light of new data. In the early twentieth century, reports filtered to the outside world about a remarkable previously unknown species of gorilla that had been discovered deep within the jungles of Africa. What a surprise for the world to uncover a new species. We must be leery, however, of legends about mysterious monsters of the deep, dragons, extraterrestrials, and other fictional creatures.

Surely we have to be skeptical about outrageous claims inflated by hucksters. Nevertheless, we need to keep an open mind about exotic species and strange events. Now that virtually the entire surface of the planet Earth has been explored, there are perhaps fewer major surprises in store for us. But scientific investigations still have been able to discover and classify several new species of plants, insects, reptiles, and animals, such as the recent discovery in Madagascar of the golden-crowned sefaka, *propithecus diadema,* a species of the lemur family.[1] Nevertheless, cryptozoology is a field that bears careful scrutiny; for it is interested in locating still undiscovered species in still unexplored corners of the globe. There were reports of mermaids off the shores of New Caledonia, which

---

1. See *Discover* magazine, January 1990, p. 22.

turned out to be white dugongs, aquatic herbivorous mammals. There are still uncorroborated reports of dinosaurs in the Congo, of Yeti in the Himalayas, and of Bigfoot in the American Northwest. All of these reports need careful investigation. One cannot foreclose inquiry. As humankind explores the planets of our solar system and perhaps other galaxies beyond, we need to be receptive to totally unexpected discoveries. The only proviso is that we utilize rigorous standards in evaluating claims. Extraordinary claims need to be supported by strong evidence, not anecdotal, fragmentary, or weak evidence. When an anomalous claim is made we need to be sensitive to the possibility that it is true and be prepared to investigate it. We cannot simply rule it out a priori on grounds that it is miraculous. On the other hand, people may have mis-perceived otherwise prosaic events and/or misinterpreted what they saw, and entirely ordinary explanations may be given for what purport to be paranormal mysteries.

Circumstantial Evidence

Much of what is known about nature may not be directly observed, but only inferred. And there may not be secondhand or thirdhand eyewitness testimony to draw upon to corroborate it. This is true of events in the present as well as of those in the past. Yet by means of circumstantial evidence, we may draw inferences about what most likely occurred. The best illustrations of the use of this method can be found in the work of fictional detectives, such as George Simenon's Inspector Maigret and Arthur Conan Doyle's Sherlock Holmes. Both dramatized the use of the method of detection to identify undiscovered criminals and murderers. To illustrate: A woman is found dead in her apartment. All the doors and windows are bolted from the inside. She is lying on the floor strangled. Interviews of the neighbors draw blank stares. No one heard or saw anything. Who was in the room with her? How was she killed? Only by gathering telltale clues could Maigret or Holmes, if they visited the scene, point to the murderer—perhaps an ex-lover who strangled her and used a looped coat-hanger (later found in his possession) to latch the door from a transom above and escape unnoticed from the room. There were no witnesses, yet there was a motive, and perhaps eventually a confession to corroborate the inference. All of this is based upon circumstantial evidence. One has to be cautious. Perhaps, the detective was mistaken; the circumstantial evidence may have been too fragmentary and the inferences in the deductive process incorrectly drawn. Perhaps the police extracted a confession from a confused jilted lover who was actually innocent.

Yet circumstantial evidence is constantly used, and necessarily so, in practical affairs. It involves the introduction of conjecture of what might have occurred. Here the basic tool of inquiry is a working hypothesis, which functions as an instrument of explanation. The hypothesis, if successful, enables us to put together the pieces of a puzzle. It does so by locating causal sequences and relating them to effects. The quest for a cause is the search for a key to unlock a mystery. Clearly, in murder cases we want to find out who the responsible culprit was, and we want to fill in details such as *when* and *where*. But we also want to know *how* and *why*. In such cases we are seeking a fairly simplified singular causal hypothesis that fits the unique data in the situation.

Circumstantial evidence is also used in the development of general theories. We do not reason in isolation, but constantly draw inferences from past experiences. Here we draw upon generalizations. We note similarities, find constant conjunctions, and uncover regularities, on the basis of which we think we are entitled to draw causal inferences. The underlying causes of a phenomenon are often discovered by the use of circumstantial evidence. Why do patients with certain symptoms get sick and die? We may discover that they were infected with the AIDS virus, which is responsible for a breakdown of the body's immune system. Statistical correlations often help point to the causality at work. We reason that whenever a person is infected with the HIV virus, he or she will most likely develop AIDS. Similarly, the use of circumstantial evidence occurs in astronomy, geology, archaeology, and history, where we attempt to fit together events from the remote past into some sort of coherent whole.

The theory of evolution is based on conjecture and inference supported by circumstantial evidence. Paleontologists attempt to infer what happened based on their interpretation of fossil remains.

Stephen Jay Gould gives a masterful account of the uses and misuses of circumstantial evidence in his *Wonderful Life*.[2] The Burgess Shale is a small limestone quarry located in the Canadian Rockies, 8,000 feet above sea level. Formed an estimated 530 million years ago, the Burgess Shale contains the fossils of an ancient sea abundant with a rich variety of life-forms. It was first discovered by the geologist/anthropologist Charles D. Walcott in 1909. Dozens of creatures were unearthed that had never before been known and are now extinct. They were well preserved over the millennia and finely detailed structures could be clearly seen. For example, among the species found were the five-eyed *opabinia,* the *sidneyia,* and the exotic *anomalocaris.* Now the key point that can be pondered is how to interpret the many diverse species found and how to explain why they became extinct. The classical Darwinian hypothesis held that the evolution of a species occurred gradually, with a tendency slowly becoming pronounced; and those that were adaptable for the species were favorable to its reproduction and survival. Moreover, it was held that evolution was progressive and that "higher forms" emerged to replace the lower ones.

Gould discounts this interpretation, and argues that chance and "Lady Luck" seem to play a role. Accidents and disasters in the environment or sudden genetic mutations within a species may radically threaten or alter a species or lead to its demise. Suddenly, new species appeared and old ones disappeared; there were punctuated equilibria, or leaps in the evolutionary chain. The dinosaurs may, for example, have been rendered extinct by a meteor shower on earth that destroyed their food supply. Thus the residue of circumstantial evidence can fit alternative schema of interpretation. What has happened in paleontology and genetics is that some of the well-established principles of Darwin were questioned and abandoned. Darwin was no doubt correct when he postulated that evolution occurs, but since his time there has been a fairly substantial revision of how it occurs, based on the introduction of new causal hypotheses that seem more useful as explanatory constructs.

---

2. Stephen Jay Gould, *Wonderful Life: The Burgess Shale and the Nature of History* (New York: W. W. Norton, 1989).

The Hypothetical-Deductive Method

The quest for causal knowledge is thus essential to our explanation of how and why things occur in the world. The sciences employ various techniques to discover probable causes: from the simplest statistical studies, where a method of isolation and variation is used to isolate causal correlations, to the more complex introduction of theoretical constructs to explain data. Here the hypothetical-deductive method is used; and it may take us rather far from immediate firsthand and secondhand testimony to the use of elaborate mathematical models in order to explain data in terms of theories. The hypotheses introduced are not unique or isolated, but connected in some way to other hypotheses. Each hypothesis is tested by reference to experimental data—to a firsthand, secondhand, or thirdhand meter-reading, for example—in a controlled laboratory setting. But any one hypothesis should bear some kind of logical relationship to others that have been similarly postulated and tested. Thus, for example, scientists have developed a general theory of disease. We know that many illnesses, such as diphtheria, yellow fever, and influenza, are caused by infecting agents, whether viruses, bacteria, or bacilli, and that these affect the immune system and may overwhelm the defense mechanisms of the body. Accordingly, it was only natural, when researchers were first confronted with new diseases, to postulate the existence of yet unobserved infecting agents. This was confirmed by experimental observation.

Here we have gone far beyond knowledge by acquaintance to knowledge that is achieved by the use of deductive inference. What is the degree of certainty with which we may affirm our scientific theories? Clearly, what we know about nature is not arrived at strictly by a deductive process; nor are the laws of nature simply discovered by a process of reasoning. Descartes, Spinoza, and other classical rationalists were mistaken about the test of clear and distinct ideas or self-evidence as the ultimate criterion of truth, for they confused analytic with synthetic propositions. David Hume pointed out that it is one thing to say that two plus two equals four—given certain axioms, postulates, and premises, we may deduce certain theorems that follow from them. It is quite another to make a claim about the empirical world, where some observation directly or indirectly is relevant to the factual truth of the assertion. That a triangle is a three-sided figure is a tautological proposition that is analytically true by definition. Our degree of certainty is no doubt highest in mathematics and logic, where we deduce theorems from premises, and judge their validity by the principle of noncontradiction. We simply seek an internally consistent system of propositions. But such a system, though valid, need not be true empirically, since the premises may be false. If all *flub-jubs* are *doohickeys,* and all *doohickeys* are *razmazatazahs,* we may infer that all *flub-jubs* are *razmazatazahs.* This syllogism is valid no matter what is meant by the nonsense words, and independent of whether or not it is factually true.

A Humean analysis vividly shows that if one strikes a billiard ball it would not be a contradiction to say that it sprouted wings and flew away. That it does not do so can only be discovered by experience. The properties of objects are discovered primarily by observation of them. Hence an appeal to inductive evidence is an essential component of any knowledge claim we make about the world, and our statements need some empirical referent. But we should not defend a simplified form of empiricism, because deductive inferences enable us to go beyond the realm of the immediate moment of direct eyewitness testimony and to postulate appearances not directly observed. Deduction is the instrument by which we transcend the present limits of our observation and infer what may be happening. The existence of the outermost planets in our solar system was postulated by astronomers before they were observed. Given the general Newtonian laws of mechanics, perturbations in planetary orbits were noted. The most likely explanation for these disturbances was that gravitational forces were being exerted on the planets by other planetary bodies not yet discovered. In 1842 Neptune was actually seen through a telescope by an astronomer, as earlier predicted by the general theory, thus confirming its reliability. Similarly for the discovery of Uranus and Pluto.

Some skeptics believe that nature is so shielded by an impenetrable veil that we cannot fathom its "hidden reality." The veil includes not only the fact that we are limited by our immediate observations, but that we are imprisoned by our conceptual postulates and cannot get beyond them. Do our theories as constructed by us in some sense describe or identify what's out there? Should it be the goal of science to do so? Some philosophers and scientists say that it is not necessary to picture reality in an isomorphic relationship to our theories so long as they are workable and we can make predictions on the basis of them, and/or apply our knowledge to technological results. A good illustration of this is the quandary that we still face in physics concerning the interpretation of highly complex theoretical statements in quantum mechanics. Are physicists describing what is out there in an objective sense, or do their theories have another function? The instrumentalist interpretations of physics, first proposed by Niels Bohr and his Copenhagen colleagues, maintained that the quantum theory involved the observer and his instruments in a theoretic system, and that it was meaningless to read in a reality over and beyond the empirical given of experiential observation in the laboratory. The only reality was that which we observed in the context of experimental inquiry. This interpretation was confirmed, said the instrumentalists, by the utility of the theory in explaining observed events and by these theories being verified by prediction. Whether or not the theory was descriptively true was less important than whether it worked. The contrary view, argued by Karl Popper,[3] is for an objective interpretation of quantum theory. Popper postulates realism and causality. In some way quantum theory, he said, described the actual behavior of collections of particles. Whose interpretation is right?

In my view, both interpretations are at the same time correct, and without contradiction. There is a real world of subatomic particles out there, but our interpretation of this is not on a one-to-one isomorphic scale, for the theories are convenient in enabling us to explain phenomena and test the predictions that are inferred from these theories. There need not be an exact parallelism between the theory and the particle or wave function. What this implies is that higher-level theoretical explanations in the sciences do not

---

3. Karl Popper, *Quantum Theory and the Schism in Physics* (London: Unwin and Hyman, 1989).

simply provide descriptions of phenomena, but are causal explanations; the fact that the experimenter is transacting with that which he studies in no way denies the existence of the phenomena independent of the observations or testing procedures of the experimenter. We attempt to come closer and closer to description wherever possible, but if the subject matter is highly complex or if the scale is too minute to be directly observed by our instruments, or too far distant, the best that we can hope for is that our constructs approximate what's out there, or at least enable us to make some sense by ordering what we observe in the laboratory.

The goal of science is twofold: (1) to develop theories that serve us as powerful instruments that we can use in understanding nature and applying this knowledge to technological uses, but also (2) to approximate as far as we can what nature really is like, in some way independent of the stuff of human experience and conceptualization. At various points in the history of science, however, we may reach an impasse, for the intellectual problems we face may be exceedingly complex. We should not give up, however, but instead should seek new solutions to these conceptual problems, which should be viewed as challenges for future inquiry.

"How *much* can we really know?" and "With what degree of *certainty* may we assert that something is true?" asks the skeptic. It is impossible to resolve this first question a priori. No one can say beforehand what can and cannot be known. As we have seen, science is a method of inquiry, not a fixed body of absolute truths; the method involves a programmatic commitment to persist in our quest to unravel nature. It is difficult, antecedent to inquiry, to maintain that this, that, or something else is totally unknowable, unfathomable, or beyond the reach of human understanding, particularly on logical grounds or because of existing technological limits. If one views the history of human thought, we find that there have been constant obstacles placed in the path of inquiry. Some skeptics have said that we could not know the innermost structure of objects—before the invention of a powerful microscope; or the chemical composition of the heavenly bodies—before spectroscopic analysis or space probes; or the interior of consciousness or of human nature. All such blocks erected on philosophical or theoretical grounds are fraught with peril. Surely we cannot affirm the contrary proposition with any degree of confidence, i.e., that the universe is or must be entirely intelligible to human understanding. The data of many past events may be totally lost without any residual evidence. The universe may be so enormous in complexity and magnitude that it defies the neurological structures of the human brain to unravel its causal history or to totally comprehend its nature. On the other hand, there are virtually limitless frontiers still to be reached. Yet there may be some unknowns or even unknowables far beyond our present or even future ability to comprehend. In a real sense, some things may transcend any conceptual human understanding of the future.

Three sensible attitudes seem to me to follow from this: First, given the history of scientific progress, we cannot say a priori what will or must transcend present human knowledge. Second, of those things that are at present unknown—although we may speculate about possible alternative dimensions of reality—we should suspend judgment until such time as we can effectively unravel them. There is a tendency for the transcendental temptation to take a leap of faith and to postulate spiritual or paranormal realities. We have every right to object on skeptical grounds to such unsubstantiated claims. Third, we nonetheless do have a substantial body of reliable knowledge, tested hypotheses and theories, on the basis of which we act and function; and negative skepticism here about this knowledge is mistaken. Although, as we have argued, limited skepticism is part and parcel of the very method of critical and intelligent scientific inquiry, some degree of certainty and conviction about the existing body of knowledge is reasonable. In any case, both certainty and doubt are essential components of any kind of reflective inquiry.

Analytic Truths

There is another domain of knowledge that can be reliably used: that which involves mathematical, geometric, or analytic reasoning, where we draw inferences within a formal system and test a series of propositions by their logical consistency. Here we do not pretend to offer any empirical claims to truth, for we are simply abiding by the rules of the game, which we have pre-established, and our theorems are deductively entailed by our axioms and postulates. They are tautologically true. Such formal truths may be said to be certain, i.e., given our basic postulates and axioms and the rules of inference governing their use. But we may change the premises and the rules and discover alternative formal systems. Here there is still a pragmatic test of convenience; for some systems are more ingenious and useful than others, and they provide us with powerful intellectual tools to fulfill our intellectual and practical purposes.

Knowing How

An additional kind of reliable knowledge that skeptics often overlook is basic to our active transaction with the world and to practical tests of convenience. I am here referring to "knowing how to do something," namely, technological knowledge. Technology is often overlooked by philosophers of science in favor of the grand theoretical systems of science. Yet it is essential to our knowledge of the world, for it illustrates our activistic interaction with nature as distinct from the passive model. A similar consideration applies to ordinary life and common sense, where we do not simply seek to know nature, but to do things within and to it. "Knowledge by doing" is not simply descriptive or explanatory knowledge, as in theoretical science, for it involves an attempt to bring something about. Such knowledge enables us to fix or repair, invent or implement, make or create things. It involves teleonomic means-end reasoning. A good illustration of this kind of knowledge is the skill and dexterity that experts in the applied sciences must develop, whether mechanics or engineers, surgeons or computer specialists.

Aristotle labeled art "an intellectual virtue," and by this he meant that we are able to develop *aretē* and *technē*, artistic and means-ends know-how. This enables us to function in the world. As I have already pointed out, the traditional epistemological models are passive. The perceiver or knower attempts to describe and/or comprehend the world out there and is enveloped in a mystery, for he or she is unable to bridge the gap between the knower and the known. But technological knowledge is the means by which we enter into the world, not simply to describe it but to modify or change it. If the faucet in the sink leaks, I may get a wrench, loosen the parts, and install a new washer. I have correctly inferred that the cause of this leak is a faulty washer, and I can fix the leak by a process of means-ends behavior, interposing a new causal sequence, as it were, on nature. There is thus a kind of practical mechanical know-how that works. If I am freezing in the winter I can get an axe, chop down a tree, light a fire, and burn the wood in the fireplace. My knowledge of the world is thus transactional. I need to understand the parameters within which nature operates, which I can use to my own advantage, intervening constantly in the sequences of events. Causal intervention is decisive in human affairs: I have a high temperature, a runny nose, and aches and pains all over. The doctor prescribes an antibiotic that helps to stem the infection. Thus we *intervene* constantly, and we learn how to do so by drilling teeth, performing surgery, constructing dams, building bridges, and so on. All of this adds to our store of reliable knowledge. And it points to the fact that the body of technological know-how does not have mere theoretical truth-value, but it is tested by the hard rock of application to the world in which we live and function.

Common Sense and Science

Science is not separate and distinct from common sense. The ordinary person in the normal course of behaving in the world must use some methods of critical reasoning as part of normal coping behavior. The scientific method is simply a more sophisticated elaboration of the procedures that we use to transact with the world. This point is vital; for skeptics and theologians alike often argue as if the inductive/deductive method is based on pure postulate and a leap of faith that it is no better or worse than, say, the leap of faith of a religious person who believes in God. One cannot demonstrate that one ought to be rational or abide by the law of contradiction, it is said, or that one ought to ground his claims to truth in the evidence, without presupposing that both logic and experience are a source of truth. A complete skeptic will thus question or doubt all standards or criteria of truth, including the scientific method; for he insists that all such methodological principles lie beyond any possible proof.

How would I respond to this totalist skeptical critique? First by admitting that one cannot "prove" the absolute validity of such a method. However, we cannot, I would argue, *prove* in any deductively necessary way anything about nature, but we can make a reasonable case. I would assert that the hypothetical/inductive/deductive method is comparatively the most effective instrument we have for advancing our knowledge of the world. But the skeptic immediately retorts that I have introduced a pragmatic criterion, implying that this method is the most *useful* or *convenient*. But why should I accept that criterion? Who cares about *effectiveness?* the skeptic asks.

How would I respond to the skeptic's probing quest for further justification? My answer is by going to common everyday life and seeing whether his darts hit the bull's eye here or whether they are in fact ludicrous. Let me begin by saying: (*a*) In everyday affairs we need to be in some kind of cognitive touch with objects in the external world, and this requires us to pay heed to the evidence as I sense and interpret it within nature. Thus the appeal to empirical observation is a precondition of any kind of functioning in nature. Without accurate knowledge by acquaintance with things, I would be unable to make my way down the street. I would be unable to tell what will nourish me or quench my thirst, or what poses a threat to my very survival. All animal behavior presupposes the precondition of being able to function in the world and to respond effectively to external stimuli. (*b*) This does not apply simply to isolated events or objects in the world *in abstracto,* for they are interpreted by reference to past experiences and in the light of future expectations. Intermixed in the very process of perception is our conceptual inference of the relationship between objects and events. Some deductive processes are inherent in the coping behavior of other animals: the wolf spells danger to the squirrel, who flees up a tree; the heat from a forest fire stimulates the deer to run as fast as it can away from the rampage.

(*c*) For higher primates, including humans, some intelligent response is required if they are to deal effectively with the challenges encountered in the environment. Ideas are tested by their results in the material world. On the rudimentary level, then, the adaptive mechanisms of human organisms presuppose at least the three criteria: (*a*) the evidence, (*b*) inferences drawn from it, and (*c*) the effectiveness of the response.

The beliefs that an organism entertains are those evaluated by a range of empirical observations that presumably correctly report and/or describe what is or is not in the environment. A fawn is impelled by an organic need to seek water in order to quench its thirst. To do so, there must be an accurate perception of the natural context, which is discovered by vision, hearing, tasting, smelling, touching, and manipulating as interactive methods of discovery. On the basis of this and past experiences, the organism makes inferences about hidden causes and/or dangers, and these inferences may be true or false. The belief functions as an internalized goad for action, in the sense that it implies a complex form of behavioral knowledge, related to the motor activity that issues from it, and on the basis of which it is prepared to act. The worm is perceived as food for the bird, and the stalking cat who lies in wait for a bird is its enemy.

In his mitigated skepticism, Hume says that our knowledge of cause and effect is based on custom, habit, and expectation, by means of which we live and function. Peirce indicated that beliefs are plans of action. Santayana refers to animal faith. All point to the same basic premise: The quest for knowledge as true belief adequately grounded is rooted in underlying coping mechanisms. Beliefs have survival value for those organisms able to function most effectively and persist. They are the tools with which human beings seek food and drink, clothing, and shelter, do battle with our adversaries, prepare to mate, protect themselves from threatening beasts, and seek repose in sleep.

The question should thus be pointed toward our coping behavior: Why cope? Why seek to be effective in arriving at beliefs that are true? The answer I would give is that, judged by their observable consequences, some methods of coping may be comparatively better than others. To question the criterion of effectiveness is to question whether a living organism should function and even survive. Why survive? the skeptic asks. Why not just give up? Why seek knowledge, slake your thirst, satisfy your hunger, or ejaculate your sperm in some welcoming vagina? Here we no doubt come to a fundamental question of value: the will to survive and to live. But if the will-to-live is not present, then there is little else that we can say. We presuppose the organism's desire to live as a root postulate of life. Without it, nothing makes much sense. The question should thus be repostulated: If one is to live and function in the world, then one needs to cope with the world, even on the most elementary perceptual level. I grant that under certain conditions, there may not be a will-to-live, as in persons seeking voluntary euthanasia or rational suicide, where the most sensible option is to hasten the dying process. Thus this postulate is not an absolute. For those wishing to live, however, there are pragmatic imperatives based in part on true beliefs. The criteria for establishing and/or evaluating truth claims are implicit in the struggle for existence. They are not arbitrarily invented by philosophers, nor imposed on organisms; they grow out of the exigencies of life itself. They are rules governing our transactions within nature, discovered in the act of living, preconditions of any intelligent response to stimuli. As such, they are not unique to the human species but are found in other species as well, embedded in both instinctual and learned behavior.

Scientific modes of inquiry accordingly are simply extensions of the ordinary methods of critical intelligence—involving accurate perception, inference, and behavioral effectiveness. We did not dream them up out of thin air. They are revealed in our active behavior within the world. We learn that building a fire will keep us warm or enable us to roast meat, that water will put out a fire or quench our thirst. We also learn that responding to stimuli in the environment requires a kind of practical intelligence: there is a kind of logic of ordinary living.

Now the term *common sense* has been used to describe coping behavior, and in a fundamental way it is the bedrock of my argument. We have to be careful about what we mean by "common sense," however. First, there is considerable ambiguity in the term *common*. It may refer to what is commonly held in a society, being identified with customary beliefs and practices. This use is deceptive, for what is commonly believed or practiced in any given society may be untrue or wrong. And we should not allow the weight of tradition to oppose nonconformist modes of belief. Often the person who rejects the sacred cows of his culture is condemned as a heretic or lampooned as a fool, lacking "common sense." Here common sense as equivalent to a conservative, conformist outlook may be mistaken, and it may be used to oppose new departures in thought. The more accurate meaning of the term *common* refers to that which is shared by human beings, whether or not they have higher education or sophisticated training. It refers to a kind of innate or natural practical capacity for understanding and reasoning. The term *sense* thus more readily points to what is present, namely sensical as distinct from nonsensical. People who have good sense are able to discern or identify what is the case, aside from any abstract or fanciful theories to the contrary, and they possess good judgment in being able to sort out the true from the fraudulent. Common sense, as I am using it, refers to critical and practical intelligence. It is based on ordinary observations of the facts, involves some reasoning capacity to interpret the facts with some sagacity, and includes the ability to judge their effects upon behavior and the world.

Let me emphasize the fact that science may flout common sense in the sense of rejecting received doctrines or customary ways of looking at the world. The Copernican theory—which held that the earth rotated on its axis and that the planets revolved around the sun—seemed to violate every standard of common, ordinary views of the world: The earth had to be flat, else we would fall off when upside down. Similarly for theories developed in quantum mechanics today, which stretch our familiar ways of looking at the world. But neither science nor ordinary behavior should be constrained by the habits of thought or the prejudices of the past, but must be open to new ways of thinking and responding. Common sense, in this sense enables us to do so: for it refers to a *method* of testing ideas, rather than fixation on a body of prevailing beliefs or encrusted dogmas. Does common sense mean that if a child puts his fallen tooth under his pillow at night and makes a wish that the Tooth Fairy will guarantee that the wish is fulfilled? On the contrary, is not the best way to decide the question of the reality of the Tooth Fairy by testing a child's wish against the actual results over a period of time. A child may wish upon a star, but the wish may not come true. The child learns from experience to be more realistic. Common sense, in the proper acceptation of the term, prefers to base its beliefs on (a) evidence, the hard facts of the case, (b) reasons and inferences carefully deduced by means of logical principles, and (c) their effectiveness as judged by the consequences. Such forms of practical thinking are ultimately the means by which the human species has survived and has come to dominate this planet.

Science roots its justifications in the ordinary procedures of rationality used in everyday life: how to repair the roof that is leaking, plan a journey, plant the crop, or harvest it? Not all behavior or knowledge can be reduced to this coping mechanism, however. For we not only cope with the world, but seek to enjoy or contemplate it for its own sake. There is a range of intrinsic behavior—meditation, contemplation, and theoretical understanding—and this is independent of any immediate utilitarian or practical goals. Not all knowledge is instrumental, and not all forms of life involve cognitive functioning. Thus speculative, metaphysical, and spiritual yearnings—though perhaps they have a deeper psychological coping function—leap out of the soil and roam the heavens in wonder and reveries. Imagination often is contra-coping; it interferes with and blocks action. Still, our speculative flights can be brought back to earth by the sharp tools of common sense. Whether or not they are expressions of pure fantasy or point to hidden dimensions of reality can only be evaluated by the hard methods of skeptical inquiry. These methods may end up with devastating results in the fields of religion and the paranormal, where practical intelligence resists easy applications of our excursions into fantasy.

Chapter 5

Objectivity and the Ethics of Belief

The Objective Method

Implicit in our discussion thus far is the recognition that there are objective criteria that we use in testing truth claims, and that these are applied effectively both in science and in ordinary life. Analogous methods, moreover, can be applied to normative domains as well. They are not only used in areas where we seek to establish what is descriptively the case, such as a fact or a cause, but what prescriptively ought to be the case when we are examining alternative courses of action. There is, I submit, a logic of practical judgment, as it is employed in the applied arts and sciences, in questions of ethics, economics, politics, and social policy. I will deal with this area explicitly in Part 4 of this book.

In what follows I will outline some of the main characteristics of the objective method of inquiry in testing claims to knowledge. This is intended as a pragmatic methodology, judged by its effectiveness in achieving results. It includes rules of inquiry and confirmation that are considered to be most convenient because of their results. I should point out that the methodology that I will define is "objectively relative"; it is not "absolutely objective." This objective method does not provide us with absolute or ready-made rules. It does not pretend to be a simple recipe book in terms of which all true beliefs may be checked off. It merely describes some general characteristics of objective inquiry, but how such inquiries work out depends on the concrete contexts under investigation. This does not deny that our standards of objectivity are no doubt influenced by the paradigms that prevail historically in different socio-cultural milieus, as Thomas S. Kuhn has pointed out,[1] and they are relative in part to what diverse communities of inquirers find persuasive. I am not unmindful of the criticisms of some skeptical philosophers of science who deny that there is an objective method of science. But to deny that there are any objective criteria for testing or validating scientific truth claims would reduce science merely to a matter of subjectivity, and it would be difficult to explain how and why it works.

First, beliefs should in principle be considered to be hypotheses; that is, they should not be taken as final or absolutely fixed or beyond revision or modification. Hypotheses should be viewed as working ideas or proposals that need verification. They are *propositions* in the colloquial sense in that they propose something to someone. They are claims that something is true, and as such, grounds must be adduced to support them. Until they are verified, confirmed, or corroborated, they should be taken as tentative. By making this statement I do not mean to deny that some beliefs may be held with strength and conviction, but these are only those that have been supported by adequate grounds and incorporated within the body of knowledge. A hypothesis lays down a possible truth; it presents a supposition or conjecture that seems reasonable in a specific context of inquiry. It may be provisionally adopted for purposes of guiding the direction of future research or as a means to draw out possible inferences that would follow if it were true. It should not be taken as a fixed form of knowledge until sufficient evidence is brought to bear to support it. This means that there must be some justification for a hypothesis if it is to be converted into a truth. A belief/hypothesis is one on which we may be prepared to act, intellectually or practically. But whether

---

1. Thomas S. Kuhn, *The Structure of Scientific Revolutions* (Chicago: University of Chicago Press, 1966; 2nd ed., 1971).

it is adopted is a function of the grounds appealed to in support of it. Hypotheses are crucial to scientific investigations. They are the theoretical constructs that direct the course of inquiry. Once confirmed, they can be integrated into our body of knowledge.

Hypotheses can be used in both pure research and applied science, in political and normative areas, and in ordinary life as well. As we shall see in Chapters 9 and 10, judgments of practice may be taken as hypotheses that have been confirmed by the consequences of our behavior.

Implicit in this is the assumption that a hypothesis must be falsifiable, at least in principle. Karl Popper held that many beliefs never reach this stage. They may be so vague or incoherent that no conceivable test could determine whether they are true or false. This would exclude many basic principles of religion and the pseudosciences that are beyond the range of disconfirmation.

Second, it is clear that before we can accept a hypothesis as true we need to offer adequate grounds that confirm it. Among these grounds is empirical evidence. There are various kinds of evidence appropriate to the hypothesis under review. Some hypotheses purport to simply describe or classify a range of data. Others seek to explain how and why the phenomenon under study occurs by providing a causal account. In all such cases there must be sufficient supporting empirical data; that is, there must be sufficient reliable testimony or observations that will confirm either the facts or the causal explanations of them.

Third, the evidence should not be simply passive, that is, a particular item of observation or information that has been recorded without activity on the part of the observer. It may involve active interaction and methods of isolating antecedents to see whether or not the effects occur. Knowledge of a fact is a function of the acts used to confirm it. Here experimenters may be involved in manipulating and controlling the data or events to uncover the causes. They attempt to discover conditional relations: whenever *a* occurs, *b* occurs; and if *a* is absent, *b* is absent. If they introduce or suppress *a*, will it make any difference as to whether *b* will occur? This range of data is experimental and operational in content and its use is best illustrated in a controlled laboratory setting. The active process of testing our ideas is essential to pragmatic instrumentalism; for ideas and beliefs are related to our behavior and do not exist in abstraction from it.

Fourth, the evidence that is appealed to should not be irreducibly subjective, private, or dependent solely on firsthand testimony. The evidence, observational and experiential, must be, wherever possible, *intersubjective;* that is, it must be such that under standard conditions similar evidence will be uncovered. This means that it must be capable of *replication* by reasonably objective and responsible inquirers. If cold fusion is discovered in one laboratory, it must be replicable in other laboratories that undertake to repeat the experiment. If a claim is to be accepted, the evidence must be open to impartial and neutral observers. The evidence cannot be anecdotal, based on hearsay, or immune to critical scrutiny by anyone repeating the steps that have been taken in order to achieve similar results.

Evidence that is intrinsically private or subjective cannot be admitted unless it is corroborated by independent impartial inquirers. Purely introspective reports are in this category, as are mystical appeals and claims to personal revelation. Although these claims may be intriguing, they surely cannot be accepted at face value. Religious prophets and seers have maintained that they have a special kind of divine calling and authority and have sought to define the truth by uttering it. Many people have been profoundly influenced by the proclamations of charismatic individuals—Moses, Jesus, Mohammed, and many others. For someone to assert that something is true simply because it is stated to be so, without additional confirming evidence, is presumptuous. Independent observers should take it with a grain of salt. If someone claims to hear voices or see visions, this is interesting as psychological drama, but it does not necessarily point to any objective outside truth. It is not by itself an opening to another realm. If the person persists, his or her claim cannot be dismissed out of hand, without further scrutiny, but we need to corroborate the private phenomenological given and/or seek to find alternative naturalistic explanations for it.

Fifth, a hypothesis cannot be treated in isolation, but must be considered in its relationship to other beliefs, especially those supported by evidence, and even those that have not been confirmed.

Here we seek to ascertain how well the belief relates to other theories or propositions that are maintained to be true. The rules of deductive logic presuppose some standards of consistency; there is an internal criterion of formal validity. No one can argue or make sense if he violates the rules of identity, contradiction, and the excluded middle. *S* must either be *P* or *not P,* and cannot be both *P* and *not P* at the same time and in the same manner. This criterion is sometimes called the rationalistic criterion; it is based on cognitive intuitions to validate premises and the deductive inferences drawn from them.

Mathematics, geometry, and calculus all are based on analytic methods of reason. In principle, one does not need to know anything about the empirical content of the statements asserted, for this is a test of formal validity. Such deductive systems are powerful tools, applicable to empirical research; they can take us beyond that which is immediately observed to other areas of knowledge. This criterion implies that any hypothesis or belief must be evaluated by its relationship to the entire body of tested principles or theories. If the latter have a high degree of support drawn from a wide range of subject matters, and the hypothesis contradicts this body of tested principles or theories, then either the hypothesis needs to be confirmed by a considerable amount of positive evidence, or the pre-existing set of principles or theories need to be modified or abandoned. Scientific revolutions occur when there is a clash between well-established theories and new data, both of which cannot be held at the same time. Logical consistency is never sufficient by itself. One always needs empirical evidence to make any claim about the world. It is a necessary though not sufficient condition of warranting a truth claim.

The story is told about a psychology class visiting an insane asylum. They were met at the door by an affable guide who took the class from case to case explaining what the psychiatric condition of each inmate was. One patient thought he was Napoleon; another, the Queen of Sheba. The guide told the group that he left the worst case until the last. He said, "Tiptoe over and peer into the room." They did, and people asked, "Well, what is the matter with him?" The guide replied, "He thinks he's Bismarck." To which a member of the group responded, "Well, what's so bad about that? It's not any crazier than any of the other psychoses." To which the guide exclaimed, stamping his feet, "No. No. No. You don't understand. *I'm* Bismarck!" No doubt, given his premise, and within his system of logic, he was perfectly rational, but the important question is whether or not his empirical facts were true. One may possess a logically coherent internal system of beliefs, yet these may at root lack adequate empirical confirmation.

Sixth, we judge beliefs by their consequences. As already indicated, a belief is a plan of action. A hypothesis is stated in conditional form. If it is true, it would enable us to make predictions that will confirm it. Whenever certain conditions are observed to be present, certain consequences will most likely follow. A prediction of a future event verifies the causal statement. The causal or conditional explanation, if confirmed, is thus deemed to be convenient to sort out and account for the data. This implies that there are further evaluative data present. Many beliefs are considered of practical use, not simply because they conform to a knowledge claim that something is the case, but because of possible behavioral or technological effects that may flow from them. These consequences may be purely or primarily intellectual and cognitive, but they also have concrete results in terms of their effects upon practice. But surely one cannot interpret all knowledge claims as equivalent to their pragmatic or operational results. This is especially difficult in theoretical areas of research, although an instrumental test is often present. It surely is present in belief and knowledge claims made in ordinary life. Not all descriptions can thus be reduced to prescriptions, even though there may be an implicit prescriptive element.

Seventh, Peirce's principle of fallibilism is central to the objective method. For if a hypothesis is only as strong as the range of evidence and reasons brought to bear to support it, then the relationship of the proposal to its ground is not one of strict formal necessity or certainty, but only probabilistic. We cannot deduce a claim from its ground, even though it is supported by it. New evidence brought to light, or alternative theories or the counter-arguments of critics, may require us to modify or abandon our hypothesis. The range of evidence is rarely complete or exhaustive. Even in those inquiries in which we think we have accounted for all the observable phenomena in a class, our research project may be subject to error, misperception, or misinformation. New ideas are at first considered heretical; when accepted, they become dogmas; in time they may become superstitions. Thus, in principle, we ought always to be willing to admit that we may be wrong. Infallible, iron-clad assertions are generally presumptive. This means that we must be prepared to revise our hypotheses in the light of criticism or the discovery of new evidence.

Some skeptics have drawn from the principle of fallibilism the mistaken conclusion that because all knowledge is prone to error, *no knowledge is reliable.* But this form of negative skepticism does not follow. If I say that in many fields of inquiry we can have high degrees of certainty, if not absolute certitude, this does not mean that we are not capable of reaching trustworthy and testable knowledge. For example, I can assert that the United States now has 100 elected senators. Here I am talking about a limited class of individuals, and I am therefore fairly confident about this. I am not willing to assert blithely that I have absolute certitude, since some mistakes may have crept in, but it is so close to certainty that I will not quibble. Similarly about any number of empirical generalizations. "The volume of a gas is inversely proportional to the pressure present." "High interest rates tend to lower capital investments, for the cost of borrowing is too high." "Advanced cancer of the spine is nearly always fatal." "Milk is nourishing for infants." These are all statements that I am prepared to make as highly probable, though not deductively certain. They are framed as conditional statements, allowing for some exceptions if the initial conditions are not present or if other conditions intervene. In any case, all that the principle of fallibilism states is that no one is infallible or can claim to be immune to criticism. And this applies in principle to any area of human knowledge, including the most developed forms of scientific inquiry. Given the history of scientific inquiry and the developments of human knowledge in gradual stages and in leaps and spurts, we have to be careful in making ultimate claims that may need to be revised in the future or even overthrown. The degree of skepticism applied to an assertion is directly related to the strength of the supporting grounds used to confirm it.

Eighth, implicit in this last point is an essential principle governing skeptical inquiry, what we may call *the need to be open to new ideas;* that is, we have to guard against any form of rigid dogmatism that would foreclose on a-priori grounds alternative explanations. There have been so many illustrations of this in the history of science, philosophy, and practically every other field of learning, that one has to be extremely cautious. This is sometimes called the "Galileo Principle," referring to the Galileo period, when the so-called scientific and theological authorities of the day refused to look at the data observed in Galileo's telescope. The heliocentric theory, which postulated the sun, rather than the earth, as the center of our solar system, was rejected by the so-called authorities of the day, who deferred to Aristotle's cosmology based on the theory of epicycles. Similar examples from science are the opposition to reports of meteor showers by a panel of leading scientific authorities, including Benjamin Franklin and Pierre Laplace at the end of the eighteenth century, who thought that the reports of stones raining from the sky were superstition (they later turned out to be meteors); the rejection of the germ theory of disease (unobservable) by the medical colleagues of Semmelweis in Vienna in the mid-nineteenth century; and the opposition by geologists to Wegener's continental-drift hypothesis in the twentieth century. One must be prepared for the possibility of radical paradigm shifts; for our fondest and most revered forms of belief—whether in science, philosophy, common sense, religion, politics, or morality—may be mistaken. Thus we need to keep an open mind, willing to give a fair and impartial hearing to every responsible idea.

There is a difference between an open mind and an open sink, however, for the latter often equates any and every idea, however ill-framed or misconceived it might be, as possibly true and entitled to an extended hearing. Some ideas lie beyond the pale of coherence and do not even provide testable hypotheses, and these may not deserve equal and exhaustive examination. Yet even here we may be mistaken. What this implies is the recognition that, since we may be in error, there is need for self-criticism not only of our theories but of our method of evaluating them. The open mind is committed to tolerance for competing hypotheses and is willing to examine and reexamine them without prejudice or blindness. The open sink implies that we abandon all standards of critical evaluation and be willing to assimilate uncritically anything and everything thrown into it. This is the "empty head syndrome." It has been said that our minds should not be so open that our brains fall out.

Although we ought always to leave the door open to new ideas and creative hypotheses, however outlandish they may at first seem, not every claimant waiting in the wings is a Galileo. Each proponent must pass muster—if he or she is to be heard and accepted—by submitting his or her ideas to objective standards of corroboration and validation. The scientific mind is radical in that it is willing to leave the door ajar for new departures in thought. It is also conservative in that it insists that unless these ideas can be supported by rigorous standards of validation and verification, we ought to either reject the claim as unlikely, improbable, or false, and lacking decisive or compelling evidence, or be prepared to suspend judgment. All that we ask is that new beliefs or hypotheses, if seriously formulated, should receive a responsible hearing from inquirers committed to objective methods of evaluation.

The Suspension of Belief

A central issue for skeptical inquiry is whether or not we are obligated to suspend our judgment about claims for which there is neither sufficient evidence nor adequate reasons. Should we always doubt that which is doubtful and assent *only* to that for which we have sufficient grounds?

Bertrand Russell states a doctrine that he says appears to be "widely paradoxical and subversive," namely, "that it is undesirable to believe a proposition when there is no ground whatever for supposing it true."[2] And W. K. Clifford, in a remarkable essay, "The Ethics of Belief," sums up his argument with an even bolder

---

2. Bertrand Russell, *Skeptical Essays* (London: Allen and Unwin, 1928), p. 11.

and more sweeping statement: "It is wrong always, everywhere, and for anyone, to believe anything upon insufficient evidence."[3]

Both of these statements lay down rules that the authors believe ought to apply in judging our beliefs. The question that can be raised is whether the rules are universal or whether they need to be examined critically by the skeptical eye.

Russell's statement is less restrictive, for it says only that it is undesirable to believe a proposition when there is *no ground whatever* for it; whereas Clifford's extends the proposal more widely to *insufficient evidence,* suggesting that the suspension of belief should apply where, although there may be some grounds, they are insufficient. It is interesting to note that William James's famous essay "The Will to Believe"[4] was written in part as a response to Clifford's declaration, to affirm that we have the *right* to believe, at least in the area of religion, when we may have some evidence, but an insufficient amount to decide either way, yet feel we must nonetheless make a choice. Should we suspend judgment in those situations where we have insufficient evidence? Or is the agnostic decision not to decide a questionable action?

Russell's rule seems to me to be so apparently persuasive that it is difficult to deny it, but then it is stated in an extremely restrictive form, for it applies only to those cases for which there are no grounds whatever. It is difficult to imagine a situation in which we have no clues or inclinations whatsoever, not even a glimmer or possibility of a fact. Here, to affirm a belief is like whistling in the dark in order to assure ourselves about something. It is conceivable that in some situations we may truly be in the dark and yet may feel that we have to make a dash or a leap if we are to survive. A belief here is pure guesswork, and we cannot possibly convince ourselves that it is true or warranted. There may be "forced momentous options," to use James's terminology, but it is sheer folly to hold that in such cases our beliefs are true.

Similarly, it is difficult to justify a belief in the face of over-

---

3. W. K. Clifford, *Contemporary Review,* 1887. See also his *Ethics of Belief and Other Essays* (London: Watts, 1947).

4. William James, *The Will to Believe and Other Essays in Popular Philosophy* (New York: Longmans, Green, 1896).

whelming evidence or reasons to the contrary. This is tenacious faith, intransigence pure and simple, where some people feel satisfied in clinging to worn-out doctrines and discredited belief systems no matter what. Basically, it is a form of irrational behavior, even fanaticism, if such beliefs are stoutly defended. It is difficult to know how to deal with the behavior of those who have beliefs that are so strong that they are unwilling to look at the evidence, defying all of the rules of logic and common sense. The best that we can say is that no one can consistently abide by such a know-nothing attitude. If generalized as a rule of conduct, eventually it will make life practically impossible. We should be aware of the fact, however, that such cases are very common in human history and still prevail today, especially in the areas of religion, politics, and ethics, where people will cling to their belief systems and, when challenged, reaffirm them in spite of the lack of evidence for them or positive evidence to the contrary. Given the need to advance human knowledge, it is a continuing struggle to defend reason and science against its irrational detractors.

When all is said and done few people will consistently defend beliefs that fall into these classes, for they tend to believe that there is at least *some* credible evidence—which critics may find insubstantial—and they will bring forth reasons to support their beliefs, even though others may consider these to be only rationalizations.

The most direct challenge concerns Clifford's rule, namely, that we ought not to accept a belief if it is based on *insufficient* evidence. That is a far more ambitious and comprehensive proposal and far more radical than Russell's.

Let us make it clear that the proposition is not descriptive, for it surely does not describe how and why people believe. Clifford's proposition, however, is implicit in our objective method delineated in the previous section; it is clearly a normative recommendation, and thus it concerns the ethics of belief. The rule is not simply true per se, but rather may be considered to be a prescription; it is thought to be an effective, valuable, and useful guide for our belief-making and belief-evaluating conduct. But, we may ask, How far should we be guided by it? If taken in its strict sense, it surely would make life very difficult, for there are many areas

131

where we may have to believe and to act in spite of insufficient evidence.

The quandary that often arises is when we ask, Under what conditions is evidence sufficient and the grounds adequate to affirm a belief? Unfortunately, there are no hard and fast rules that we can lay down a priori. In a deep sense it depends on the particular context of inquiry, the unique facts of the case, and whether the relevant reasons adduced to support the hypothesis or theory are considered to be sufficient.

Concerning matters of fact, we very rarely, if ever, are able to apply strict rules of deductive inference; in most such cases we do not have proof, only probabilities. Accordingly, there are degrees of certainty, and the adequacy of the grounds cannot be simply deduced from the premises. Only the evaluative mind of the inquirer or inquirers can determine which beliefs are well formulated. No doubt the most sensible statement to make is that we should seek to arrive at beliefs where the evidence is such that no reasonable person would doubt the claim. Therefore, if we do not have absolute certitude in ordinary life or science, at least we may have reasonable certitude; or negatively, we may affirm that something is the case in the sense that it is beyond any reasonable doubt.

There are an enormous number of situations in life in which we have adequate grounds to accept something as true. For example, in cases of firsthand direct testimony. The illustration that I alluded to in an earlier chapter is that I may affirm that my hand is now casting a shadow over the desk; and I can confirm this statement if I so desire (though in most cases it is simply not necessary) by moving my hand from one angle to another or by calling in another person to corroborate my observations, or I may even take a photograph of my hand. It would in such cases be unnecessary to gild the lily or to engage in quibbles about whether my hand is casting a shadow, since we have adequate grounds to affirm this statement and any reasonable person would understand that, except, perhaps, a perverse student of philosophy who has just read George Berkeley!

In regard to secondhand testimony, if someone tells me that an event occurred, for instance, that a fire truck was in the street, and this is reiterated by two or three other persons I think are trustworthy witnesses, then I may decide that their statements constitute adequate grounds for the claim. If I am puzzled, I may even dash out to see what is going on. Secondhand testimony thus, under certain conditions, may be taken as a reliable source of knowledge, and at some point no sensible person would continue to reasonably doubt the claim. Of course they may be mistaken, the loud siren and beeping lights may be that of a police car or a helicopter; but in principle at least we can in many different ways confirm the accuracy of the observation and correctly report that it is a fire truck. Here at some point the evidence may be said to be sufficient.

Similarly, degrees of certainty attach to various other knowledge claims, though there is a class of beliefs where the sufficiency of the evidence may be open to dispute, at least in principle. For example, in cases of detective work where circumstantial evidence is appealed to, or in cases of the historical reconstruction of past events, where the evidence may be only fragmentary or sketchy, the hypothesis in error, and the research investigator mistaken. Here we can only decide on the basis of the best evidence available, but it may not be sufficient.

This is demonstrated vividly in both ordinary life and modern science, where often the ground for establishing or verifying a hypothesis is only probable. In the context of scientific research, given the criticism of peer review, we need to be extremely cautious and only talk about probabilities. New theories, when first introduced, are only at the level of conjecture, and they will await refutation or confirmation by further research and replication.

As I write this, the question of whether cold fusion exists is still up in the air, although the problem in time will most likely be resolved. The research controversy vividly demonstrates the constructive role that skepticism plays in the course of inquiry. Professors Stanley Pons and Martin Fleischmann, two chemists, asserted that they had achieved cold fusion in their laboratory at the University of Utah. They said that when they inserted bars of palladium in heavy water they detected a discharge of energy over and beyond what could be accounted for normally. This suggested a kind of fusion process at work. If their experiments were accurately conducted, this would mark an astounding breakthrough in science and might have enormous technological applications.

Were there adequate grounds for this theory? Skeptics would reply, only if the experiments could be replicated independently in other laboratories in the world. Here matters became very heated, for although a few scientists said that they got similar results elsewhere, repeated efforts to replicate the experiment under controlled laboratory conditions proved fruitless. Was the design of Pons and Fleischmann's experiment faulty? Did others follow the same protocol? Were there other explanations for what Pons and Fleischmann reported? Obviously what is directly in dispute is the sufficiency of the evidence and the adequacy of their grounds: the theory as well as the data. Presumably one should suspend judgment until some consensus is reached within the scientific community. At this point Pons and Fleischmann insist they are correct, and many scientists unable to replicate their work are unconvinced and remain skeptics. As the search for alternative sources of energy is ongoing, one can say that the reasonable course to pursue is to suspend judgment but to keep investigating on the outside chance that something important may be occurring. Throughout the sciences there are competing claims and alternative theories. Often it is difficult at one stage of inquiry to determine which hypothesis is more reasonably true and which is not, and we can simply suspend judgment and await the results of further research.

In many cases in life, however, we may not be able simply to be suspended in midair until all the evidence is in. For example, imagine that a patient is brought into an emergency room in a crisis situation. The patient is unconscious, breathing is rapid, the pulse is very weak, the blood pressure is low. The doctor has to quickly diagnose the case if rescue efforts are to be successful. And here there may not be time to determine the exact nature of the illness. Was the patient suffering a diabetic coma; had he taken an overdose of cocaine; was he asphyxiated by a gas leak; did he have a heart attack, or was there some other cause? Obviously the doctor has to act on the *best evidence available*. In James's sense, the decision is a forced and momentous one. To delay treatment because one has not made a complete and exhaustive study may have dire consequences. Thus one postulates a hypothesis that guides further diagnosis and possible remedies, but these may have to be abandoned as new symptoms are observed.

The same thing is true in ordinary life, even about the most prosaic matters. If a person's car breaks down, it may be due to a faulty battery, or the car may have run out of gas, or the fuel line may be blocked. The average person can test each of these possible conjectures, working with the best available evidence.

If a field commander in a wartime situation wonders what the opposing army is up to, he may send out reconnaissance patrols. Reports are brought back that enemy troops and tanks are being brought to the front. Is this a sign of a possible new assault, or are these only defensive maneuvers taken by the enemy? One may not be able to formulate a hypothesis that is readily sustainable by the evidence available. It is like a jigsaw puzzle with some of the pieces missing; one has to fill in the empty spaces as best one can. Thus I wish to modify Russell's and Clifford's rules of inquiry.

Let us agree with Russell that in principle it is wrong to believe something if there are no grounds whatsoever for the claim. No doubt one can think of urgent cases where we have to act, but here we have mere conjecture, not belief. Furthermore, we may even agree that in principle it is wrong to believe that something is the case without adequate grounds—the stronger rule of Clifford. Although this ideal as an ideal does not seem unreasonable, in many questions it is unattainable. For example, some inquirers may dispute whether or not the grounds are adequate or the evidence sufficient, and in some cases they may not feel sufficiently convinced either way to make a prudent assessment. In these cases we ought as a practical necessity, where we have to formulate a belief, do so on the basis of the *best available evidence*. Here we formulate beliefs in terms of the level of probability and certitude appropriate to the context, and our decision, given the circumstances, is the most reasonable, though it may be open to amendment or revision.

In all of the cases above, belief is not equivalent to complete certitude, but only to degrees of certitude. Thus in such cases we should readily admit that we have examined the situation and we think, given the available evidence, that this is most likely warranted as probable or true. On the other hand, we may be mistaken and new evidence or additional considerations may be brought to light and we may have to revise our judgment later.

Beliefs are relative, directly or indirectly, to *praxis,* or conduct. Where the evidence is only tenuous, we can suspend judgment and confess that we simply do not know. For example, we can suspend judgment about the rodent population of Outer Mongolia (assuming that we are not Mongolians, or grain merchants exporting our products there). And we can suspend judgment about the temperature of the star Sirius or the precise date when Asians crossed the land bridge over the Bering Sea to the North American continent. These are questions that may intrigue us, and although we may have hunches or opinions, there is no problem in suspending judgment here. This is different from those beliefs that are directly related to our conduct and where there is an urgent practical necessity that we act; and so we believe on the basis of the most likely evidence, though it may not have been fully confirmed or corroborated.

It is when one enters areas such as religion, ethics, politics, or economics, that questions of conviction and skepticism become especially relevant. For we are living in a social climate where claims are bandied about and demands are made for our commitment or devotion to many causes, and disagreements may become heated. If we do not have sufficient evidence or reasonable grounds on the basis of which we may believe and act, what options are open to us? In the public arena we often need to act on the best evidence then available, and yet this evidence may not be fully convincing. It is the beginning of wisdom to recognize these shortcomings and not leap in with cocksuredness and insist that what we believe is right or true no matter what the grounds.

Part Three

The Paranormal, Religion, and Fantasy

Chapter 6

Skepticism and the Paranormal

The Definition of the Paranormal

A good illustration of the application of objective methods is their use in examining paranormal claims. The term *paranormal* has been applied to a range of phenomena that allegedly cannot be explained by using the concepts and theories of science, for it refers either to a "transcendental" realm or to extraordinary "psychic" powers. Is it possible to deal with paranormal phenomena objectively; are they amenable to experimental science? Should skepticism apply, and in what sense? Perhaps we should begin by attempting to define "paranormal." I am not certain, however, that the term is entirely meaningful, at least in the sense that it has been used.

The spiritualist movement in the nineteenth century dealt with strange phenomena that were claimed to point to the existence of disembodied spirits. Spiritualists alleged that trance mediums were able to communicate with discarnate beings. The Society for Psychical Research was established in England in the late nineteenth century by philosophers and scientists in order to investigate such phenomena scientifically. Many psychical researchers were disturbed by the theory of evolution, which they thought undermined the theistic worldview. Psychical phenomena suggested that there were other dimensions to the universe besides the purely materialistic. The Society at first focused on the question of survival after death, which many hoped they could demonstrate empirically. In addition to mediumistic reports, they examined ghostly hauntings and reports of apparitions and poltergeists as evidence for discarnate survival. These inquiries were later broadened to include studies of telepathy, clairvoyance, precognition, and hypnotism. After 25 years of research, both William James and Henry Sidgwick expressed dissatisfaction at the progress in achieving results, for they soon discovered that the field was given to fraud and dupery at the hands of charlatans.[1]

Nevertheless, it was believed there were ways of perceiving information that were extrasensory in character; hence the term *extrasensory perception* (ESP) came into vogue. In an effort to develop strictly experimental controls, *parapsychology* became popular in the 1920s, especially through the efforts of Joseph Banks Rhine. The term *parapsychology* referred to studies that went on along side of and/or in addition to laboratory psychology, for many or most academic psychologists were highly skeptical of "psychical research" and either refused to deal with the subject or rejected it outright. The intention of parapsychologists was to use the best techniques of laboratory science and statistical methods in order to prove the existence of clairvoyance, telepathy, precognition, and psychokinesis (PK). The survival question was laid aside, and the focus was more narrow. Nonetheless, Rhine said that in dealing with ESP and PK he was attempting to demonstrate the existence of phenomena that could not be explained in terms of normal science, which he said was physicalist in its bias.

Parapsychology has proved to be highly controversial. Many of its critics maintain that little or no progress has been made since its inception and that parapsychologists have failed to demonstrate the reality of ESP or PK and have not even provided a single replicable experiment that could decisively resolve the ques-

---

1. See especially "The Final Impressions of a Psychical Researcher," Chapter 7 of *William James on Psychical Research,* ed. by Gardner Murphy and Robert O. Ballou (New York: Viking Press, 1960).

tion. Rhine thought that he had found certain individuals with psychic powers who when tested were able to make correct guesses, at above or below chance, as to the symbols on Zener cards being turned over by an experimenter on the other side of a screen. Many skeptics disputed his results because they thought that they could be parsimoniously accounted for by prosaic explanations, such as sensory leakage, ill-designed experiments, the questionable interpretations of hits, fraud, and so on. Many alleged experiments hailed as breakthroughs by parapsychologists were later shown to be flawed. This was especially true of the work of S. G. Soal in Britain, who claimed he had decisively proved the reality of precognition, but his results were thrown out by the scientific community when it was discovered that he had tampered with the data.[2] Some more careful inquirers have used the more neutral term "psi" to describe what was being studied, without necessarily reading in extrasensory or paranormal causes.

The term *paranormal,* used in the context of psychical research, was later extended over and beyond parapsychology to deal with a wide range of phenomena independent of the survival after death hypothesis, ESP, precognition, or PK. Indeed, it referred to many kinds of phenomena that allegedly could not be explained by the existing body of scientific principles, yet seemed to be mysterious and/or inexplicable. The net was widely flung, so that it now pertained to reincarnation, channeling, levitation, astral projection, firewalking, psychic healing, demonic possession, and so on. But it has now gone even further, to include many other fascinating topics—UFO abductions, ancient astronauts, the correlation between professional achievement and planetary configurations at the time of birth, and many apparent pseudosciences, such as astrology, numerology, Tarot cards, and biorhythms.

The term *paranormal* has now taken on at least two different kinds of meaning. First, it is used to refer to reports of various anomalies, i.e., strange or unusual phenomena that do not come

---

2. See Paul Kurtz, ed., *A Skeptic's Handbook of Parapsychology* (Buffalo, N.Y: Prometheus Books, 1985), and Paul Kurtz, *The Transcendental Temptation,* (Buffalo, N.Y: Prometheus Books, 1986), for extensive discussions of these and other issues in parapsychology.

under any normal classifications and are thus abnormal or exceptional. The universe described by science and understood by common sense is based on regularities encountered in experience and amenable to general laws. But there are many surprising and even shocking reports of idiosyncratic and weird facts. For example, dragonlike sea serpents in Loch Ness or Lake George, the spontaneous combustion of human beings who suddenly are consumed by flames, hailstorms in the middle of July, a rainfall of turtles, and the Abominable Snowman in the Himalayas.

The provocative accounts of the bizarre intrigue us. Are the reports to be taken as true or false? We have our commonsense view of how the world operates; many of these anomalies offend our expectations, and some appear to be highly improbable, given the body of scientific knowledge that we have assembled. But there would be nothing amiss if we were to discover that some or most, or perhaps all, of the phenomena mentioned above actually did exist, even though they appear to be very unlikely. If confirmed they could be catalogued and included in encyclopedias of knowledge. They would be not much different from reports of freak accidents—such as the crash of an airplane into the Empire State Building, or the sinking of the *Titanic*. Nor would they be any less intriguing than a total solar eclipse, the discovery of the comet Kahoutek approaching Earth's orbit, the blizzard of 1888, or the rings around Neptune discovered by Voyager II, or more dismaying than the atomic destruction of Hiroshima and Nagasaki and the San Francisco earthquakes. The body of information that we have is a function of our first- and second-hand testimony, circumstantial evidence, and the use of the hypothetical-deductive method, and we simply would need to add other interesting facts to our list of discoveries. Skeptics cannot a priori exclude such claims. This would be dogmatism of the worst sort. We need only to be assured that accounts of out-of-the-ordinary phenomena have a sufficient degree of credible eyewitness testimony to establish their truth claims. We need, of course, to be skeptical about taking such reports at face value without careful checking. But we also need an open mind, for what is deemed surprising or bizarre to one generation can be accepted as proved fact by the next.

Some accounts of anomalies, however, strain our credulity.

They are so extraordinary that we would need extraordinary evidence, well-established by rigorous observation, before we were to accept them. For example, a talking horse who can respond to and communicate with others verbally, a 2,500-year-old mummy who suddenly awakens from his slumber and returns to life, a person who can levitate 50 feet above the ground and hover in midair, the reanimation of a man 72 hours after his death where rigor mortis had set in and brain death had been confirmed, the regression of a person to a previous life and the progression forward to a future life, the ability of a woman to leave her body and travel to the surface of Jupiter and to report what she discovered there, the report of an adult male being raped a dozen times by Succubus, a satanic preternatural demon, the ability to peer into the future and provide an entirely accurate prediction of the Dow Jones Industrial Average ten years from now, day by day; or the power to bend and break a three-inch steel bar by a person's mind alone.

Now these phenomena are of a different class than the previous list of anomalies, not because they are exotic and unexpected but because they violate (*a*) the general principles by which we view the world, and (*b*) the known laws and regularities as discovered by science. They come under the heading of "paranormal" events because they are not in keeping with our expectations of how human beings function in nature. Such extraordinary claims conflict with our knowledge of the world in a fundamental way. It would be difficult to make room for them without radically altering our basic conceptual framework about how the world operates.

It is this second class of events that suggests that the term *paranormal* is being used as equivalent not simply to the anomalous or unusual but to the *supernormal, occult,* or *supernatural.* In other words, they seem to indicate another realm of being, a heretofore hidden dimension of existence, a transcendental form of reality. Are both kinds of reality genuine: (1) the natural world as described by science and common sense, and (2) a non-natural or other-worldly mode of existence? We are told that this second kind of reality is so puzzling and inexplicable that the science we now possess breaks down when one tries to investigate it. Is the paranormal beyond objective scientific inquiry?

What should be the response of the skeptic? One possible answer might be to reject all of these claims a priori, maintaining that they are in principle "impossible" because they contradict known laws. Now there are, I suppose, some claims that would be labeled "logically impossible," or at least as so incoherent and unintelligible that they make no sense at all, such as a square circle, a four-sided triangle, or a married bachelor. These would be analytically self-contradictory because they violate the meanings of the concepts used. But there is always a danger in generalizing a refutation to paranormal claims. For what is possible or impossible about empirical claims is not purely analytic, but is relative to an existing body of knowledge and the level of scientific advance at any one time in history. What is viewed as "impossible" in any one age may be believed in the next. The terms *possible* and *impossible* are appropriately used in the context of purely formal systems. The more relevant language to use in evaluating extraordinary paranormal claims is that of "probable" or "improbable," "likely" or "unlikely."

We can indeed question paranormal claims if they fit into the "improbable" or "unlikely" class, as I think all of the above-mentioned instances do. However, we cannot say that something is improbable on a priori grounds antecedent to any kind of inquiry. This form of skepticism would be rightly objected to by paranormal believers as a form of dogmatism. For each claim needs to be examined on its own merits without bias or prejudice, and there is surely the danger that reductive physicalists will rule out of court all paranormal claims without giving them a fair hearing. There are other kinds of phenomena that are not quite as extreme: for example, clairvoyance, i.e., that some people can see or hear some events at a remote distance, or when they are shielded from any possible direct sensory input; and precognition, i.e., that some people can know some events will occur in the future; or telepathy, i.e., that two persons can read each other's thoughts and feelings; or psychokinesis, i.e., that the mind can influence or alter physical objects. These claims allege that the mind is capable of "psychic" abilities, though they may be only modest or weak in character.

Should these phenomena be ruled out because they threaten the physicalist framework of contemporary science, which would require that some energy be transmitted from the source to the perceiver's brain? Philosophers have analyzed the coherence between physical theories and alleged extrasensory functions in order to determine whether the latter should be rejected because they are inconsistent with physical laws. I submit that one should be dubious about purely a priori formal methods of evaluation, because if a phenomenon is found to be genuine, then it is the antecedent conceptual system that will have to be modified. The data must not be sacrificed at the altar of preconceived notions of logical coherence.

There are two actual questions in regard to paranormal claims. First is the evidential one. We ask: Do the facts exist as reported, have the phenomena been properly described, and are there observable effects? Second, if we do reliably establish the reality of the facts, how do we explain or account for them?

In reference to the first question, I have discovered, after years of examining the evidence for alleged phenomena, that the evidential claims invariably do not survive rigorous scrutiny. In other words, there is often misperception or misinformation about the rudimentary facts of the case. Indeed, the field of paranormal inquiry is notorious for the intrusion of the "transcendental temptation." There is for many people a predisposition to accept a psychic reality. They tend to read mystical overtones into their prosaic experiences.

For example, many people interpret their dreams as psychic or precognitive. If a person dreams that an uncle has died, and he does shortly thereafter have a fatal heart attack, does this prove precognition—particularly if the uncle was quite elderly and likely to die? A person may be fearful that a friend or relative will have an automobile accident, and if this does happen, the person may believe that this confirms his or her psychic ability. Some people think they are telepathic. If they are able to anticipate what a friend says before he does so, they too may believe that they are psychic. In such cases, I often query the person: "Have you ever had dreams that did not come true, or premonitions and worries that were not fulfilled?" "Yes," is usually the reply. "Then what is the basic probability of some such dream or premonition being fulfilled? Could the hit have been due to coincidence?" My wife had told me many times that she dreamt that her grandmother had died. She finally did at the age of 94, but that did not prove my wife's ability to prophesy. A parent will often worry about his or her child having an accident, and nothing may happen. A dream or premonition may be emphasized after the fact, if it turns out to have been correct. Those that are not are usually forgotten. It is not an unreasonable inference to fear the death of an aging grandparent and to dream about it; or to worry about a young son's speeding to a skiing resort and having an accident.

The ability to read another person's mind can likewise be explained in natural terms. Being familiar with the person's personality and past behavior, we are able to interpret his or her thoughts and moods in the present. At the very least, we can read behavior by visual cues: a person may be quiet, or look depressed, or, conversely, be animated and lively. Thus intrinsic to the so-called factual observation is the assumed interposition of a paranormal explanation. The "psychic" account both colors the perception of events and interprets their meanings at the same time.

This is all the more true about secondhand or thirdhand testimony. It is not uncommon to be offered confused or contradictory "eyewitness testimony" of the same event. Careful checking often demonstrates that the observations were mistaken. The great controversy about parapsychology today concerns the reality of psychic phenomena, whether they have been shown to exist experimentally. And here the primary obligation of the skeptic is to engage in careful, dispassionate investigation of the data. We proceed further until we can ascertain whether the reports of such occurrences are accurate, and whether the phenomena can be replicated under controlled conditions. Before we engage in conceptual acceptance or rejection, we need to know whether the facts occurred as reported. We need to ask, Have the alleged sightings of Yeti in the Himalayas or of the Lake George monster been confirmed by a sufficient number of credible witnesses? We cannot dismiss the reports out of hand; but we do have a right to demand that they be carefully authenticated. Concerning the existence of clairvoyance, precognition, telepathy, or psychokinesis, we have all the more need to be cautious; for when new concepts wreak havoc with well-established principles of perception, we have a right to expect that the evidence be unambiguous. Where the claims are extraordinary, as in the case of a clinically dead person's being reanimated, a person's being able to regress to an earlier life or being exorcised of a demon, we need very substantial evidence indeed. Anecdotal reports by unreliable or contradictory witnesses are inadequate. We need replication of the phenomena under strict conditions of observation by dispassionate investigators.

But let us suppose that the reports of an event, by firsthand or secondhand testimony or by the use of circumstantial evidence, have been established as trustworthy and the claims are said to be reliable. At that point the second question comes to the fore. How may one explain the phenomenon that has been observed? What kind of causal account can be given for it? And it is here that the application of skeptical doubt again needs to be applied; namely, we need to seek for the *cause* of the phenomenon. To say that there is no known cause, that we are faced with a mystery, or that present scientific categories fail us is to confess our ignorance of how and why what was observed occurred. *To then leap in and attribute it to a paranormal or occult cause is illegitimate.* It is similar to invoking a miracle to explain what we do not understand, or attempting to offer an explanation in physics by attributing it to an "occult" cause. Does this mean that I am ruling out paranormal explanations by definition and that I am rejecting any explanation that invokes a paranormal cause? If so, am I doing exactly what I said is illegitimate, namely, rejecting the paranormal on a priori grounds? The solution to this query depends on what is meant by the term *paranormal.* Let me suggest some possible definitions:

1. First, by "paranormal" one may mean that some strange or unusual phenomenon may fit one or more of the following conditions: (*a*) its existence may be totally different from any other kind we know of, (*b*) it may be different from our normal expectations of the world and its objects, or (*c*) it may be inexplicable in terms of ordinary common sense.

Now none of these conditions is decisive. To discover something of a different kind of existence does not preclude its being admitted to serious consideration. Similarly for the violation of our normal expectations of the world and its objects. It is the discovery of new facts that may lead to new advances. Darwin observed strange forms of life in the Galapagos Islands that no one ever before observed. This led him to postulate new hypotheses to account for what he had seen; hence the theory of evolution. Even though what has occurred is inexplicable in terms of ordinary common sense, this should not prevent us from introducing alternative hypotheses to explain it. Indeed, science can only proceed by overthrowing the *commonly* held views of the world and introducing daring new theories, and this is precisely what happens in the history of thought. So this cannot be held as a decisive objection to admitting the phenomenon; although prima facie, if we do uncover such an unusual phenomenon, I reiterate, our reports of it need to be highly reliable. Similarly, the causal explanations need *not* conform to what is ordinarily believed. It may be totally unlike anything we have commonly believed until now. This conflict between the observed phenomenon and the present theories of the universe or of common sense does not *ipso facto* make it paranormal. However, if we can violate common sense in regard to the *content* of theories, we are still limited to common sense in using the ordinary methods of reason and evidence in appraising them, and here the standards of common sense and critical intelligence are continuous with scientific methods as they are understood and used.

2. A second definition of a paranormal phenomenon is (*a*) that it is inexplicable in terms of current theories, or (*b*) that it can be explained scientifically only by a major revision of our existing theories. But this would mean that the paranormal is relative to the level of scientific knowledge at any one time in history, and therefore what was held to be a "paranormal mystery" at one time may later be solved and moved into the realm of normal or natural scientific knowledge. Examples of this are abundant: The principles of Newtonian science were modified by relativity physics and quantum mechanics. The view that the continents on our planet were fixed was later revised by geologists to allow for continental drift. There thus have been many revisions of basic theories in science. This does not pose a special problem. Therefore the paranormal here is redundant, for it simply suggests a relativistic notion, as a function of the stages of scientific inquiry. By this

I mean that new concepts and hypotheses may need to be introduced to account for the novel or unexpected event uncovered. But this does not qualify it as "paranormal."

3. A third possible meaning of the "paranormal" is that there is *no known cause* to account for a phenomenon; hence it must be paranormal. In this sense, the term *paranormal phenomenon* is equivalent to *miracle*. But here again the term is only a substitute for our ignorance. When AIDS was first discovered, medical researchers were puzzled. What caused it? Surely, because we did not know the cause did not mean that there was no cause, or that it was thereby paranormal. Eventually a virus was identified as the probable cause, and an HIV test was devised to determine which individuals were infected. Once we can causally explain a phenomenon, it is admitted into the body of scientific knowledge and hence has no paranormal quality to it. So this sense of "paranormal" is used mistakenly.

4. There is still a fourth definition of the paranormal lurking in the background, and many people who use the term apparently are assuming this conception, namely, that there is a cause but that (*a*) it is nonmaterial, nonphysical, and has some kind of spiritual, mental, or idealistic dimensions, and/or (*b*) it is nonnatural or supernatural in character. Now it is this interpretation of the paranormal that, I submit, is what really underlies the attraction of the paranormal for many people. For it postulates a transcendental dimension to the universe and human behavior, and it further supposes that such nonnatural causes, outside of the world of nature, are leaking into the universe and bringing about strange effects. For example, there is a significant difference in saying that the parapsychologist deals with neutral psi phenomena versus claiming that ESP or psychokinesis is responsible for it, if the latter is taken as paranormal or contra-causal. I have no objection to the former approach to describe above- and below-chance guessing as *psi*. I do, however, have serious doubts about the invoking of an occult contra-causal explanation that has not been independently verified. There may be other causal accounts to fit the data, and this tends to beg the question of its cause. In any case, even if ESP and psychokinesis were introduced as new forces of causality *within* nature, they would not be paranormal but normal. If we can con-

firm a causal hypothesis, in whatever form it takes, it would be "natural."

Now definitions 3 and 4 above have been offered throughout the history of inquiry; but they have often served as obstacles to further research. We have been constantly admonished that this, that, or something else is inexplicable, unknowable, or unfathomable to human understanding and that our knowledge of the phenomenon is thereby limited. Interestingly, this posture belies an a priori kind of agnosticism or skepticism, for it expresses a belief that certain questions are beyond reason or experience or nature. My response to all of this is that to invoke the "paranormal" in this way is to block further inquiry and to leap in with an unknowable occult cause. This does not deny that there are certain areas of research that are extremely difficult to resolve and certain research projects that remain puzzling. But surely we are not entitled to foreclose inquiry a priori without the continued critical quest for natural explanations.

A spiritual or nonphysicalist cause presupposes a generalized philosophic-theological approach to the universe that is basically religious. One can ask: Is a religious outlook really lurking in the background of those who present a paranormal explanation? And is the quest for the paranormal really a quest of the transcendental temptation for something beyond the natural world?

For these reasons, I find the concept of the "paranormal" basically fruitless. For to say that something is paranormal means either that one does not know what the cause is (this often is the case in science) or that there is no cause (this is a very doubtful thesis) or that the cause is nonnatural (this has not been demonstrated and it presupposes what needs to be demonstrated). I am thus skeptical of definitions 3 and 4 of the term *paranormal*. A far better locution would be to say that we are willing to investigate reports of anomalous or unusual events and leave it at that, thus seeking wherever possible natural explanations for them. The paranormal in this sense would simply refer to that which is unusual or surprising in the first sense (1 above), without attributing it to paranormal causes, and we would not be precluded from developing new scientific causal theories (2 above) within the parameters of scientific research.

It would perhaps be useful to illustrate my general skepticism of any special kind of paranormal causality by examining concrete areas of research. When I say that I am skeptical, I do not mean that the phenomena should not be studied. I affirm that they should. Nor that we should not have an open mind about them; I insist that we should. Nor even that anomalous factors will not be uncovered; they still continue to intrigue us. I merely object to attributing a *para*normal cause to them; for once a cause is discovered, it can be incorporated into the science of nature, which may be more complicated than first thought, and this becomes a normal part of the theoretical-conceptual framework. I will deal with two main areas of research—reincarnation and faith healing—with which I have had some direct acquaintance. I do not intend my discussion to be exhaustive on either of these topics, but am dealing selectively with certain kinds of evidence to illustrate my thesis.

Reincarnation

The first area for examination is the doctrine of reincarnation. This is an ancient belief system that has persisted for a very long time in human culture. It was prominent in Hindu and Buddhist literature, in ancient Egyptian sources, and in Greek philosophy. However, the word *reincarnation* did not come into usage until the mid-nineteenth century, when some Western writers introduced it. There has been renewed interest in reincarnation in the twentieth century because some parapsychologists have attempted to find scientific evidence to support it. Thus a classical supernatural concept has been converted into a paranormal claim.

The earlier terms used to depict this belief were *metempsychosis* (from *meta,* beyond, over) and *empsychoun,* (from *em,* to animate; and *psyche,* or soul). "Metempsychosis" refers to the passing of the soul at death into another living thing, whether in human, animal, or plant form. This doctrine developed from a widely held belief of many primitive religions. Human beings, it was held, had souls connected in some way to breath, which was separated from a person's body at sleep, and decisively at death. Animals and plants were likewise possessed of souls, and they even had human

151

sentiments and powers. Upon death, the soul could be transferred from one organism to another. In the Hindu spiritual writings, another doctrine was added, *the transmigration of the soul,* which was dependent upon a person's behavior in his or her past lives. After death, the individual soul entered a new plane of existence. *Karma,* the moral conduct of a soul in the past, determined the nature of its future existence, happiness or misery, as it assumed different bodies. According to the doctrine of reincarnation, the soul exists eternally, and it will continue to be reborn in new bodies. The soul can only be released from the endless cycle of births and deaths by earning it. This series of incarnations will continue until the soul is finally released. For Buddhists, the ultimate quest is to achieve a state of Nirvana, or nothingness, to become part of the absolute consciousness. This can be obtained by leading good lives and achieving a state of enlightenment.

These doctrines took on special meaning in philosophy because of their use by Socrates and Plato, who were influenced by the Pythagoreans. In the *Republic,* Plato recounts "the myth of Er." Er returns to life twelve days after his death and relates to us a tale of another world. Er says that after dying he went to a special place to receive judgment. There he witnessed souls returning from Hades, and he accompanied them when they chose new lives, whether animal or human: Orpheus became a swan, Thamyris a nightingale, and Atalanta an athlete.

Plato develops the same theory in other dialogues. In the *Phaedo,* Socrates is depicted in his final days awaiting death and implying the doctrine of the transmigration of souls. Socrates disclaims any fear of death, and he attempts to demonstrate reincarnation and immortality by reference to the theory of ideas. If there is a realm of timeless essences, he asserts, then the separable existence of the soul after death is meaningful. This theory was related to Plato's bifurcation of the universe into two realms: a material world of appearances in space and time, and an ideal world of eternal essences. In the *Meno,* Plato draws upon the doctrine of mnemesis, or memory recall of what we knew in a prior existence, to further support the theory of reincarnation.

Reincarnation is based upon a dualistic account of human nature; namely, living things are divisible into two parts, a physical body and a psychical dimension. The soul existed before the birth of the body, and upon the death of the physical body it persisted in some form until, after an interval of time, it would occupy still another material body.

Two criticisms have been introduced by skeptics. The first concerns linguistic definition. Does it make any sense to talk of a separate or "discarnate" self, able to change bodies? Or is such language totally nonsensical? Some analytic philosophers have said that this proposition masks a basic kind of incoherence. For how can the mind, self, or soul see, hear, or experience any thoughts or feelings without sense organs, a brain, and a nervous system? Thus a disembodied, floating, psychic self is a purely speculative conjecture. The soul should be interpreted as a functional concept related to forms of behavior. To translate it into a noun and declare it to be a separable entity is to commit a basic category mistake.

Analogously, one can ask the question, "What is the 'corporation'?" The proper response is that the corporation is not a real entity, separate or distinct from the buildings, offices, or factories, board of directors, employees, customers, and their mutual transactions that make it up. The corporation is a "legal fiction" recognized by the state, but it should not be reified as a special being with an independent existence. Similarly for soul language, which, like God language, is vacuous. We should adopt a position similar to "igtheism,"[3] i.e., "igsoulism"; the concept of a separable soul is unintelligible.

This skeptical critique is a powerful one. But one must be careful that one does not attempt to deny forms of existence by a priori linguistic definition, because the reincarnationist is not simply making a linguistic statement but a factual claim; and whether or not the use of the word *soul* (as a separable being) is meaningful depends upon whether or not we can find evidence to support this use. In my view, linguistic analyses presuppose empirical grounds and cannot be appealed to independently of evidential considerations. Igsoulists believe the "disembodied soul" is meaningless because they do not think an independent soul exists.

We thus need to ask the question, Is there adequate evidence

---

3. See my discussion of this in Chapter 7.

for the belief that the soul exists separate from the body *and* has had prior existence? I will not deal with the question of post-mortem survival here, but will only focus on prior existence. It is interesting that the Judeo-Christian tradition rejects the doctrine of reincarnation, though it does assume, of course, its own article of faith in the future survival of the soul. This view entails the doctrine of "special creation": God infuses a soul into the embryo. The immortal soul is thus created out of nothing at the moment of conception. Reincarnation theory does not require such a speculative leap. By postulating preexistence, however, it has its own unanswered difficulties.

The theory of the transmigration of the soul has been described as superior to that of the Judeo-Christian soul; for among other things, it enables us to explain the moral inequalities, unredeemed injustices, and manifold evils encountered in human life, attributing many of the inequities of this life to compensation for the errors of our prior existence. The real question, however, is whether it is true. Namely, is there any *evidence* for prior existence? Does the claim have any scientific credibility?

In recent years, a considerable amount of effort has been devoted to this investigation by parapsychologists. Belief in re-incarnation has enjoyed a revival in part because of alleged new empirical data that have been uncovered. Reincarnation, then, is not taken as simply an article of faith, but needs to be justified by the evidence to be accepted as true. What is the strongest evidence adduced by its proponents to support the hypothesis that the soul pre-existed?: the alleged memories of its past existence. In other words, some individuals claim to be able to recall their prior lives.

Memories of Young Children

The first kind of reincarnation research is based primarily on the memories of young children, who, often just learning how to talk, recount to their parents and others in their immediate circle in-credible tales of previous lives. As they grow older their memory fades from consciousness. A large body of evidence for pre-existence has been assembled by Ian Stevenson, who claimed in 1977 that he had collected data on 1,600 cases.[4] Stevenson is a professor of psychiatry at the University of Virginia Medical School and a former president of the Parapsychological Association. In his study, *Twenty Cases Suggestive of Reincarnation,* he focuses on cases derived from India, Ceylon, Brazil, Lebanon, and Alaskan Eskimos. All of these children were born into families that believed in reincarnation. In a review article in the *Handbook of Parapsychology* he concentrates on one case, that of a young boy, Kemal Andawar (a pseudonym), in Lebanon. I will deal with this case by way of illustration. Presumably Stevenson believes the evidence in the case to be rather strong.

Kemal was born on May 17, 1966, in the small village of El Kalaa, 15 miles east of Beirut. His parents, Fuad and Samiha Andawar, were both members of the Druse religion. When Kemal was two years old, someone mentioned the name of Dr. Arif Eldary in his presence, upon which Kemal blurted, "Arif is my brother!" When he was three years old, he began to say that he was Abu Naef, that his family's name was Eldary, and that he had at one time lived in Hammana, a village five miles away. Kemal gradually related other details about his former life. He said that his wife was named Edma, that he had three sons, Naef, Abbas, and Ramez, that he had a sister, Afafe, and a brother, Adnan.

Kemal related that in his former life he had traveled to other countries, had lived outside of Lebanon, had been wealthy, and lived in a house with a tile roof. He claimed that he had been killed by a falling concrete block when the car he was riding in struck a wall of cement blocks. There was no doubt in the family's mind that Kemal was referring to Faruq Eldary, a businessman who had lived and traveled abroad frequently and had died in an auto accident in Lebanon on August 19, 1965. Kemal's father, on one occasion, took the child to Hammana to confirm some of the events, and they even visited the house of the deceased.

---

4. Ian Stevenson, "Reincarnation: Field Studies and Theoretical Issues," in *Handbook of Parapsychology,* ed. by Benjamin B. Wolman (New York: Van Nostrand, Reinhold, 1977), pp. 631-663. See also Ian Stevenson, *Twenty Cases Suggestive of Reincarnation* (Charlottesville: University Press of Virginia, 1980).

Stevenson investigated the case during a visit to Lebanon in early 1972, and again in 1973. At that time, the Kemal child was about six years old and still talking about his previous life, and he responded to questions about it—although it was claimed that his memories were beginning to fade. Stevenson questioned many people in the immediate family and their neighbors, and he visited the former home of Faruq Eldary. Although he maintains that the evidence points to reincarnation in this "typical case," Stevenson recognizes some weaknesses in the data.

In reviewing his published account, one can easily encounter serious gaps in a paranormal explanation. Alternative, naturalistic causes can fit the data without the need to postulate reincarnation. First, the Druses believe in reincarnation. It might thus be expected that the members of the family, devout believers, would tend to highlight responses of their son—consciously or unconsciously—and to read paranormal significance into otherwise random events. The innocent child, in his turn, would be amenable to suggestion; responding to his parents' questions, he would reinforce his belief in a previous life. Moreover, he might pick up tidbits of information proffered by his parents and other relatives, friends, and neighbors. Interestingly, it turns out that the family had some prior acquaintance with Faruq, the deceased man, and his family. The Eldary family was well known in the area, and the child's parents had known members of his family and had even attended Faruq's funeral. There was much that Kemal claimed not to have remembered about his previous life. Stevenson says that of 28 statements made by Kemal, 17 were correct, 10 were in error, and one was doubtful. For example, according to his family, the man died, not due to a falling cement block, but from a heart attack on his way to the hospital.

Although this case might impress one already inclined to believe in reincarnation, it is hardly persuasive for the skeptic. Similarly for the other cases cited by reincarnationists. Not all of them can be so easily unraveled, for we do not have all of the facts. In some cases, birthmarks are interpreted as remnants of previous mishaps; for example, a red blotch on a person's back is believed to be the place where that person had been stabbed in a former incarnation, or a scarlike appearance around the neck is believed to indicate a beheading. Because of the culture-bound character of most of the cases, one has to be cautious about reading in a paranormal explanation. The popularity of reincarnation in India leads many children to imagine they were mythical figures, gods, or heroes of the past, replete with their birthmarks. Stevenson notes that generally the subject lives within 15 miles of the deceased— which suggests either that souls do not like to travel far from the place of death or that the tale woven within the family fabric is colored by the environmental context. Since most of these cases appear in cultural climates already heavily preconditioned to accept reincarnation, there is a strong temptation for the people involved to believe in it and to look around for facts to bolster the belief.

Stevenson himself suggests at least three alternative, naturalistic explanations to account for the facts of such cases of remembrance:

1. *Fraud.* Some cases have been dishonestly contrived for notoriety or financial gain on the part of adults. Once children find that they receive so much attention and adulation, they may engage in play-acting, adding to and embellishing a story for the benefit of the adults who seem agog at what is said.

2. *Paramnesia.* The memories of the affected persons may be mingled and confused and the parents or relatives may attribute to the children more knowledge than they actually have.

3. *Cryptomnesia.* Alleged recollected facts may have been derived by means of cues, and/or items of information about the deceased may be stored in the unconscious memory, without knowledge of its true source, and volunteered as evidence of a previous life. Given the notorious unreliability of the testimony of children, these explanations would appear to better account for the data than the postulation of prior lives.

Hypnotic Regression

Another kind of "evidence" for previous lives comes from adults, not children. First, some people claim to have out-of-body experiences, which suddenly triggered, bring them back to earlier existences.[5] These accounts are largely anecdotal, subjective accounts,

---

5. See Frederick Lenz, *Lifetimes: True Accounts of Reincarnation* (Indianapolis: Bobbs Merrill, 1979).

and it is difficult to evaluate the objective facts of such reports. Another kind of alleged evidence that has received considerable attention involves the use of hypnosis. When patients are placed in a "trance," they are supposedly able to recall their previous lives. It is at least possible to subject this testimony to some independent, controlled observations that, in many instances, enable us to evaluate the accuracy of the alleged historical facts recounted.

The use of hypnotic regression came to the fore in the well-publicized Bridey Murphy case.[6] Virginia Tighe (or Ruth Simmons, the pseudonym used to protect her identity), a Denver, Colorado, housewife, claimed to recall her life as Bridey Murphy in Cork, Ireland, in the early nineteenth century. Under hypnosis, Tighe spoke with an Irish accent and described her previous life in great detail. This case has been much examined by skeptics, who uncovered normal influences in Tighe's childhood and adolescence that could account for her hypnotic renditions. A neighbor who had grown up in Ireland and whose maiden name was Bridey Murphy had regaled Tighe with stories about her life in Ireland. Moreover, Virginia Tighe had learned to speak in an Irish brogue for a part she played in a high school play.

A much more impressive body of data was assembled by a British hypnotherapist, Arnall Bloxham, who over the years had recorded on audiotape more than 400 subjects whom he had put under hypnosis. These are now known as the Bloxham tapes. Bloxham was a firm believer in reincarnation. I will illustrate the data by reference to one subject who especially impressed investigators. The regression of Jane Evans, a Welsh housewife, is detailed in the book *More Lives Than One?* by Jeffrey Iverson.[7] Evans described six past lives. They were so rich in historical detail and so diverse that many otherwise neutral observers were deeply impressed. Evans, under hypnosis, said that she was (1) a lady-in-waiting to Catherine of Aragon in the 1500s, (2) a London seamstress named Anne Tasker, who lived in the 1700s, (3) a Des Moines, Iowa, nun, Sister Grace, who died in the 1920s, (4) Livonia,

---

6. Morey Bernstein, *The Search for Bridey Murphy* (Garden City, N.J.: Doubleday, 1956).

7. Jeffrey Iverson, *More Lives Than One?* (London: Pan Books, 1977).

who lived near York in the third century as a member of the entourage of the Roman governor of Britain, Constantius, (5) Rebecca, wife of a rich Jewish money-lender, again in York, in 1189, and (6) in medieval France in 1450 as a young Egyptian servant named Alison, in the household of Jacques Coeur, a famous merchant prince.

Melvin Harris, a skeptical paranormal investigator, has examined Bloxham's Jane Evans tapes in meticulous detail.[8] Harris believes that he can explain Evans's "memories" in terms of cryptomnesia (or source amnesia) without postulating reincarnation. Let us focus on the fifth life of Jane Evans. Bloxham usually began by asking his subject to go back in time to a past life. Jane Evans begins to recall her earlier incarnation as Rebecca, known as the Jewess of York, who was supposedly killed in 1190. The tale began to unfold in 1189, as Rebecca, who was married to Joseph, the money-lender. They lived in the north of the city where "most of the wealthy Jews lived." The period was one of great trouble for the Jews, who were subject to pogroms. Isaac of Coney Street had been killed by a marauding band, and Rebecca and her family were fearful. By the spring of 1190, as the dangers increased, the family was prepared to flee, when an armed mob raided the house next door and killed its occupants. Rebecca, Joseph, and their two children fled for their lives, finding refuge in a church, where they hid in a cellar. At a distance they could hear the mob screaming and setting fire to the homes of Jews. Their sanctuary within the church was short-lived, for a priest and a clerk revealed their whereabouts to soldiers who had come to the church looking for them. At this point in her hypnotic regression, Jane Evans became "almost incoherent with terror." The soldiers seized her daughter; she whispered "Dark . . . dark," and then she allegedly died.

Harris maintained that the facts described above could be attributed to cryptomnesia and creative imagination, and that the tale of Rebecca was a product of Jane Evans's fantasies, which careful factual checking showed to be wrong. Apparently there

---

8. Melvin Harris, "Are 'Past Life' Regressions Evidence of Reincarnation?" *Free Inquiry,* Fall 1986 (vol. 6, no. 4).

had been a pogrom in York in 1190, which was common historical knowledge, but most of the Jews died in the York Castle Keep. According to Harris, there is no evidence of the church crypt. Jane Evans claimed four times that the Jews were compelled to wear yellow badges, but such badges were not introduced until the next century, and they were not yellow (as were the badges worn by Jews in Germany and France), but two oblong white stripes similar to Moses' tablet. Another error was the claim that there was a "special Jewish quarter" in York, for the Jews lived all over the city. Harris concludes that Jane Evans was able to retain vivid stories in her unconscious—from films, books, and/or magazine articles that she had seen or read—and that she had identified with one of the characters. Rebecca was a fictionalized character that Evans brought forth in hypnotic session.

Harris further demonstrated that Jane Evans's tale of Livonia, a Roman wife, which began in 286 in Britain, was taken directly from a best-selling novel by Louis De Wohl, *The Living Wood,* published in 1947. But Livonia also is a fictionalized character. Harris is likewise able to trace the life of Alison, the teenaged servant in Jacques Coeur's household in fifteenth-century France. Coeur was counsellor to Charles VII. Jane Evans knew a great deal about Agnes Sorel, the mistress of Charles VII, and she was able to describe Coeur's resplendent chateau and the tomb of Agnes Sorel in a church. But all of those facts were in H. D. Sedgwick's *A Short History of France,* published in 1930, in Dame Joan Evans's *Life in Medieval France,* and in other books. Harris maintains that Jane Evans's "past life" was derived from the novel *The Moneyman,* by C. B. Costain, which is based on Coeur's life. Of particular interest is the fact that Jane Evans's "Alison" never mentions that her master was married and had five children. The reason for this is that, as the novelist Costain tells us, he had decided not to mention Coeur's family in his novel—and so they do not appear in Jane Evans's regression.

Dr. Reima Kampman, a Finnish psychiatrist at the University of Oulu, says that some people provide impressive items of information when put under hypnotic regression. But when the same subjects are re-hypnotized, they sometimes explain how and from where they derived their information in their present life.

They point to the books they have read, films they have seen, and so on. This again suggests that much information is lodged in the brain, consciously forgotten, but retrieved during a hypnotic session.[9] Thus it is possible to give a naturalistic account of Jane Evans's stories without postulating a prior existence in any of her historical permutations.

I recently was involved in examining the claims of Dr. Brian Weiss, who, in his book *Many Lives, Many Masters,* describes his extensive therapeutic relationship with a single patient, whom he calls Catherine, and whom he submitted to extensive past life regression.[10] Weiss was so impressed by Catherine's tales that he began using hypnotic regression as a therapeutic technique for other patients. I debated Dr. Weiss on Sally Jessy Raphael's national television program in 1989. Weiss brought three of his patients with him, all of whom claimed he had regressed them to earlier lives. One of Weiss's patients, Linda Adler, recounted the many past lives she had lived. She claimed that she had been a man who was hanged during the Middle Ages, and also a young soldier who was thrown off a tower to drown in the water below. Dr. Weiss appeared to hypnotize Adler onstage by saying that he would put her in a deeper state of focused concentration. He asked her to go back to her previous life. This time she said that she was a young girl and that the year was 1632. The transcript of this hypnotic regression is as follows:

> Sally Jessy Raphael: . . . On the air, Dr. Weiss has attempted to hypnotize Linda Adler. Explain what you're doing, Dr. Weiss.
> Brian Weiss: Linda's in a deeper state now. Hypnosis is a state of focused concentration, and she's very focused now, and in a moment I'm going to touch her on her forehead—this is something that we have worked on earlier—and she's going to go into an even deeper state and try to remember some events from a previous lifetime. I'm going to do that now. I'm talking more quietly because I want to keep the mood level.

---

9. D. Scott Rogo, *Psychic Breakthroughs Today* (Wellingsborough, England: The Aquarian Press, 1987), p. 193.

10. See Brian Weiss, *Many Lives, Many Masters* (New York: Simon and Schuster, 1988).

Linda, you're in a deeper state now. I'm going to touch you on your forehead, and you'll go to a very very deep state of focused concentration and you will be able to go back to a previous life and to remember, to see the scene, to visualize, and to talk about it, all the while maintaining the deeper state. I'm going to touch you on your forehead now.

Now, Linda, you'll be able to talk to me and to describe what you're seeing.

Linda Adler: [*Long pause, with occasional starts, moans, and other noises*] It's—um—outside. [*Mild gasp.*] It's a big—um—[*Pause. Gasp.*] big space, and it's very early in the morning. There's nobody there, and there's a bunch—um—of people [*Gasp.*] and there's one that I'm looking at, and he's—um—his arms and legs and head are in this thing, this wooden thing.

Weiss: And you're seeing him?

Adler: I see him.

Weiss: Can you see yourself there? Can you tell me how old you are there?

Adler: A little girl.

Weiss: A little girl? He's in this device with his arms and his head, and you're watching him?

Adler: There's other ones, too. They're all, all like in this semicircle in this—this big space. There's pigeons. And in the back, this big building made out of stone, real tall.

Weiss: Are you able to see any year? Do you know—? [*Pause*]

Adler: 1632.

Weiss: 1632. Is there anything special about this person that you picked out of all the others in this—in these devices?

Adler: He's my father.

Weiss: Your father?

Adler: . . . I come there [*Gasp*] in the morning to see him. [*Cries*] He looks terrible. [*Weeps*]

Weiss: Has he done something to be in that, to be punished in this way?

Adler: I don't know.

Weiss: You don't know.

Adler: I think it has something to do with being poor.

Weiss: I want you to look closely at your father now. It's okay. Look closely at your father, and see if you recognize him as someone from your current life.

Adler: Yeah, I do.

Weiss: You do?

Adler: It's Bruce.

Weiss: Bruce? That's your friend, Bruce?

Adler: I don't know how long he's been there, but, but he can't, he can't talk to me. He's like—. [*Pause*]

Raphael: Dr. Weiss, can she—, can she hear me? . . .

Weiss: I don't know. We can guess.

Raphael: Can I get you, while we're talking, would it disturb you if you awakened her?

Weiss: No, I can awaken her.

Raphael: Can you?

Weiss: I'd rather, because she's becoming very upset here . . . .

It is clear from this episode: (*a*) that Weiss is asking leading questions of Adler, and that these suggestions color and bias the rendition, and (*b*) that she is able to relate people that she saw in the past to events of the present, in this case her father in an earlier life to someone that she knows in the present world, namely Bruce. (*c*) She even later mentioned in the program the film *Monty Python and the Holy Grail* in referring to the seventeenth-century scene, which suggests that a fictional motion pitture is transformed and taken as a real experience. All of this indicates that there is a cryptomnesic characteristic to the hypnotic session. However, a complication emerges in this case because Linda Adler, I was later to discover, was herself a psychotherapist who uses the same techniques and is hardly an objective or impartial subject. When she came out of the state of alleged hypnosis she remembered exactly what had transpired, which raises further doubts as to whether the "trance" was genuine.

Why did someone from the present appear in the past? Weiss confirms that for his patients, friends and relatives seem to reincarnate in the same area and time frame. "People stay within the same group" and come back in "the immediate circle," Weiss says, which again suggests that the person being hypnotized is drawing upon present experiences and reinterpreting it in past terms.

When Linda Adler was asked when this remembered event occurred, she replied "1632." But how did she know? "It just flashed," she later said in response to a question from a member of the audience. Interestingly, in the book *Many Lives, Many Masters* (p. 30), Catherine at one time was regressed by Weiss back to the year "1568 B.C." How she would know it was B.C. at that time is hard to imagine, unless she was interpolating from the present.

On the Sally Jessy Raphael program, Weiss said that he, up to that point, had regressed approximately 40 patients and that the strongest evidence for reincarnation is the therapeutic value of the encounter. He introduced Dr. Umberto Montez, a colleague from Miami, who claims he had been suffering from back pain for more than ten years, until Dr. Weiss regressed him back to two previous lives. In one case he was an old man on a battlefield in France with a severe back deformity; and in the other, a child who also had a back deformity. Ever since these regressions, Montez maintained, he has been relieved of these symptoms.

I raised the question of whether, if this technique worked, it was perhaps due simply to the placebo effect. Were people being relieved of psychosomatic illnesses? Weiss denied the placebo effect explanation. He claimed he was able to effect cures of many symptoms—not only panic attacks, phobias, and depression, but also asthma, migraine headaches and arthritis. Only the reincarnation thesis, he said, explained his results.

What are we to make of the introduction of the reincarnation thesis to account for therapeutic effects? Is an occult cause at work here, or is there indeed some placebo influence? The skeptic would look for a psychological and/or natural physical cause, without invoking a paranormal explanation. I am merely suggesting this because one would need detailed investigations of Dr. Weiss's cases to make a reasonable judgment. We need to ask whether or not alternative, naturalistic causes will explain the data. In particular, we may ask, how reliable is Wiess's hypnosis as a method of ferreting out hidden and unknown facts about the past that lie deeply buried in the unconscious? There is no doubt that hypnosis can be a useful technique and can be used in many ways. It may help individuals remember otherwise forgotten experiences. It may also be useful in certain cases as a method of therapy. Ever since the days of Mesmer, hypnosis has intrigued those who have observed it as well as the scientific researchers who have attempted to explain it.

However, a powerful skeptical critique of hypnosis has developed, and it needs to be acknowledged: It is not at all certain that those who are hypnotized go into a special "trance state" or that they can be held under the "magnetic" influence of the hypnotist. There are many psychological explanations that cast doubt on both the accuracy and the power of hypnosis.

The "Hypnosis" Controversy

Kreskin, who performs as a mentalist and has "hypnotized" thousands of people, does not believe that the "hypnotic trance" state exists. Yet he has been able to demonstrate the power of suggestion and the willingness of subjects to follow his commands. Hypnosis, he maintains, is a perfectly natural psychological phenomenon and there is no need to postulate a supernatural or occult explanation for it.[11]

It is said that hypnosis has been effectively used by police authorities and the courts to assist them in uncovering facts about crimes. Its use is based on the belief that hypnosis in some mysterious way is able to improve one's memory and reveal hidden facts about the past. The psychologist Robert Baker, of the University of Kentucky, in his book *They Call It Hypnosis,*[12] shows how unreliable hypnosis often is. Other leading psychologists, such as Theodore X. Barber and Martin Orne, maintain that hypnosis does put subjects in a more relaxed state where they are able to concentrate and perhaps better able to remember. Subjects often recall what they believe to be true, but their memory may be clouded by mixtures derived from their imagination. Research indicates that human memory is often fluid and inexact; it is not like a direct transcript or video recorder, but reconstructive. And here other psychological processes intervene; for some individuals con-

---

11. Kreskin, *Secrets of the Amazing Kreskin* (Buffalo, N.Y.: Prometheus Books, 1991).

12. Robert Baker, *They Call It Hypnosis* (Buffalo, N.Y.: Prometheus Books, 1990).

fabulation, fantasy, and creative imagination may better explain their descriptions of past lives.

I have myself applied this technique on selected subjects. When I asked students in my classroom to go back to a previous life, I began by telling them to select a period in history that especially intrigued them, and to imagine that they are there. In some cases I was amazed at the vivid stories they told. For example, one member of an audience where I was giving a lecture recounted his life as a Roman chariot driver and gave intimate descriptions of his leather gear. Another recounted his life in Egypt by the Pyramids. A woman went back to her life in a primitive tribe during the Neanderthal period; she was seated in a circle and eating raw meat with others. In no case had I "hypnotized" these subjects, but just asked them to allow their creative imaginations to roam. I also attempted to progress people to a future life, and those with a science fiction imagination spun out tales of space travel. It was clear that my suggestions—like Dr. Weiss's or any other hypnotist's— had an inordinate role in directing the course of the sessions.

Baker, who has regressed or progressed more than five hundred individuals, relates how his instructions to the group beforehand colors the result. If he begins his sessions by confidently stating that regressive hypnosis is a valuable method of uncovering past lives, 90 percent of his subjects are able to go back and "retrieve" a past life. If, on the other hand, he is skeptical of the claims and tells them so, 90 percent cannot or will not tell such tales. Of special interest is the fact that a certain percentage of people have "fantasy-prone" personalities (an estimated 4 to 6 percent of the population) with extremely rich imaginations. They spend a good deal of time in fantasizing and daydreaming and are able to produce superb stories. They are able to "hallucinate" readily, especially during hypnotic sessions. These people are not psychotic, and are otherwise as well-adjusted as the general population. But they also allow their fantasies to develop under the power of suggestion by a hypnotist. Thus we need not invoke paranormal or occult explanations for what is a purely psychological occurrence. In the psychodrama of give-and-take with a hypnotist, these fantasies can be lively and internally consistent and even may seem real to the person experiencing them.

Most regressions can occur with only a brief contact session between the hypnotist and the subject. However, Jonathan Venn, a clinical psychologist, conducted 60 hypnotic sessions with a subject over an 18-month period and was able to analyze the results in great detail.[13] He found many inconsistencies and factual errors in the regressions. The subject was "Matthew," a 26-year-old optometrist's assistant from Oklahoma. According to Venn, Matthew had tremendous "hypnotic virtuosity." He "regressed" to the personality of Jacques Gionne Trecaulte, a French aviator in World War I, who he maintained had been machine-gunned in the chest by a German pilot in August 1914 over Mons, France. His sessions became so intense that Matthew would clutch at his chest, complain of pain, break out in a sweat, and scream. Matthew had chest pains prior to his hypnotic sessions, and indeed had gone to hospital emergency rooms several times complaining of cardiac trouble. Apparently the *belief* that he had been machine-gunned in a previous life had an abreactive effect and helped cure him of what Venn believes were psychosomatic symptoms. Was the placebo effect at work or did the actual regression to an earlier life enable Matthew to be cured? The former interpretation, said Venn, better fits the facts.

Jacques Trecaulte had uttered 47 statements during the hypnotic sessions that could be checked for their historical accuracy. This Venn set out to do by investigating original source material in France. Of the 30 facts that could be verified by local sources, 16 turned out to be true and 14 false. The 17 remaining claims, which could be checked by reference to foreign archives, all turned out to be untrue. For example, machine guns were not put into airplanes until October 1914 (not in August, when he claimed to have been injured). Moreover, some of the towns that he cited did not exist. Nor could the name of Jacques Trecaulte be located in the military archives in Paris or in Theonville, the city where he allegedly was born, married, and lived. Venn concludes that Matthew's past life had no basis in fact and was not a paranormal event, but that Matthew had learned about World War I and

13. Jonathan Venn, "Hypnosis and Reincarnation: A Critique and Case Study," *Skeptical Inquirer,* vol. 12 no. 4, Summer 1988.

French life from books, television, and comic books (he was an avid reader of these). The best explanation to fit the data was source amnesia, or cryptomnesia. Matthew was unaware of the source of his fantasies, but they could be traced to specific influences and some degree of confabulation.

Another telling empirical objection to the "reincarnation hypothesis" should be raised. Peter J. Reveen, a stage performer known as "Reveen the Impossibilist," was able to regress hundreds of volunteers in his act. He says that he is effective only if his subjects are led to believe that he has no doubt about the reality of reincarnation.[14] Reveen was able to elicit, night after night, dozens of entertaining descriptions of past lives. He encountered one serious problem: On one particular night, more than one person claimed to be the same historical personality. Two men claimed to be King Henry VIII of England. And at another show both a man and a woman maintained that they had been Christopher Columbus. Thus, if nothing else raises a conceptual problem, how could more than one soul have occupied the same body?

Nicholas Spanos, also a psychologist, points out that after more than a century of research the scientific community still does not agree about the "hypnotic trance." On a comparative behavioristic scale, nonhypnotic control subjects who are encouraged to perform do just as well as those who allegedly "go into a trance state." Spanos maintains that suggestions by the hypnotist play a role in the process, that they function as tacit requests to become involved in a "make-believe situation." Good hypnotic subjects understand the requests and employ their acting skills to comply with them. Subjects who behave as *if* they had previous selves are acting out a fantasy, as if it were true, or at least they become so absorbed in the interaction with the hypnotist that they behave as if they believe it.[15]

---

14. Peter J. Reveen, "Fantasizing Under Hypnosis: Some Experimental Evidence," *Skeptical Inquirer*, vol. 12 no. 2, Winter 1987/1988.

15. Nicholas P. Spanos, "Past-Life Hypnotic Regression: A Critical View," *Skeptical Inquirer*, ibid.

Conceptual Difficulties

Thus far I have been dealing with flaws in the empirical data, but philosophers have also introduced serious conceptual problems.[16] The most important question asked is, How is it possible for a "separate soul"—in the mind's eye, as it were—to exist independent of a nervous system or brain? How could there be perception of sights, sounds, and smells, without sense organs? How could there be memory without brain cells in which to store these bits of information? Presumably the physical body and the nervous system would both die simultaneously.

Those who offer a dualistic theory of human nature have never shown that they are talking in meaningful terms when they postulate a separable noncorporeal soul. But without a brain or nervous system, how is memory and perception possible? The evidence for the dependence of the functions of the mind on the physical state of the body is massive. For example, Alzheimer's disease strikes many elderly persons. The disease leads to a severe decline in intellectual and psychological functions. It indicates that mind states are clearly functions of brain states. There are other forms of physiological evidence to spook "the ghost in the machine" doctrine: stroke victims with damage to certain portions of the brain are unable to perform specific functions. Destruction of certain areas of the brain can lead to paralysis, with speech or other vital functions seriously impaired. While it is granted that different portions of the brain may take over some functions, there is no evidence that if a large enough portion of the brain is destroyed, any cognitive, perceptual, or memory functions can ever be restored. And brain death clearly leads to the death of the person's self as we know it and as we know and understand such human beings to be. Similarly, at the other end of the scale, the fetus growing in the mother's womb is not created at the moment of conception, but depends on the growth of the brain stem and the nervous system, and it is only in the later part of the growth process that psychological functions begin to appear. Thus the reincarnationist's

---

16. See especially Paul Edwards's four-part series, "The Case Against Reincarnation," *Free Inquiry,* beginning with vol. 6 no. 4 (1986).

postulation of the separable existence of a soul independent of a body seems to fly in the face of all the evidence we have of what it means to be a human being. Personality is a function both of a person's psychological self-awareness, or consciousness, and of his or her physiological state.

There are many other serious conceptual difficulties with reincarnation. Why do the "souls" of adults that are "reborn" come back as infants, having forgotten their previous lives? If the doctrine of Karma is to be most effective, one might think that they should remember their previous existence, or at least begin as adults, aware of their former moral misdeeds so that they could put into practice what they learned from experience and thus morally improve and hasten their release to Nirvana.

Moreover, the population of the human species is increasing at a very rapid rate. Since close to six billion humans now exist and there were only two hundred million at about the time of Christ (a thirty-fold increase), would there not be a lack of sufficient souls from the past to make up the deficiency?

Still another objection concerns what happens to a person's soul from the time of his death until it occupies another body. Again, the soul would exist either as a disembodied mind (as Plato thought) or as an astral body, which is a completely mystifying conception, for we do not learn from its proponents what this could possibly mean and whether or not and to what extent this entity would be material or nonmaterial. In any case, we do not have to postulate any kind of astral plane in order to account for out-of-body experiences (OBEs), which some people experience and which can be explained as a psychological and physiological phenomenon, without invoking a paranormal or occult explanation.[17]

Thus reincarnation, I submit, is an implausible doctrine. It is based upon a paranormal interpretation of human existence. We have raised two questions: (1) What does it mean to say that the soul can pre-exist? (2) What is the evidence for the claim? In both instances we are led to a skeptical conclusion. The dualistic concept of the soul independent of the body is confused and incoherent, but aside from that, the demand for evidence has not

---

17. See Susan Blackmore, *Beyond the Body* (London: Heinemann, 1982).

been satisfied. Neither the appeal to the memory of young children nor the efforts to hypnotically regress subjects to past lives can stand up under careful analysis, and hypnotic regression may be interpreted in naturalistic terms. Thus we do not have sufficiently good reasons to believe in the reality of reincarnation. This does not mean that we should foreclose the examination of any new data that supporters of the theory will bring forth, though on the basis of what has already transpired, reincarnation appears to be more a matter of faith than of empirical warrant, and it is highly unlikely to be true.

Faith Healing

We will now examine another area in which the paranormal is said to be at work. I am here referring to faith healing. This is such a vast field that I will only focus on what have been purported to be "miraculous cures"; that is, when people who are seriously ill are allegedly restored to health by divine intervention. My discussion will not be exhaustive but will illustrate the main point I wish to raise: How should an open-minded skeptical inquirer interpret such claims?

Faith healing is as old as religion itself. Historically, the medicine man, shaman, or sorcerer was capable of appealing to the spirit world, whether beneficent or evil, to set aside the order of nature, untap mysterious cleansing forces, and achieve wondrous things. Faith healing was widely used in primitive cultures before the development of modern medicine. No doubt it had important psychological and sociological functions. Obviously there were quacks and charlatans who deceived innocent people who were desperate for some help. On the other hand, many people were no doubt comforted by the healers, who offered balm to ease their pain and suffering. Faith healers provided an outlet for those unable to cope with adversity and illness who did not know where else to turn. People are always troubled by disease, and if they can find no medical help, even today they may turn to faith healers.

Indubitably, the strong belief that one can be healed by a charismatic healer or magnetic personality may for some people

171

have a powerful effect. In many cases, sick persons will after a period of time recover without medical treatment—though shamans will often take credit for their new-found health. Moreover, some of the ancient herbs and medicines developed over long periods of time may have curative powers, as Native American tribes have learned. But perhaps more important, and more directly, is the power of the placebo effect. Some illnesses are due to stress and anxiety, and some anxious persons may be restored to health by belief in an individual or process, a cleansing ritual or ceremony. The person's psychological state thus can have a positive effect in curing some illnesses.

The real question is not about psychosomatic illnesses, but whether or not and to what extent people may be cured of entirely organic and physiological disorders by "miraculous" means. Can a person's limbs mend more rapidly? Can he or she be cured of cancer, diabetes, or psychosis by divine intervention? It is these questions that I wish to focus on in the light of the most recent scientific data.

Biblical Miracles

No doubt the persistence of belief in faith healing has its roots in religious convictions. There are hundreds of accounts of faith healing in the Old and New Testaments. Jesus Christ first established his reputation on the basis of the claim that he was a wonder worker who could heal people of otherwise inexplicable or intolerable afflictions. Our knowledge of Jesus' ministry is dependent entirely on a questionable source, i.e., the New Testament. The letters of Paul were written many years after the death of Jesus. Paul did not know him directly. Likewise, the four Gospels were most likely written some 35 to 70 years after Jesus' death. Much of the New Testament was transmitted by an oral tradition, whose accuracy is unreliable. Since none of the Gospel writers knew Jesus directly, their accounts of his faith healing are based on secondhand and thirdhand testimony. Any earlier accounts of Jesus' ministry or his sayings have been lost.

The Gospel according to Matthew tells us that Jesus' fame spread widely and that ". . . sufferers from every kind of illness, racked with pain, possessed by devils, epileptic, or paralyzed, were all brought to him, and he cured them."[18]

We read the following account of his healing:

> After he had come down from the hill he was followed by a great crowd. And now a leper approached him, bowed low, and said, "Sir, if only you will, you can cleanse me." Jesus stretched out his hand, touched him, and said, "Indeed I will; be clean again." And his leprosy was cured immediately. Then Jesus said to him, "Be sure you tell nobody; but go and show yourself to the priest, and make the offering laid down by Moses for your cleansing; that will certify the cure."[19]

Unfortunately there is no way at this date to corroborate (a) that the man had leprosy, or what other condition he may have suffered from, or (b) that he was cured immediately and permanently.

According to Matthew, when Jesus had entered Capernaum, a centurion came up to ask for help. " 'Sir,' he said, 'a boy of mine lies at home paralyzed and racked with pain.' "[20] Jesus replied that he would accompany him to cure the boy, but the centurion responded that it was not necessary to visit him directly, only say the word.

"Then Jesus said to the centurion, 'Go home now; because of your faith, so let it be.' At that moment the boy recovered."[21] Again, no notion of what condition the child was suffering from and no account of the cure.

We read on: "Jesus then went to Peter's house and found Peter's mother-in-law in bed with fever. So he took her by the hand; the fever left her, and she got up and waited on him."[22] Was she suffering from the flu, or was it an intermittent fever or a more serious illness? Nary a word from the Gospel author.

---

18. Matt. 4:24-25, *The New English Bible* (Cambridge University Press, 1972).
19. Matt. 8:1-4.
20. Ibid., 8:5ff.
21. Ibid., 8:13.
22. Ibid., 8:14-15.

In the next passage, we read, "When evening fell, they brought to him many who were possessed by devils; and he drove the spirits out with the word and healed all who were sick. . . ."[23]

The New Testament writers attributed illnesses to possession by demons. Jesus was said to have driven the devil out of two men and sent them into "a herd of pigs," who rushed over a high ledge and perished in the lake below. Here we are told that the two men were violent "madmen" who were relieved of their illness. Hardly an accurate diagnosis of their psychotic disorders. Is this to be taken seriously by a modern-day reader?

We read further that "some men brought him a paralyzed man lying on a bed. Seeing their faith, Jesus said to him that his sins were forgiven. And he turned to the man and said, " 'Stand up, take your bed and go home.' Thereupon the man got up, and went off home."[24] Was the man only partially paralyzed and able to walk or hobble, or completely paralyzed? And if the latter, was the paralysis due to hysteria, a psychosomatic condition?

In other accounts Jesus allegedly cures a woman who had "suffered from hemorrhages for 12 years." We may ask, Which part of her body was bleeding? And we are told that Jesus cured her "instantly" when she touched the edge of his cloak.[25] Similarly for two blind men whose sight he restored, and a dumb person who recovered his speech when the "devil was cast out." Indeed, the New Testament tells us that Jesus is constantly exorcising people's demons and their illnesses, and that "it is only by Beelzebub, prince of devils, that this man drives the devils out."[26] Thus we may ask, What were the conditions that the patients suffered, and how reliable are the accounts of their cures?

In the Gospel according to Mark, which probably preceded the writings of Matthew, we have similar tales of faith healing.

"On another occasion when he went to synagogue, there was a man in the congregation who had a withered arm."[27] Jesus was

---

23. Ibid., 8:16.
24. Ibid., 9:6-8.
25. Ibid., 9:20-22.
26. Ibid., 12:24ff.
27. Mark 3:1ff.

able to "restore" the arm. What was the ailment that he was suffering from? Was it a birth defect or a curable malady?

Luke tells us that Jesus healed a man suffering from dropsy or edema, an abnormal accumulation of serus fluid in the body.[28] Similarly, no diagnosis or follow-up descriptions of the therapy.

One account of Jesus' faith healing is particularly pathetic, for the patient seems to manifest epilepsy. In Mark, we read that a father describes to Jesus the symptoms of his son's illness. "He is possessed by a spirit which makes him speechless. Whenever it attacks him, it dashes him to the ground and he foams at the mouth, grinds his teeth, and goes rigid."[29] Apparently the disciples of Jesus were unable to help this boy by exorcism. They brought him to Jesus, ". . . and as soon as the spirit saw him it threw the boy into convulsions, and he fell on the ground and rolled about foaming at the mouth."[30] The father tells Jesus that the boy has been like that since childhood. Jesus rebukes the unclean spirit: " '. . . I command you, come out of him and never go back!' After crying aloud and racking him fiercely, it came out; and the boy looked like a corpse. . . . But Jesus took his hand and raised him to his feet, and he stood up."[31] Jesus later tells his disciples pointedly that "there is no means of casting this sort out but prayer." Was the boy permanently cured of epilepsy, or has the fit simply passed? If this was epilepsy, surely a cure was not feasible, since the illness is not psychosomatic.

A careful reading of the accounts of faith healing in the New Testament can only lead to skepticism. We are dealing with a fairly primitive nomadic and agricultural civilization that knew very little about the causes of diseases or psychotic behavior and only possessed rudimentary means of therapy. None of the miraculous cures are adequately documented. Where there is a placebo effect, a strong psychological factor might intervene to provide some remedy, but there is no reliable basis for judging whether the diagnoses are accurate and the remedies permanent, or whether

---

28. Luke 14:1-4.
29. Mark, 9:17-18.
30. Mark, 9:20.
31. Mark, 9:25-29.

they were due to natural psychological factors or were indeed supernatural. In any case, the biblical record is inadequate. Is the only response to the question dependent on a sheer act of faith? Can it be claimed that, if one believed in God and that Jesus was divine, all things followed, including miraculous cures? But how can we accept these premises in the context of medical science, especially since empirical claims were made?[32]

One point of special interest here is the fact that many skeptics of the paranormal have said that they do not wish to deal with religious questions, which are based primarily on faith, but only with those claims that have some modicum of empirical data. I would respond that this position is an evasion and that the skeptical method should not simply be applied in an arbitrary way only to those questions that are deemed convenient to deal with and not to those that might offend the sacred cows of society. Undoubtedly many skeptics consider it dangerous, politically or socially, to apply skepticism to traditional biblical claims. I would argue in response that the Bible should be read as any other book, using the best tools of scholarly and scientific criticism; and if one does so, then the accounts of faith healing in the New Testament are highly dubious. Some timid skeptics may refuse to invade the main sanctum of faith and they may seek to preserve the territorial hegemony of religion, but this seems to me to be an indefensible position to adopt.

Miraculous Cures at Lourdes

The appeal to miraculous cures is found throughout the entire history of Christianity. A particularly graphic and well-known illustration can be found in the shrine of the Virgin Mary at Lourdes, a small town at the foot of the Pyrenees in southwestern France. The shrine has been recognized by the Catholic church since 1862, four years after an illiterate and asthmatic village girl of fourteen, Bernadette Soubirous, claimed that she had had visions of the Virgin Mary. At first considered deranged, in time Bernadette was

---

32. For a fuller analysis of my treatment of Jesus, see *The Transcendental Temptation*, Chapter 7, "The Jesus Myth."

proclaimed a saint, although she died in her thirties of cancer. Since that time, tens of millions have visited Lourdes, prayed before the shrine, and bathed in its waters. Lourdes has become a mecca for the desperately ill.

There have been approximately six thousand claimed recoveries among those who have visited Lourdes, but the church has officially recognized only sixty-four as "miracles." The Catholic church established the *Bureau des Constatations Medicales* to examine all claims of cures. One of these allegedly occurred in 1970, when Serge Perrin of Angers, France, was said to have regained his sight. The odds of a "cure" are about that for winning a lottery, one in a million, yet people continue to flock to the shrine, and many return time and again. For example, Paul Russell of Kendall Park, New Jersey, lost the use of one arm and both legs in an automobile accident in 1972 and has made a pilgrimage to Lourdes year after year. The town has only 18,000 inhabitants, but over 400 hotels—more than any other city in France except Paris and Nice—testifying to the fact that belief in faith healing is still strong today. Indeed, every afternoon at four o'clock, throngs of the sick and handicapped enter the valley of the grotto of the Virgin Mary for prayer, song, and hope for recovery.

In the nineteenth century the Catholic press sensationalized many alleged miracles. In response, skeptics like Emile Zola visited Lourdes and exposed several cures as fraudulent. The strongest defender of the shrine was Alexis Carrel, a Nobel Prize winner in physiology and medicine in 1912, who had been converted after a visit to the shrine in 1903.

According to the *Bureau des Constatations Medicales,* for a cure to be accepted (1) the person's medical condition must have been certified by exact medical diagnosis beforehand; (2) the condition must have been organic; (3) it must have been regarded as either incurable or treatable only by lengthy therapy; and (4) a complete recovery must have occurred at the time of the visit to the shrine.

What of the alleged sixty-four cases that fulfilled these criteria? Dr. Donald West examined eleven of the most recent cases deemed miraculous and found flaws in every one of them. He noted the inadequate clinical facilities and documentation by the *Bureau.*

There were several dubious examples of cures of malignant tumors, many inadequately verified cases of tuberculosis, and a preponderance of elderly spinsters who had allegedly received physical benefits. After evaluating all of the available evidence and the medical records provided to the Catholic commissioner, West concludes: "There are no cases of lost eyes or amputated legs sprouting anew. . . . The cures claimed mostly consist in a sudden tipping of the balance in favour of the patient, whose recuperative powers seemed suddenly to reassert themselves."[33] There have not been any totally *neutral* investigations in which controlled studies of the Lourdes pilgrims have been conducted. Without this documentation, one must be skeptical about the claims.

One point often overlooked: How many people have been harmed by their visits to Lourdes? The conditions of the baths are unsanitary and substandard. My wife, who grew up in France, reports that she accompanied her classmates to Lourdes as a young girl and that when they visited the shrine they were each placed in a tub of cold, running water, following the immersion of people with all sorts of afflictions, including open sores. How many people may have contracted infectious diseases at Lourdes cannot be easily calculated.

Recent Empirical Studies of Faith Healing

Let us thus turn our attention to more recent, scientific studies where the possibility of independent scientific controls and empirical verification is possible. Has faith healing been demonstrated to work in any of these cases? The first is *Faith Healing,*[34] by Louis Rose, a British clinical psychologist. In this book, Rose reports his investigation of faith-healers in Britain, such as Harry Edwards and Christopher Woodward, as well as Christian Science practitioners. His studies include not only religious faith healers, but "psychic healers" as well. According to Rose, what is needed in order to accept faith healing as genuine is incontrovertible evidence

---

33. Donald West, *Eleven Lourdes Miracles* (New York: Helex, 1957), 172:12-13.

34. Louis Rose, *Faith Healing* (London: Pelican, 1968).

that stands up under meticulous scrutiny. The basic problem, however, is that there is an abysmal lack of hard data, including follow-up studies, in support of the faith-healing hypothesis. After examining literally hundreds of cases of purported cures over the years, Rose narrowed his quest to a search for just a handful of cases, perhaps only a single case, "in which the intervention of a faith-healer had led to an irrefutable case."[35] It would have to be a cure not in the vague sense that the patient felt better or in the sense that a progressive disease had been limited but "in the sense that as a result of the healer's work alone, a demonstrated pathological state had been entirely eliminated." It is important to point out that some illnesses are misdiagnosed, some (such as cancer) may go into remission, and some simply run their course and cure themselves in time. What is needed are definitive illustrations of healers' cures.

Rose examined in detail 95 instances of purported cures. In 58 cases, it was impossible to see medical or other records to evaluate the "cure." In 22 cases the records were at such variance with the claims that it was considered useless to proceed with an investigation. In other cases, temporary improvement was followed by a relapse, or improvement occurred concurrent with orthodox medical treatment. Here is Rose's evaluation of some typical cases:

> M.R., a boy aged 9, was suffering from pseudohypertrophic muscular dystrophy. When Rose examined him in December 1951 he was free of spinal deformity. He later visited Mr. Edwards (the faith healer) who told him he "would get better and that he had straightened his back." The family general practitioner wrote in February 1953: "I am sorry to report that in my opinion the condition is very definitely worse."[36]

> Mrs. M.H. was the subject of an article in a well-known pictorial magazine: the patient sent in her own history. According to her, after several X-ray and anesthetic examinations the hospital could do nothing more for her; she had been obliged to continue wearing her surgical belt for thirteen more years and could not get out of

---

35. Ibid., p. 175.
36. Ibid., p. 164.

bed without it, but in 1949 she went to a healer at whose hands she claimed she was "cured." When Rose examined the hospital records, they revealed that Mrs. M.H. had had an appendectomy in 1934 and a curetage for cervical erosion. In 1936 there was a barium investigation revealing nothing more than visceroptosis and in 1943 there was a further examination, all with negative findings. Her doctor subsequently wrote in terms which did not substantiate her claims, or those of the publication, that she had been seriously ill, and he gave his opinion that there was a large factor of functional exaggeration.[37]

J.K., a young boy, was, according to the headlines of a tabloid, "permanently cured": "Psychic healing succeeded when doctors failed," it read. "He was given up by professors and doctors who examined him as a hopelessly incurable case. He was born paralyzed in legs and arms, he was dumb and he had a distended stomach. After four years he received one treatment and the paralysis left him," the account continued, "the next morning he spoke and could run. . . . J. has now grown into a fine young man, leading a normal, happy life." In answer to Rose's request, the hospital concerned reported that J.R. was an in-patient for two months in 1934, suffering from rickets, and was discharged "improved." From September 1934 to February 1935 he was treated for coeliac disease, chicken-pox and whooping cough and again discharged "improved." From December 1948 to February 1949 he was suffering from Brodie's abscess of the ankle and was discharged with satisfactory results. There was no record of any other disability, temporary or permanent.[38]

Mr. R.B. A biopsy was carried out on this patient in June 1953, and a week later Mr. B. was informed that he was suffering from cancer of the larynx, calling for a major operation. Mr. B. applied to Harry Edwards for direct healing, and during the interview his hoarse voice began to improve in quality and gain in volume. Then, on 21 July 1953, Mr. B. was re-examined under an anaesthetic in hospital and informed that the pathologist's report was at variance with the previous one. Independent examination was arranged and a later report ran: "In all Mr. B. has been examined by five throat

---

37. Ibid., pp. 156-157.
38. Ibid., p. 157.

specialists, one of whom is considered the greatest authority on cancer in this country. The two specialists who examined him after he had had the direct healing from Mr. Edwards both reported 'no cancer now.' " One of the surgeons wrote to Rose in December 1953: "I doubt if anyone will give a definite reply. . . . My own belief is that it was pure fortunate coincidence that this man had a piece removed for biopsy and it had happened to contain all of the carcinomatous tissues."[39]

Rose concluded his study by saying that he could not find a single unambiguous case in which a "miracle" cure had been demonstrated.

Another interesting study is by Inge Strauch, who got in touch with the patients of Kurt Trampler, a well-known German healer. Strauch asked them to evaluate their "cures" subjectively: 39 percent reported improvement; 22 percent, temporary improvement; 29 percent, no improvement; and 10 percent, a deterioration of their conditions. Strauch was able to obtain the medical documents of 247 of their patients. Only 9 percent of them showed any objective improvement (2 percent temporary improvement), 75 percent showed no change, and 44 percent showed deterioration. Strauch concluded that no miracles had occurred, but that what Trampler was able to produce was "subjective changes" in his patients' attitudes.[40]

The study by William Nolen, a surgeon from Minnesota, is most instructive. In his book, *Healing: A Doctor in Search of a Miracle*,[41] Nolen recounts the growth of his interest in various forms of faith-healing and his investigation of its effectiveness. Probably the most popular faith-healer a generation ago was Kathryn Kuhlman. Nolen visited her healing sessions, where hundreds, even thousands, of afflicted people would come forth and be declared healed. He describes what occurred in one alleged "cure": "At one point a young man with liver cancer staggered down the

---

39. Ibid., p. 158.
40. Inge Strauch, "Medical Aspects of 'Mental' Healing," *International Journal of Parapsychology*, 5, 1963, pp. 135-165; 170; 149.
41. William Nolen, *Healing: A Doctor in Search of a Miracle* (New York: Random House, 1975).

aisle in a vain attempt to claim a 'cure.' He was turned away, gently. . . . When he collapsed into a chair I could see his bulging abdomen—as tumor-laden as it had been earlier."[42] Nolen concludes that "all the desperately ill patients who had been in wheelchairs were still in wheelchairs. In fact, [the] man with . . . kidney cancer in his spine and hip . . . was now back in his wheelchair. His 'cure,' even if only a hysterical one, had been extremely short-lived."[43]

Dr. Nolen was able to record the names and addresses of twenty-three people who were allegedly miraculously healed by Kuhlman. He followed up on these cases. One woman had been announced by Kuhlman to have been cured of lung cancer, but the disease persisted. Another woman with cancer of the spine had discarded her brace and followed Kuhlman's command to run across the stage. The next day her backbone collapsed. Four months later she was dead. Nolen's follow-up studies showed that none of the patients he examined who had been claimed as "cures" at the service "had in fact been miraculously cured of anything by either Kathryn Kuhlman or the Holy Ghost."[44] The more Nolen studied the results of Kuhlman's miracle services, the more doubtful he became that "any good she was doing could possibly outweigh the misery she was causing."[45]

In the course of his investigation, Nolen also tracked down many other healers, and their patients who had supposedly been cured, but still to no avail. There were no miracles to be found. Nolen thus raises the question, Does faith-healing help people? And he concludes that in cases of functional disorder or psychosomatic illness it may be of some help—particularly where suggestion plays a role and the autonomous voluntary nervous system is involved. Even here, though, patients may be only temporarily relieved of symptoms. Whether there are any long-lasting cures is another matter. However, any pretense of a cure does not apply to organic diseases. It has not been shown that one can grow

---

42. Ibid., p. 59.
43. Ibid., p. 60.
44. Ibid., p. 81.
45. Ibid., p. 89.

a limb or cure a diseased gall-bladder or a hernia by willing it. Nolen recognizes that many cases of cancer in remission do occur. There are far fewer cases where the cancer disappears entirely. It is estimated, he says, that perhaps only one in ten thousand cases of cancer, or perhaps as few as one in one hundred thousand, actually are spontaneously regressed. We don't always know the causes for this, he observed, but we have no evidence at all that they are due to miracles or to the intervention of a faith-healer.

An interesting investigation of faith healers was done by the conjurer James Randi. His work was supported by the Committee for the Scientific Examination of Religion. I worked with Randi throughout this project.

Our study focused primarily on modern-day fundamentalist faith healers,[46] including Ernest Angley, W. V. Grant, Peter Popoff, Oral Roberts, Pat Robertson, and others. Faith healing had become an extremely popular part of the religious landscape, with the faith healers regularly appearing on television. They appeared in huge amphitheaters or convention centers packed with thousands of fervent and often desperate people seeking miraculous healings. Many of these latter-day faith healers claimed that they cured hundreds, even thousands, of people every night. They were not talking about ordinary cures of ulcers, alcoholism, arthritis, and other such maladies, but of death-threatening illnesses like terminal cancer, advanced diabetes, multiple sclerosis, and arteriosclerosis.

As we watched their theatrical performances we were stunned at the great number of sincere and deeply shaken believers who claimed that they were cured. People would throw away their crutches or get out of wheelchairs and walk; many claimed that their afflictions had been overcome. The first faith healer we witnessed directly was Ernest Angley. James Randi, myself, and a team of four others journeyed to his electronic church in Akron, Ohio. We were deeply impressed by the dramatic display, which went on for five hours, involving music, song, and prayers. Hun-

---

46. This work has been written up in *Free Inquiry* magazine; see especially the Spring 1986 special issue on "An Investigation of Faith Healing," and articles in Summer and Fall 1986 issues. See also James Randi, *The Faith Healers* (Buffalo, N.Y.: Prometheus Books, 1987).

dreds of people came forward to attest to their cures. Our procedure was to follow out of the auditorium as many of those as we could, to get their names and addresses, and later, if possible, their doctors' names and addresses, in order to do follow-up studies.

What we discovered was disheartening. First, many faith healers were all too willing and able to deceive gullible audiences. For example, the Reverend W. V. Grant, brought in a truckload of wheelchairs with him. When an aged or deformed person hobbled in, often he or she would be invited to sit in a wheelchair and be rolled up front. During the height of the faith healing service, these people would be called upon to "be healed" and to stand up and push their own chairs. We followed one case, a man from Rochester, New York, who the audience was led to believe had been "healed" by Grant. Our follow-up study revealed that there was no improvement in his condition. Another woman, from Syracuse, New York, who Grant had pronounced cured of cancer, died two weeks later.

Indeed, after several months of firsthand investigation, James Randi could find no single, incontrovertible case of a miraculous cure. In some cases he found outright deception. Some of the faith healers led the audience to believe that they could read minds or receive revelations from God. But later Randi discovered how Peter Popoff, a popular televangelist, used a tiny radio receiver hidden in his ear to receive information transmitted by his wife backstage that she had previously been given by participants. Popoff would tell the person his name, address, ailment, and doctor. But all of this had been compiled earlier. W. V. Grant had developed a memory system and used cue cards that he peeked at during the ceremony, and this was his alleged pipeline to God.

I do not doubt that faith healing can provide a tremendous psychological uplift for some people. Attending a session can be a passionately charged cathartic event, and many people are tremendously moved by it. For some, the placebo effect has some curative power—if they truly believe in the power of the healer. But if it does, its impact is entirely naturalistic, for it is the power of suggestion that has a significant effect on the person who is moved. There is no occult cause at work.

There is a growing body of literature on holistic medicine,

testifying to the healing powers of the mind in curing some illnesses. Norman Cousins argues that his debilitating illness was conquered by his attitude.[47] Similarly, Dr. Bernie Siegel maintains the importance of mind over illnesses.[48] These are all debatable issues, and skeptics discount this evidence, maintaining that it is anecdotal and has not been submitted to carefully controlled clinical testing. Psychosomatic illnesses, they admit, are often based on stress and can be improved by reducing anxiety. That these methods apply to overtly organic or physical illness, however, is still open to question. Andrew Neher, in *The Psychology of Transcendence,* demonstrates that psychosomatic illnesses can be induced by stress and can be "learned" and "unlearned."[49] Suggestion can have a powerful effect on the learning process.

Lawrence LeShan reports the following case:

> The most dramatic single result I had occurred when a man I knew asked me to do a distance healing for an extremely painful condition requiring immediate and intensive surgery. I promised to do the healing that night and the next morning when he awoke a "miraculous cure" had occurred. The medical specialist was astounded, and offered to send me pre and post healing X-rays and to sponsor publication in a scientific journal. It would have been the psychic healing case of the century except for one small detail. In the press of overwork, I had forgotten to do the healing![50]

Jerome Frank describes another placebo cure:

> . . . Three hospitalized female patients, all in their 60s, . . . had not been helped by medical treatment. One woman was suffering from chronic gallbladder inflammation; the second had failed to recuperate after an operation for pancreatitis and was wasting away; and the

47. Norman Cousins, *Anatomy of an Illness as Perceived by a Patient* (New York: Norton, 1979).

48. Bernie S. Siegel, *Love, Medicine and Miracles* (New York: HarperCollins, 1986).

49. Andrew Neher, *The Psychology of Transcendence* (Englewood Cliffs, N.J.: Prentice Hall, 1980).

50. Quoted from Lawrence LeShan, *The Medium, the Mystic, and the Physicist* (New York: Viking, 1974), in Neher, ibid., p. 165.

third had inoperable cancer of the uterus, along with edema of the legs and anemia. As an experiment, the doctor called in a faith healer—who practiced his wonders on an absentee basis—without informing the patients. After 12 healing sessions there was no change in the patients' conditions. Then the doctor told the patients that the faith healer, who was described in glowing terms, would be working for them each morning for three days, when in fact he would not be. The three women experienced an immediate lessening of symptoms, and all were able to leave the hospital within a week's time.[51]

Neher points out that various normal mechanisms may operate in such situations: (1) *Some diseases are self-limiting,* i.e., as natural physiological defense mechanisms intervene to restore the body's health. There are also natural remissions of some diseases. (2) *Some attitude changes are mistaken for organic changes.* A change in subjective attitude leads many patients to believe that they are cured, when no organic cure has occurred. (3) *Ignorance of the role of psychological factors may lead some to postulate a paranormal cause.* Individuals may be totally unaware of the placebo effect that suggestion may have on their illnesses, and not appreciate the psychosomatic character of illnesses or therapy. (4) *Charlatan healers.* Some healers deceive and defraud innocent people.[52]

Edgar Cayce: Diagnosing Illnesses Psychically

We will continue our discussion of "psychic medicine" by evaluating one of the most famous psychics of the twentieth century, Edgar Cayce (1877-1945). Cayce has developed a large following. What is unique about Cayce is his claim to be able to diagnose and cure illnesses by going into a "trance state." Channeling is a fairly typical paranormal phenomenon that has attracted considerable interest. Channelers claim to go into a trance and to communicate with discarnate entities on the "other side" who allegedly convey

---

51. Quoted from Jerome Frank, "The Medical Power of Faith" (*Human Nature,* August 1978, pp. 40, 47), in Neher, ibid., p. 165. See also Jerome Frank, *Persuasion and Healing* (New York: Schocken, 1963).

52. Neher, ibid., p. 172-173.

special or hidden knowledge. Cayce was a rural healer from Kentucky who never received any schooling beyond the ninth grade, yet he claimed to have extraordinary paranormal powers. His first cure was of himself. According to legend, after being struck by a baseball, he went into a trance and instructed his mother to apply a poultice of certain medicines. It was said that the wound was healed by the next day. He began to apply his methods to friends and relatives, claiming that he was able to cure his wife of tuberculosis and hemorrhages, and to restore the sight in one of his son's eyes, damaged in an accident, despite opposition from the doctors treating him.

The method he used was as follows: Lying on a couch in his home, he would go into a so-called trance state. We have no way of knowing whether this was feigned or genuine. He claimed to have been able to see the health problem of the patient, diagnose the conditions, and recommend a remedy. Many of his therapies were homespun and they were based in part on some questionable methods of homeopathy and chiropractic. This included a massage of muscles and joints, enemas, castor oil packs, and the ingesting of vegetables, grape juice, and syrups. Some of his nostrums were odd. For example, for the treatment of scleroderma he recommended: ". . . a compound combined in this manner. . . . To two ounces of cocoa butter . . . add Russian white oil, sassafras oil, witch hazel."[53] Another of Cayce's dieting recommendations was to avoid "quantities of starches . . . no apples raw, no bananas raw."[54]

There are more than 14,000 Readings in the files of the Association for Research and Enlightenment, founded in 1931 by Cayce in Virginia Beach. This Association is now directed by his sons and his disciples. They maintain that ministers, physicians,

---

53. Thomas Sugrue, *There Is a River: The Story of Edgar Cayce* (New York: Dell Publishing Company), 1970, p. 366.

54. Ibid., p. 371. Interestingly, much of Cayce's health advice is considered quackery. He failed to warn his patients of the dangers of caffeine and nicotine. He told his disciples that "coffee is a fluid," that "smoking in moderation to most bodies is healthful." Nor did he warn his patients about the excessive use of sugar. No doubt he was imbibing the medical advice of his day, where the dangers of caffeine, nicotine, and sugar were not fully recognized, rather than offering transcendent truths.

and psychiatrists now consult these readings "to assist them in curing patients." They are on topics from adenoiditis, alcoholism, and apoplexy to hemorrhoids, multiple sclerosis, and sterility. Moreover, the Virginia Beach center maintains testimonials from thousands of grateful followers who attest to having been cured by Cayce's readings. Were these due to the placebo effect and the power of suggestion, or were they genuine cures?

The key question for the skeptical investigator is whether there was sufficient corroboration of Cayce's claims. There would need to be some independent diagnosis of illnesses by reference to medical records and the evaluation of his patients after the treatment to see whether Cayce's remedies were actually effective. That this was done is doubtful.

Cayce did not physically examine most of his patients directly. Nor did he use X-rays, blood tests, urinalysis, or other diagnostic tests. To say that he was able to accurately diagnose the cause of the symptoms stretches one's credulity. Without independent clinically controlled tests, most of his medical expertise must be read with skepticism. The skeptical inquirer needs to keep an open mind and not preclude or foreclose judgment a priori. Nonetheless, given the paucity of independent confirmation we can only be dubious. Considerable skepticism about the other aspects of Cayce's psychic powers is especially relevant. Since he claimed to be able to prophesy the future, we can independently evaluate his success rate. Alas, most of his specific prophecies turned out to be false.

Jess Stearn, author of *Edgar Cayce, the Sleeping Prophet,*[55] and a disciple, maintained that Cayce was "the most fantastically gifted prophet of all time!" Andrew Neher had one of his students research Cayce's batting average and discovered numerous errors. Cayce predicted that "Russia, the United States, Japan, and England or the United Kingdom would be broken up by 1936; war and a shifting of the Earth's axis would also occur in 1936; a force to make iron swim and stone float would be discovered in 1958. . . . Hitler would not be destroyed by the exercise of power; Atlantis would rise again in 1968 or 1969; by the mid-1970s many lands,

---

55. Jess Stearn, *Edgar Cayce, the Sleeping Prophet* (New York: Bantam, 1968).

including the southern portion of Carolina and Georgia, would disappear; . . . and from 1943 to 1968 rule in China would become more Christian and democratic."[56] None of these predictions were fulfilled.

Of special interest to the appraisal of Cayce is the fact that he was a strong believer in reincarnation, and indeed claimed to be able to regress himself to earlier periods in history. His trance state allowed another entity from a previous life to enter into his consciousness. Cayce was only the channel for this spiritual source, he said. The trance state took Cayce through seventeen incarnations.

In the book, *Many Happy Returns: The Lives of Edgar Cayce,*[57] W. H. Church points out serious discrepancies in the record of the dates of Cayce's previous incarnations. Of special interest is Cayce's claim that the entity's Egyptian incarnation was in the time of "Ra Ta" (Cayce's Reading 5748-6). This supposedly occurred some 10,500 years B.C.E., but Church points out that the precise date varies in several readings. Cayce claims that the construction of the Great Pyramid was from 10,490-10,390 B.C.E., but as far as we are aware, the pyramids of Egypt were built thousands of years later than that, so that if Cayce's historical dating is correct, the findings of archaeology are incorrect. Church also finds some difficulties with Cayce's Persian cycle, as "Uhjltd," a nomadic ruler. No specific dates are given, though it appears to be 8000 to 9000 B.C.E. In Cayce's Readings 1097-2 and 3356-1, however, the Persian incarnation seems to occur *after* an incarnation in the days of Moses (c. 1300 B.C.E.), and, in another, later than the Babylonian Exile of the Israelites (c. 600 B.C.E.).[58]

There are other examples of incarnations given out of sequence in the various readings. Cayce apparently was not clear about the known historical record, nor did he remember always what he had said before, and was therefore inconsistent. This points to fabrication and/or cryptomnesia on his part, though his defenders claim that he was "sincere." Of special interest is Cayce's

---

56. Neher, op. cit., p. 160.
57. W. H. Church, *Many Happy Returns: The Lives of Edgar Cayce* (New York: Harper and Row, 1971).
58. Ibid., p. 23.

incarnation during the reign of "Amicius" of Atlantis, the lost continent. Reading 364-3 tells us that Amicius's reign was 100,000 years before the days of Rama in India, which refers to an incarnation of 103,000 B.C.E. If Cayce is correct, then he existed before Neanderthal Man as a highly civilized being on a lost continent.[59] So we can reasonably ask whether we are dealing with genuine history or pure fiction? The most plausible explanation for Cayce's trance states is that they were renderings of his fantasies, consciously or unconsciously spun out of his imagination, and not regression to previous lives. But in providing this interpretation, skeptics of course have to be careful or they may be accused of dogmatic debunking by paranormalists. Nonetheless, based on our detailed examination of reincarnation and of Cayce's claim to be a healer, the most likely explanation for Cayce's paranormal feats, if they occurred, would be naturalistic, and he and his followers have failed to make the case that he had occult powers.

Conclusion

What I have attempted to establish in this chapter is that there is no basis for postulating a paranormal realm. There are surely things that we do not presently know and may indeed never know. These may be far beyond the ken of human perception or inquiry. But to claim that there are no natural causes for the anomalous phenomena that we encounter, or to claim that the causes are irremediably "occult," is only a substitute for our ignorance. If there is no known cause, this does not allow us to attribute a hidden or mysterious cause or a transcendental source.

I have illustrated this from two areas that have fascinated human beings: (1) The possibility of the prior or separate existence of the human soul and its reincarnation. I cannot find sufficient evidence or convincing arguments as adequate ground for this claim. (2) The effectiveness of faith healing and other "miraculous cures." If human beings become ill, the presence of disease and death may be explained in terms of infectious agents, immune disorders,

---

59. Ibid., p. 35.

processes of aging and/or accidents. Cures of psychosomatic maladies, if they occur, may be causally explained on natural grounds as due to the placebo effect or other psychological influences, without attributing them to mysterious psychic or paranormal forces.

The only sensible approach of the skeptic is an open mind about any such claims, a commitment to careful investigation of the alleged phenomena, and an inquiry into possible causal factors as to how or why they occur. But this procedure is perfectly consistent with naturalistic science, and it does not involve a leap beyond the range of observable phenomena, nor the postulation of phenomena outside of the naturalistic universe.

I may be mistaken; perhaps persistent and careful inquiry into paranormal claims will uncover data that point to human psychic power and transcendental realities. Should this be demonstrated on scientific grounds, it would not invalidate my thesis, which is that objective methods of inquiry, including skepticism as part of the process, is still the most reliable way of establishing truth claims, no matter what the field.

Chapter 7

Religious Unbelief

Many skeptical investigators today who are willing to use scientific methods to examine paranormal claims are reluctant to extend their critiques to religious claims. The paranormal, we are told, is amenable to skeptical criticism, but religion is not. Is skepticism relevant to religion? And if not, why not? Since psychics, astrologers, and UFOlogists are not socially powerful, skeptics do not endanger social institutions by debunking their efforts. However, it appears that skeptics threaten the very fabric of established institutions when they attempt to enter the domain of religion. Nevertheless, it is intriguing to find that the processes of credulity and gullibility that are encountered in the paranormal realm are similar to those at work in religion.

There are many definitions of the term *religion,* and there is a good deal of disagreement about its meaning. Some liberal theologians would like to stretch the term so far that it applies to any expression of an "ultimate concern"—any commitment to a set of ideal ends—including those of secular humanists and other unbelievers. But this functional definition of "religion," I submit, involves a misuse of language. "Religion," in my view, should be used to refer to those systems of faith that venerate an occult, supernatural, or divine being. It is confusing to use it so widely that it refers to virtually everything. I have introduced the term *eupraxophy* to designate nonreligious belief systems that present a naturalistic cosmic outlook and a humanistic life stance.[1]

In this chapter I will concentrate primarily on theistic religion, as expressed by Christianity, Islam, and Judaism. These religions postulate the existence of a divine creator of the universe who promises eternal salvation. What should be the appropriate response of skeptical inquirers to this? I wish to explore three possible positions of the unbelievers: (1) igtheism, (2) atheism, and (3) agnosticism. Historically, it has been extremely difficult for skeptics to openly admit that they are unbelievers, and many renowned thinkers have attempted to conceal their irreligion. At least two basic questions have emerged in the debate between theists and unbelievers: First, What is the meaning of the concept "God"? and, second, What is the justification for the claim that such a being "exists"?

Igtheism

The first issue concerns definition. Before we can ascertain whether x exists, one needs to understand what x denotes, designates, or connotes. Whatever God is, what does it mean to say that "God exists"? Contemporary analytic philosophers have devoted considerable attention to analyzing God-talk. Skeptics believe that those who use God-language are inextricably mired in paradox, for traditional monotheistic religions present us with the concept of an ultimate being who transcends the categories of human experience and understanding. Aquinas maintained that he could demonstrate that God exists, and he pointed to what he thought were some of his properties; but the ultimate "essence" of God, he said, is unknowable by human understanding. Here faith must supplement reason, which is inadequate to penetrate the veiled mystery of divine reality.

There are at least two basic senses of "God." First, that he *transcends* any of our normal channels of perception and cognition. Second, that he is *immanent* in nature and that he reveals himself

---

1. Paul Kurtz, *Eupraxophy: Living Without Religion* (Buffalo, N.Y.: Prometheus Books, 1989).

to man at some times in history. It is this first sense, of God as an infinite, omnipresent, omnipotent being, that is most troubling, since it resists any kind of identifiable definition. Kant pointed out, in his *Critique of Pure Reason,* that this concept of God is vacuous since, as a noumenal being, he lacks any observable phenomenal content. As such, we may ask, what are theologians attempting to assert in maintaining that such a being "of which none greater can be conceived" exists? Are they making a meaningful statement that is capable of validation or confirmation?

In one sense of the term, "God" is referred to as the "ground of being," the "source" and "creator" of the universe, its ultimate "cause." But here the terms *ground, source, creator,* and *cause* are being used metaphorically, for such terms only make sense within the range of human experience and transaction; but when their meanings are extended outside of these boundaries they elude comprehension. When we say that "x is a cause" we are making a conditional statement of implicitly observable and/or behavioral phenomena, but x as a transcendent cause exceeds our grasp and hence involves pure postulation. We do, of course, introduce constructs in mathematics. We talk about infinity or an infinite series. But here we are clearly dealing with a set of ideal concepts, and we deduce inferences from them without the further assumption that these postulated concepts exist in actual fact.

The concept of a transcendental divine being is indefinable. The terms used to describe its properties are only analogical; these have poetic and metaphoric force and function as stimuli to moral behavior, but they have no literal or descriptive meaning per se. It therefore makes no sense to ask whether God exists, for the God referent is without experiential content.

A similar problem concerns the term *exists.* For to say that something exists makes no sense unless we specify under what conditions and in what sense it exists. Claims to existence must have some concrete particularity. We may say that "pebbles exist in the garden," or that "molecules are observable in living cells." Here we specify the spatial and temporal dimensions of the entities under observation. But God allegedly is beyond space and time. We say that the "poem exists in someone's imagination" or that "it is published in a book of poetry." Or "the giant exists in the story *Jack and the Beanstalk* as part of a mythic fairy tale." What do we mean when we say that "God exists" if we cannot specify the conditions under which he exists or identify what kind of being we are dealing with. To talk about "God the Father" as the "maker and ruler of the universe" thus is a transactionally meaningless concept. I have introduced the term *igtheism,* because the kind of theistic being discussed by theologians and philosophers is irreducibly unintelligible. Here *ig* is derived from "ignorant," for we are totally incapable of knowing what is meant by "theism" when we use the term "God" to denote a transcendent being or the "ground" of being. The argument by theologians (such as Tillich) that God-language must be viewed symbolically or metaphorically is, in my view, a great dodge. Murky language is invoked to read in something ambiguous, which if clearly specified would appear to be false. But this semantic fog of untranslatable metaphors does not really advance the apologetic of theists. Not only is all such language clearly nonfalsifiable—for there is no way that we can ever know whether it is true or false since we do not have any but the vaguest conception of what is meant—but it is also basically unintelligible.

No doubt believers will criticize my argument as "positivistic," to which I reply: If we make a claim to know something about the universe, then we must use words in a descriptive or referential sense; and there are reasonable standards that we have to follow if we are to make sense. To talk about God in a transcendent sense is to utter indefinable, even nonsensical language. In saying this I am surely not unmindful of the fact that religious language is very rich in nuance. Indeed, religious beliefs have a multiplicity of functions. God-talk may be used in an expressive and evocative way, in that it may provoke our most passionate feelings about our encounters with brute reality. It may be used in a ceremonial or performative way in celebrating certain rites of passage, such as birth, marriage, and death. Here God is the poetic-legal symbol used to "sanctify" or certify an event or relationship as valid before society. Or God can be used in an imperative-normative way; that is, when some people say that God declares that "adultery is wrong," they mean that "thou shalt not commit adultery," or when they say that "you shall not suffer a witch to live," they mean that you should burn witches at the stake. Here God-talk has moral implications and takes on the force of law. Indeed, in some fundamental sense God-language is really a sanction for the deepest moral beliefs and values of a culture. People feel so profoundly committed to what they think is good or bad, right or wrong, just or unjust, that they ascribe their moral code to some divinity, and they maintain that anyone who violates it is wicked. Many believers say that abortion or divorce is wrong because God is against it. But what they are really saying is that their postulated God is against it because they are against it.

I surely do not deny that religious language has many functions and meanings. My only point here is that the phrase "God exists" is at the very least intended as a statement that has existential import, and that the theist in this sense is making a "factual" claim, which by definition is "nonfactual" in that God exceeds the category of observable fact. That is why I can maintain, as a skeptic, that I am an *igtheist,* for I do not understand what the theist is talking about. I cannot say whether or not such a being exists since I do not comprehend what is being asserted. I have little objection to a Spinozistic conception of God as equivalent to the "laws of nature," other than to say that this is a misuse of the theistic conception, especially if God is not a person, the creator of the universe, or concerned with our destiny. Thus God surely cannot be an object of worship, since theistic definitions postulate the need for pious veneration of such a being in an effort to move him in our behalf—though Spinoza leaves room for a kind of intellectual love of the vast cosmic universe. In any case, Spinoza's use of the term is simply a linguistic redefinition of a classical term, one that is perhaps thought to be less offensive by those fearful of public condemnation for atheism.

There is, however, still another meaning to the term *God* that avoids these objections and yet is in some sense meaningful (whether or not it is true is another matter): it refers to God as an immanent being. This anthropomorphic God is the kind of being feared and loved by the authors of the Bible. To talk about God the Father, or God the Son, or to say that Man is created in the image of God at least gives some empirical referents to go by in order to determine whether such a being exists. To say that Moses en-

197

countered Jehovah on Mount Sinai or that Jesus is the Son of God is not to utter statements of total transcendence. There are surely semantic problems in Christianity concerning "the Trinity," i.e., the relationship between God the Father, God the Son, and the Holy Spirit. This language has its own intrinsic ambiguity and presents paradoxes that presumably only the faithful are capable of imbibing. Whatever the Trinity means, God in the above senses, as encountered in the Old and New Testaments, at least, takes on a kind of historical character, for the transcendent being allegedly enters into history, reveals himself to the prophets or disciples, and performs miracles, and these claims at least give some quasi-empirical content to the concept "God." These uses of God-language, as I have said, overcome the indictment of the igtheist who claims that God-talk that is purely transcendental is without content. These uses do not violate the standards of meaningful language, for they are not beyond all possible experience. The question that is relevant is whether there is sufficient evidence and reason to believe in God in the sense of historical immanence.

Let us move the discussion to another stage and *assume* for purposes of argument only that the God of traditional theology is fully comprehensible and meaningful. God here is the creator and ground of the universe, an infinite, omniscient, omnipotent being, a law giver, the source of justice and the good. He is supernatural in the sense that he transcends nature as its source or ground. As I have said, I doubt that these ascriptions to God make sense. The question that we will have to deal with is the second one, whether such a being exists (whatever "God" refers to), or whether it is reasonable to disbelieve in such a being.

Atheism

A possible skeptical posture to take here is that of the atheist. Atheism means literally the negative of theism: *non-* or *not* theism. Atheists clearly are unbelievers, for they reject belief in such a God. They think that the proposition "God exists" is false, unlikely, or improbable. Thus atheists *disbelieve* in God. Now what I wish to consider here is not whether someone is or is not a disbeliever in God, but the *grounds* for his state of disbelief. It is entirely conceivable that some people are second- or third-generation atheists; that is, they might have been brought up within an atheistic family and simply imbibed atheism at their parents' or grandparents' knees. This form of atheism, like theism, is based on custom and tradition, and the disbeliefs of one's ancestors are simply accepted. This form of atheism may be akin to unquestioning faith, for it may be based upon cultural conditioning.

Similarly, atheism may be a product primarily of strong passion and feeling. Some people may have been so bruised by the trappings of religious institutions that they are repelled by religious faith on emotional grounds. Some individuals may, for example, reject the whole doctrine and litany of God because they reject the Roman Catholic hierarchy and its repressive attitude toward women, birth control, and abortion. Others may reject Orthodox Judaism because they find its rituals archaic and unappealing. Or still others may be disgusted by Protestant fundamentalism because they may abhor its Puritan phobias of sexuality or be offended by the skullduggery of televangelists. Much irreligion in today's world has psychological or sociological causes.

Or one may become an atheist primarily on political or ideological grounds. Many Marxists rejected religious belief because it was the "opiate of the masses," or the "sigh of the oppressed," or because it was often used by entrenched social classes to maintain their economic privileges. Atheism went hand in hand with the revolutionary struggle for social justice. Some such forms of atheism, however, may be as dogmatic as theism. One can think of the brutal suppression of religious believers at the hands of Stalin and the battle waged against the Russian Orthodox church by communist "true unbelievers" who sought to destroy its influence in the Soviet Union.

These forms of intolerant unbelief are unjustifiable as grounds for atheism per se. No doubt the churches are political institutions, and they express social doctrines that many may reject. In the *anciens regimes* of Europe and Latin America, authoritarian ecclesiastical institutions were often allied with the dominant wealthy classes and resisted the genuine grievances of peasants and workers. Interestingly, in recent times the Roman Catholic church, smarting from radical critiques of its ideological position, shifted to a defense of democracy, especially in its attack on the communist regimes in Eastern Europe. It has persistently defended its moral doctrines, however, and opposed reproductive freedom—birth control, sterilization, artificial insemination, and abortion. Opposition to repressive church policies on ideological or moral grounds is surely justifiable. However, our interest here is not in these grounds for the rejection of religious beliefs, but rather in atheism itself as a form of disbelief in God. Here we need to ask, What are the grounds for that?

We may distinguish two kinds of atheism. The first may be called *dogmatic* or *totalistic* negative disbelief. "God does not exist" says the dogmatic atheist, and that is all there is to it. This form of atheism expresses a form of fervent disbelief, the adamant conviction that atheism is simply true and needs no justification. For this kind of atheism, the case is closed. These atheists need not, they say, give reasons or evidence for their attitudes. They may accept the materialistic world-view as they interpret it and consider theism insupportable in the light of it. They exude a kind of revulsion toward theism, which they consider false, perhaps even pernicious.

Many atheists will no doubt demur and say that I am being unfair to their cause and that I have introduced a straw man. Yet I have encountered innumerable people who fit this description. Their objections to God may be idiosyncratic, based on personal psychological, sociological, or political objections. No doubt there is some ground for their attitude, for atheists have been brutally oppressed in the history of civilization. They were considered blasphemous, immoral infidels by their detractors, and often condemned to the stake. It is only in the modern period, in democratic societies, that they have come to enjoy the same rights as believers. Many are thus reacting to the kinds of religious intolerance and repression that atheists have suffered in the past. Nonetheless, I submit that this kind of position, whether held by atheists or theists, is mistaken; for it tilts in the direction of absolute, closed-minded dogmatism.

Since theism has had such a powerful hold on human imagination, the most sensible posture to take, I submit, is to examine carefully the case for and against God's existence, and to base one's lack of belief in God, if that is what one is led to, upon this examination. Thus atheism makes sense only if it is a *reasoned* position, arrived at after long and intelligent inquiry. Disbelief needs to be justified as a meaningful alternative to theism.

The basic question concerns the existence of God, and as we have seen, some philosophers and theologians have differed about the meaning of the term *God.* Some have argued that it is not an all-powerful or infinite God, but a finite God, or an anthropomorphized God playing a role in cooperation with us in helping to create a better universe. Atheists, as I define them, are those who reject *all* of these multifarious attributes of God. If knowledge refers to beliefs that are justified in some objective way and held to be true, then it also refers to negative beliefs that are said to be true, reasonable, or probable—if they are justified. If we say, after carefully examining the case for and against God's existence, that we believe that God does not exist, hence we disbelieve theism, then atheism is a form of justified knowledge, much the same as other forms of knowledge. There is a caveat that has to be added to this, however, for I submit that the existence of God has not been *dis*proved in an absolutistic sense, but simply that his existence is so highly unlikely or improbable that atheism is more likely to be true than theism. Why do I say this? Because the case for God has not been conclusively demonstrated, and alternative naturalistic explanations of the universe and human life seem better able to fit the data.

A key logical consideration here is that if someone makes a claim, especially if it is an important one, then the burden of proof is upon him or her to show why it ought to be accepted as true. One cannot simply revert to a statement of faith. The fact that someone strongly believes that something is the case and dogmatically asserts it is only a description of his or her own psychological state of mind; it tells us nothing about the world. Appeals to subjective passion, inner emotion, or intuition hardly offer sufficient justifications for a claim. If one were to demand validation for every and any private intuition, then we would open the floodgates to a plurality of conflicting idiosyncratic truths, and pure chaos would reign. On the contrary, if someone seriously maintains that something is the case about the universe, then he or she is called upon to support this statement by reference to the grounds for the belief.

Similarly, is the fact that a person's cultural tradition upholds certain religious beliefs and practices as true, and that he or she has been brought up to accept this faith, a sufficient warrant for such beliefs. If we were to accept custom as the basis for truth claims, would we not have to allow manifold truths—even if contradictory or factually false? We would then have to accept any and all claims to truth, such as the Mormon belief that an ancient tribe of Hebrews settled on the North American continent thousands of years ago, the Muslim belief in the prophetic legitimacy of Mohammed, and the Christian belief in the Second Coming. It is evident that an appeal to a set of ecclesiastical authorities or traditions that declare one faith system to be true rather than the next does not ipso facto make it so. This is hardly an adequate ground to establish the truths of a religion, especially since so-called religious authorities vehemently disagree about which is legitimate or illegitimate.

Now some religionists, in response to the arguments above, turn the tables and ask, "Can the atheist *disprove* that God exists?" "If you cannot demonstrate the negative," they say, "then we are entitled to believe the affirmative." But this line of argument is highly questionable. For example, if some people believe that mermaids exist, and I ask them for the evidence and reasons for their assertion, they may ask me to disprove the statement. I can accept this challenge and send out search parties to scour the oceans. If all of the reports come back negative, they may still be unconvinced. It is only if we were to drain all the oceans and find them empty, an insuperable practical difficulty, that we might have proved the negative. But these people might still insist that mermaids exist in the deep silt that is left, or somewhere else, or that I have killed them off by my tampering, or even that they are "paranormal" phenomena that elude any quest for evidence, and that they will continue to believe that mermaids exist. Often we can refute an affirmative statement by finding one negative instance. The universal statement that "All crows are black" can be disconfirmed by finding one instance of a pink crow, though if we have still not found one, and all that we have seen are black, one might still leave open the possibility that a pink crow may turn up. Similarly, does one believe that the gods from Mount Olympus—Zeus, Cronus, Athena, Icarus, Daedalus, and the other divine beings—exist? The polytheistic religion of the ancient Hellenes is most likely mythological. Similarly for Isis or Osiris of the ancient Egyptian religion. But try to disprove that such deities exist, and one enters into the same kind of impasse. The logical point is that unless one can find adequate grounds to establish a claim we are not entitled to hold it; moreover we cannot insist that it is incumbent on those who challenge the belief to first disprove it.

A curious argument against the atheist is that offered by the philosopher Alvin Plantinga, who has asserted that the theist does not have to bear the burden of proof to justify God's existence.[2] Plantinga does not believe that one can find an adequate foundationalist basis for knowledge. This being the case, it is not unreasonable for Christians to believe in God, which itself is a basic belief, not needing any further justification. But if Plantinga's argument were to be generalized then why could not *anyone* argue in similar fashion that their beliefs were basic, and not in need of justification. Muslims or Buddhists might simply proclaim the truths of Islam or Buddhism and deny the need to support their beliefs. Similarly, those who believe in reincarnation, or even Santa Claus, might insist that their beliefs were true and that the burden of proof would not be upon them to justify them. Would they also be entitled to hold their beliefs without any demonstration? Who is to pick and choose which need justification and which do not? Plantinga's response leaves one in a quandary, for in a sense anything goes, and one belief might be as true as the next, so long as, I suppose, it were deeply held with conviction and commitment. Although belief in God is not irrational per se, in that many honest and sincere men and women have attempted to justify their beliefs historically (although they may be mistaken

---

2. Alvin Plantinga and Nicholas Wolterstorff, eds., *Faith and Rationality* (Notre Dame, Ind.: Indiana University Press, 1986); James E. Tomberlin and Peter van Inwagen, eds., *Alvin Plantinga* (Dordrecht, Holland: D. Reidel, 1985).

in their proofs), I submit that Plantinga's move borders on irrationality. At the very least, he should defend the belief that we do not have to justify our beliefs at all—which, I submit, is an unreasonable philosophical position to take.[3]

Now very few religious believers will simply appeal to their mere faith states without any effort at argument. Nor will many claim their beliefs true without resort to any evidence at all. There no doubt have been religious zealots in the history of thought who have simply asserted their beliefs (such as Tertullian) even though others found them absurd, contradictory, and nonevidential.[4] But usually elaborate efforts have been offered by philosophers and theologians over the millennia to justify their beliefs. In what follows, I wish to outline some of the key arguments adduced, and the kinds of criticisms that have been made by skeptics. I should point out that the kind of atheism defended in this chapter may be mistaken. Perhaps there is a kind of eloquent truth that religious believers have discovered about the universe. Even though their specific cultural expressions differ, perhaps there is a common transcendental realm that they have tapped. Perhaps atheists and unbelievers are religiously blind about this realm. What we need is an open mind willing to examine the claim and a fair-minded investigation to see if there is any reliable knowledge at all that can be garnered. If there are truths, they can be arrived at by using skepticism as part of the method of inquiry.

Appeals to Experience

The first kind of justification that has been appealed to is based on the firsthand testimony of alleged witnesses. There are four kinds that need to be examined by the skeptical eye.

---

3. For a good critique of this argument, see Keith Parsons, *God and the Burden of Proof* (Buffalo, N.Y.: Prometheus Books, 1989).

4. I have discussed the appeals to custom, emotion, authority, faith, subjectivity, intuition, and the burden of proof argument in *The Transcendental Temptation* (Buffalo, N.Y.: Prometheus Books, 1986, Chapter 5), and so will not further pursue this argument here.

Revelation

Most of the major theistic documents draw upon revelations received from On High: Jacob, Abraham, Moses, and the other prophets in the Old Testament, Jesus and Paul in the New Testament, Mohammed in the Koran, Joseph Smith in the Book of Mormon, and Mary Baker Eddy in *Science and Health,* and so on. A root question to be asked of all such revelations is whether the testimony (*a*) has been corroborated by independent, impartial observers, and (*b*) whether alternative naturalistic and psychological explanations can account for the alleged experiences, such as the hearing of voices and or the seeing of visions. If one accepts revelation at face value, then it is relevant to ask which ones should be taken as veridical? For the legitimacy of the person who reveals the message has been disputed by other prophets, in which case they cancel each other out. That revelations are messages from God is doubtful. Most likely, they are the internalized soliloquies spun out of the human imagination. The fact that so many people have been willing to accept them as divinely inspired is a remarkable commentary on human gullibility, but the strength of the propensity to believe suggests that there is a deep-seated temptation at work.

The accounts of prophecies and revelations in the Bible are clearly uncorroborated. In the Old Testament, divine commandments often appear in the form of dreams. These are allegedly conveyed to the prophets by God. In the case of Moses, the voice from Jehovah, the burning bush, and the Ten Commandments were delivered to him alone on Mount Sinai. No one was able to check the authenticity of the revelations. New Testament revelations are likewise questionable, for they were transcribed 30 to 70 years after the death of Jesus, according to biblical scholars, and none of the Gospels were written by disciples who knew Jesus directly. Based on an oral tradition, the so-called testimonials are often contradictory, especially the accounts of Jesus' ministry, his virgin birth, and his resurrection. These so-called sacred books more likely are fictionalized stories penned by propagandists for a faith, rather than objective historical documents. The Koran is supposed to record the pronouncements of Mohammed, which were allegedly delivered to him by Gabriel, the messenger of Allah.

But the first set of revelations were received by Mohammed while he was alone in the hills and caves of Hirja, outside of Mecca, and later his revelations were rendered to meet practical moral and political problems; and thus they did not have the benefit of intersubjective corroboration.[5]

Miracles

The appeal to miracles has been adduced by believers to demonstrate that God intervenes in history and sets aside the laws of nature; and this is taken as a sign of the divine hand at work. Volcanic eruptions, floods, victories in time of war, and the sudden remission of illnesses have all been seen by believers as miraculous occurrences. David Hume has forcibly argued that the term *miracle* is often a substitute for ignorance of the real causes at work. If the events are favorable to human interests, he argued, this can be attributed to coincidence rather than divine intervention, and further investigations usually demonstrate that the alleged miraculous effects were due to natural causes. For Hume, whether we should admit that there has been a violation of the laws of nature is a question of probabilities. No miracle has ever been attested to by men and women of sufficient education and good judgment, says Hume, nor have any been observed under rigorously controlled conditions. Miracles are drawn from anecdotal hearsay by fairly primitive and superstitious peoples. Accordingly, before we are prepared to accept a miracle and thus overturn the natural regularities discerned in nature, we should demand extraordinary evidence for the miracle. Until we have a preponderance of evidence, we ought to reject such uncorroborated claims.

The appeal to ancient documents as evidential begs the question. Believers maintain that we should accept the Bible or the Koran because it records the prophecies of the prophets. Believers claim that the New Testament is true, because prophecies made in the Old Testament are fulfilled in the New. The skeptical response to this claim is that the Gospel writers were here presenting fic-

---

5. For a further extended discussion of these questions, see *The Transcendental Temptation,* op. cit.

tionalized accounts as fact. For example, some New Testament disciples maintain that the coming of Christ is foretold by Isaiah in the Old Testament, when he prophesied that a child would be born of a virgin. But the writers of the New Testament were undoubtedly well-versed in the Old Testament and so after the fact wrote and interpreted the New Testament in the light of it.[6] We may ask the question, How do we know that these were not inspired by God? The more likely interpretation is that they were etched by men seeking salvation, not by the finger of God. Naturalistic and historical accounts of how they were written undermine the claim that they were divinely revealed. The alleged miraculous powers of Moses, Jesus, and Mohammed were simply creative figments of human imagination, not evidence of God's presence in history.

Mystical Experience

Some believers report a special kind of intense experience in which they claim a divine being makes its presence known. This kind of experience appears in many different religious traditions—Buddhist, Christian, Muslim, Jewish, Hindu, and others. It is, however, a fairly rare occurrence within human experience. The practical question to raise is whether those who have not had such experiences should accept the secondhand testimony of those who claim they have. There are serious objections to doing so, and largely because the experience, almost by definition, resists any kind of independent corroboration. Mysticism is irremediably introspective and subjective. According to mystics as diverse as St. Theresa, St. John of the Cross, Meister Eckhart, and Plotinus, such an experience begins by a process of introversion or turning within to the "inner self." The knowledge allegedly derived is immediate and direct, and it is not mediated by representative ideas, cognitive or discursive symbols. It is, we are told, indubitable in its force, yet ineffable. Such experiences are seen to involve an involuntary and unconscious trancelike state that may culminate

---

6. See Randel Helms, *Gospel Fictions* (Buffalo, N.Y.: Prometheus Books, 1988).

in a kind of ecstatic bliss, a sense of peace, blessedness, or joy. Mystics often have the impression that they have left their bodies. For many there is a loss of awareness of the world of space, time, and material objects, and even self-hood, as they are enveloped by a new awareness of reality. They interpret this as caused by a divine power beyond themselves.

The skeptic can raise two practical questions: First, did the person who claims to have undergone such an encounter actually experience it as reported? We have no reason in general to question these phenomenological accounts. Second, and more pertinent, how shall they be interpreted? Did the mystic in some way come into contact with the absolute Godhead? Was the cause of this experience supernatural, or can one find alternative, prosaic naturalistic causal interpretations of it? The latter explanations are parsimonious. There are psychological causes, biochemical conditions, and socio-logical influences that may induce such experiences in some individuals. Indeed, experiences similar to the mystic rendition seem to be found in certain kinds of psychiatric disorders, and in some cases may be induced by psychedelic drugs.

It is difficult to know how to deal with such private claims if one has not had a similar experience. Perhaps the mystics are able to sharpen their sensibilities so that they can transcend the limits of normal perception or cognition, and those of us who have not had the benefit of such experiences may be spiritually blind. On the other hand, the mystic state may involve an abnormal distortion of perception, an unreliable altered state of consciousness. It is difficult to say so definitively. But because of the inherent problem of replication, we ought to be skeptical of the claim. This is all the more so when we realize that mystics tend to interpret their experiences in terms of the cultural and religious traditions within their environment. Thus the appeal to mysticism does not provide adequate evidence for the claim that God exists.

Religious Experience

There is still another kind of experience that some theists maintain provides an appropriate basis for belief in God. This range of evidence is not an intrinsically private or mystical experience, for it is commonly shared by a large number of human beings. I am here referring to the varieties of religious experience that sundry individuals past and present have reported as providing them sustenance in life. It assumes many forms. The belief in God, for many individuals, offers meaning and hope, a kind of psychological uplift. It enables individuals to endure adversity and tragedy, such as the death of a loved one. Many individuals say that on joining a monastery or entering a magnificent cathedral they are inspired by a sense of awe and piety. Singing hymns in unison with others and participating in common prayer and devotional services infuse a kind of aesthetic reverence. Many believers report that there is a healing power of religious belief. Life was empty, they were prey to drugs or alcohol, or addicted to sex. Belief in God had great therapeutic value for them, and it provided the motivation to overcome life's pitfalls and to persevere.

All that this testimony demonstrates, I submit, is that the commitment to a set of beliefs can infuse the individual with a reinforced sense of purpose in life. The beliefs offer therapy to the grieving heart, or help sustain an otherwise miserable or purposeless existence. They do not confirm the truth of the belief or validate its descriptive claim. Similar kinds of psychological support can be given by contradictory and mutually exclusive belief systems. Fascists and communists were as aroused and inspired by their ideological commitments as Christians or Muslims. But not all of these belief systems can be true at the same time. A religious experience in this sense refers primarily to the power of a set of convictions in a person's life; they do not affirm the truth of the claim per se.

Deductive Proofs

There have been many attempts to demonstrate the existence of God by philosophical argument. Three main proofs have been offered.

Ontological Argument

The ontological argument employs a formalistic method of proof that proceeds by the tautological analysis of the meaning of the concept of God. The ontologist begins with the idea of God, "a being of which none greater can be conceived." According to St. Anselm, if we assume that such a being does not exist, then he could not be a being of which none greater can be conceived, for finite beings do exist and would be greater. Therefore, the existence of God must be part of the essence of God, for to deny it is to assert a contradiction.

It is surprising that so many philosophers and theologians have been convinced by this argument, for its specious character is readily evident. The ontological argument assumes precisely what it sets out to prove. The very fact that some individuals have an idea of God that entails existence as part of its meaning does not necessarily demonstrate that the idea must exist independent of the concept in their minds. Not everyone has this idea of God, however; and it is not implanted in us innately. Moreover, why not assume that a being of which none greater can be conceived transcends the limits of existence and has achieved nonbeing, or Nirvana, which the Buddhists maintain is the highest state of reality. The basic fallacy of the ontological argument is that it is dealing with purely analytic statements, but whether they apply to the real world out there can only be determined by experience. To use a predefined concept to demonstrate the existence of God is to beg the question. Therefore, the ontological argument fails to convince those who do not have a prior belief in God.

Cosmological Argument

The line of reasoning of the cosmological argument is perhaps the most pervasive in the history of thought. The cosmological argument begins with the question, How explain the existence of motion, cause and effect, contingency, and necessity? We have two options, according to Aquinas: Either we can trace motion, causality, and contingency back through an infinite regress—but this, he affirms, would make the universe "unintelligible," for there would be no beginning, hence no proximate cause and no effect—or we can postulate an unmoved mover, first cause, or absolutely necessary being who has created the universe, and which, he asserts, everyone believes to be God.

Aquinas's argument only pushes our ignorance back one step, for one can always ask, What caused this being? That question is illegitimate, we are told. But why is it any more illegitimate than asking for the cause of the universe? Aquinas has postulated an infinite unknowable God, but this is not any less unintelligible than an infinite regress. Moreover, there are other possible options: Why not say that the universe is infinite, without beginning or end (God is alleged to be infinite), or that matter, mass, or energy are eternal, or that the universe is a product of chance, or that there are constant processes of creation going on? In any case, to use the term *cause* in a transcendental sense is to stretch its meaning inadmissibly. Causal explanations make sense within the natural world, where antecedent conditions can be isolated and are empirically observable. They make little sense when we extrapolate them outside the universe and endow them with transcendent meaning. The skeptic does not think that we can develop reliable knowledge about matters that extend beyond the present range of the natural sciences, but that we must suspend judgment about the "origin" of the universe. One clever variant of the cosmological argument is to say that it does not prove that God is the creator in time of the universe, but merely the ground of being; for without God to sustain the universe, all would collapse. This argument is equally specious, for it is a claim that remains unverified. Why does the universe require such a sustaining being? If so, does not that sustainer need to be sustained, and so on?

What about the "big bang," the expanding universe theory in current favor in astronomy and physics? This theory provides a useful mathematical explanatory model that is introduced to explain what appears to be a receding universe, but it tells us nothing about what existed before the big bang, nor as yet whether or not at some point in the future the universe is likely to implode and repeat the cycle. There are alternative, competing theories in contemporary physics and astronomy; for example the plasmic model, in which the universe is much older than the estimated

15 billion-year time-frame of the big-bang theory. In any case, none of these physical explanations say anything about whether there is a divine being at work in the universe, and even if one takes "God" to be equivalent to the laws of nature (à la Spinoza), such a being is not a personal god who demands worship and has provided a scheme of salvation. In regard to the human species, the theory of evolution seems to provide a more reasonable explanation for the emergence of life than does the creationist theory.

"Why should there be something rather than nothing?" asks Heidegger. Does this question make sense? Perhaps our universe (there may be a plurality of universes) is eternal and there is no beginning or end in time. No doubt the wisest posture to take is to confess that we cannot at present solve this question, and to suspend judgment. To leap in and to assert that the universe was created by divine fiat is to move far beyond the present range of verifiable evidence. In the last analysis, the cosmological argument reduces to the ontological argument, and this, as we have seen, is reduced to pure postulation. The cosmologist has assumed what he sets out to prove and has not demonstrated the existence of God. Hence skepticism about his proof seems to be a reasonable response.

Teleological, Analogical, or Design Argument

A familiar argument that is often introduced to prove the existence of God is the postulation that what appears to be order in nature is evidence of a divine intelligence. In the Thomistic vernacular this is known as the teleological argument, and it draws upon the assumption that there are teleological ends at work in nature. We observe things that have occurred with regularity and happen always, or for the most part, says Aquinas. Moreover, there seem to be means-ends causal sequences: the egg becomes the chick, which matures into a full-grown chicken; the river seeks its delta; the rain falls so that the corn may grow. How do we explain these lawlike patterns that are encountered, asks Aristotle, except by analogical reasoning. We note human intelligence and art at work. The carpenter constructs a house, each part fulfills its function: the roof provides shelter from the elements; a fireplace, fire and warmth; windows, light; and doors, an entrance and exit. In similar fashion, we can only attribute the observed teleological processes to a divine intelligence. According to Aristotle's argument, much the same as an archer shoots an arrow into the air aiming at a bull's eye, so God or the gods have imparted purposes to all physical and biological systems in nature.

Modern physics rejects teleological explanation. Aristotle's final causality collapsed under experimental investigation in the natural sciences. We need postulate no final causes, said Galileo; nature operates by material and efficient causes. Similarly, Darwinian theories of evolution provide a resounding blow to vitalistic causality in biology. Species are not fixed; they do not manifest natural ends or functions. Chance, genetic mutations, differential reproduction, and adaptation better explain the evolution of species. The human species was not created in the image of God, nor is it necessarily the highest form of life. Other highly complex forms of life have not survived; those that have done so are the result of adaptation and also a degree of luck or chance.

The teleological argument was replaced in the eighteenth century by the design argument. Deists argued that the universe is much like a mechanical device, such as a clock. God created it, but he does not intervene in history. The clock ticks away with deterministic precision and necessity. We discover what appears to be a perfect symmetry and harmony in the parts, which points to a design or plan. But it is not possible to explain this without postulating a designer who drafted the blueprint. Therefore, we may infer that God exists.

The skeptics reject both forms of the argument. They reject the use of teleological explanations in the natural sciences and opt for the evolutionary model rather than the creationist theory. In response to the argument from design, they say that we cannot discover a universal order in nature. Moreover, order does not imply design or the existence of a draftsman. Indeed, nature is often the scene of conflict, chaos, and disorder. Species struggle for survival, there are cosmic collisions, star systems come into being, explode, or begin to cool down. We cannot read purpose or design into natural processes. Nature is neutral and manifests no preferences. "Ah," replies the theist, "perhaps there is a deeper order in nature." To which the skeptic retorts, Why draw only a selective analogy between nature and human intelligence? Human beings make many mistakes. For example, they may bungle and botch in building a house, why not reason analogically that God is likewise given to error? It usually takes several carpenters to build a house, not one; perhaps this is evidence for polytheism? The universe is so vast that perhaps it needs a multiplicity of Gods to create and sustain it.

The believer again replies that God is perfect, the ideal standard of absolute goodness and justice, and is not capable of error. How are we to explain the existence of evil in the universe? asks the skeptic. If we use the cosmological and design arguments we begin with certain observed facts that we encounter in nature—motion, cause and effect, contingency, and order—and we reason back to God, who is alleged to be responsible for these. But what about other "facts": conflicts, accidents, disease, cruelty, suffering, and pain? How explain these? Using such arguments, said Hume, we can only assume that God is either impotent or malevolent. "Evil is only human," says the believer, "not divine. If there is cruelty or suffering it is due to man's omissions or commissions, not to God's." What about the slender colt that is torn to shreds by the predator? Why does God often allow good people to suffer and the wicked to succeed and become rich and prosperous? Why does God allow one-third of all pregnancies to end in miscarriages, thus killing helpless fetuses? Why does God, as the super-abortionist, not save these innocent souls? Why does God permit these terrible things to happen? If he is all-good and all-powerful, why can't he mitigate and, indeed, prevent evil?

The efforts of believers to save their ship have been ingenious, but they boil down to no more than rationalizations introduced ad hoc to bail out a leaking argument. Many deny that evil exists. They argue that from the cosmic standpoint all will turn out to be good in the end (the Buddhists' position). But is this not sheer whistling in the dark? We are all dead in the end, so why assume that everything will turn out for the best in the long run? "What appears to be evil," they say, "is only seen from our limited vantage point; it may, from a deeper view, turn out to be good." (At least our rotting corpses will feed the worms and fertilize the soil!) But if we cannot read evil into the universe, then are we entitled to read in good? The claim that all existence, as an expression of God, is ultimately good is thus wishful presumption. All human purposes may turn out to be for naught in the end. The problem of evil is not a problem for the atheist; for the universe is neither good nor evil, but just *is*. It is only a problem for theists who constantly attribute to nature their fondest dreams and their intense longings for eternal salvation.

Another effort by theists to save the case is to deny the reality of natural evil. "Evil is due only to man's sin," we are told, "and this follows from his own free will and his acts of omission or commission." In the first case, to deny that the tragedies that befall the human and animal kingdom are evil betrays a gross moral insensitivity. How justify the torment, suffering, and death of an infant from an incurable disease or a natural disaster (such as an earthquake or a tornado). To blame the parents or other human beings, and to say that God is not responsible, is to close one's eyes to suffering. Not everything can be attributed to human choice. Granted, we should find a cure for cancer and build safer buildings, but why blame men and women for acts of omission, when God— if he exists—should surely take part of the blame. After all, it is his show, "creating Man in his own image." The rationalization continues, "Man must have a genuine choice between good and evil." But if God has the same freedom of choice, why does he not choose evil as Man does; and as long as God has programmed us, why does he not make us strong enough to know the good, as he does, and to resist evil, as he likewise is able to do?

Another attempted escape hatch is to argue in terms of "privation," i.e., that evil is due to the defects of the materials that exist, as potentialities are fulfilled there is a "lack," or evil, in a natural process. But this is a form of poetic teleology that hardly makes explanatory sense on scientific grounds. We may ask, If God created the materials with which he has to work, why could he not have overcome privation? Thus all efforts to escape the problem of evil are irreconcilable with the cosmological and teleological forms of analogical arguments, and are especially paradoxical for those who choose to use this method of reasoning. At which point believers retreat to an act of faith (as did Job in the Old Testament) and ask, "Who can explain the ways of God to Man?" and affirm that "we have faith that God will make right all things in the end." But this is hardly an adequate response, for the believers are again assuming that God is good and just. But they can't make a valid exception in their argument; for if from what is observed in nature they infer a divine creator, then they end up with a paradox in being unable to account for evil. Their God is hardly a morally commendable being. Either he is a cruel, heartless, and malevolent demon, or he is finite and impotent, unable to stamp out or prevent many kinds of evil from tarnishing his creation. The design argument clearly demonstrates that the believers who use it wish to have their cake and eat it too, and that they are again assuming what they wish to prove. They have introduced ad-hoc rationalizations to dispute any paradoxes that emerge. But they have ended up in hopeless confusion and contradiction with a God whose ways are ultimately unintelligible to us.

The Positive Case for Atheism

Atheism does not simply present a negative critique of the case for God, but it seeks to set forth a positive alternative conception of the universe. There is thus a strong set of arguments in favor of atheism that needs to be stated. Historically atheism was given tremendous impetus with the development of modern science. I am here referring to the naturalistic and/or materialistic view of nature that emerged in the sciences. As a result, a comprehensive theory of nature was developed, involving generalizations from the natural sciences. It stated that the physical system of nature had no need for teleological purposes, as Aquinas and the medievalists believed, and that nature could be explained in terms of the laws of physics and chemistry, biology and astronomy, without invoking occult causes. The explanatory principles of the natural sciences are being progressively developed and are changing in the light of discoveries of new data and theories, but they also provide a coherent, nontheistic, general interpretation of nature. The naturalistic/materialistic view draws on the biological sciences and depends especially upon the theory of evolution, developed by Darwin and other naturalists in the nineteenth and twentieth centuries. Instead of fixed species created in one act by God, with human beings at the apex, human life could be accounted for in terms of natural evolutionary processes. Similarly, social institutions and human psychology could be interpreted in terms of natural causes. Thus the atheistic/naturalistic/cosmic outlook provides a comprehensive alternative interpretation of nature, and it better fits the facts of observation as an explanatory model. Accordingly, there is considerable evidence for a nontheistic *weltanschauung*.

In the great struggle ensuing between religion and science, religion had to give way at almost every point, conceding the Copernican, Darwinian, and behavioral revolutions of thought, and the classical edifice erected by theologians collapsed.

Most theologians today—save backwater remnants of fundamentalist thinking—no longer dispute scientific interpretations of nature and the human species. They may, for example, accept the theory of evolution, but they still wish to leave some room for religious piety. There are, they claim, two ways of knowing: that of science and that of religion. Religion allegedly explains the "ultimate" origins of the universe and deals with the mysteries of being still unknown.

I question these efforts to rescue the theistic view of reality, for science constantly undermines religious faith. Religionists attempt to save their systems of faith by postulating an ultimate metaphysical origin to the universe; and they are willing to push the age of the universe back from the biblical account of 10,000 years to 15 billion years. God is still a *deus ex machina,* however, for he intervenes at times in history. These claims, I submit, are unsubstantiated, and are merely a last-ditch effort to rescue religious faith. My main point is that, although the burden-of-proof argument is the ground for resisting theism, the naturalistic world-view has an enormous body of empirical evidence to support it, and so it is not simply a case of proving the negative. Without *disproving* the existence of God, it is possible to demonstrate the validity of the alternative naturalistic framework by pointing to the substantial body of tested naturalistic principles.

Agnosticism

A new form of unbelief, particularly since the nineteenth century, is agnosticism. This position was popularized by T. H. Huxley, Leslie Stephen, Clarence Darrow, among others.[7] Some critics have considered agnosticism to be a polite form of atheism, maintaining that agnostics are fearful of taking a decisive stand because of possible social ostracism. There are three forms of agnosticism that may be delineated.

In the first sense, agnosticism is the negative of gnosticism, i.e., it states that certain things are basically unknown or unknowable. God, or the transcendental reality, cannot be known by the finite mind of man. The absolute transcends both the forms of possible experience and the categories of our understanding. In this sense some religious believers can at the same time be agnostics—for they are simply confessing their inability to know God. Some fideists profess faith in God, yet believe that his essence and majesty is incomprehensible to us. This form of agnosticism leaves open more questions than it resolves, for if such a being is ultimately beyond human comprehension, how or on what basis can we affirm that he exists? To merely state that we have faith is to beg the question.

A second kind of agnosticism is especially popular today, and many people who are unwilling or unable to say whether or not they are theists or atheists maintain that they simply do not know which position is true. This form of agnosticism is similar to classical Pyrrhonistic skepticism. Having examined the arguments adduced in favor of the God hypothesis, they are uncertain as to the claim; on the other hand they do not think that God has been disproved by the atheists. Therefore they say that it is impossible to ever know such ultimate truths and that they will remain neutral and suspend judgment.

This position does not appear to me to be tenable, surely not after the centuries of arguments between theists and atheists. One or another side of the debate seems to have the stronger

---

7. See especially Thomas H. Huxley, "Agnosticism and Christianity," volume 5 of *Collected Essays* (New York: Appleton, 1894).

case. Given the burden-of-proof argument, I submit that atheism, as the lack of belief in theism, seems the more reasonable case, and God's existence is very unlikely. One might ask, Do angels exist in the universe? What would be the agnostic's response to this query? These beautiful mythological figures, I submit, are figments of the human imagination, and it is highly unlikely that they exist in some rarified mystical-spiritual universe; at least no credible evidence exists to support that speculative conjecture. I have not decisively disproved that angels exist; nevertheless I think it is unreasonable to take the position of the neutral agnostic and say that it is still an open question and that the truth may lie in either direction. I can be an *a*-angelist or *non*-angelist without being accused of being a dogmatist. There are many other questions for which we do not have sufficient evidence either way, and here the agnostic's stance is not unreasonable. For example, Does intelligent life exist in other galaxies? Or do other stars have planetary systems similar to ours? These are interesting questions that depend upon further investigation to resolve. But the second form of agnosticism as applied to the God question seems to me to be fundamentally untenable.

There is still a third form of agnosticism, actually the form introduced and defended by Huxley, and this is, in my judgment, its most compelling form. Huxley wrote:

> Agnosticism is not a creed, but a method, the essence of which lies in the rigorous application of a single principle. . . . Positively the principle may be expressed as in matters of intellect, follow your reason as far as it can take you without other consideration. And negatively, in matters of the intellect, do not pretend conclusions are certain that are not demonstrated or demonstrable.[8]

In the nineteenth century agnosticism was similar to rationalism, "a commitment to reason and evidence as a basis for belief." This form of agnosticism expresses a basic methodological principle of constructive skeptical inquiry, as I defended it earlier; that is, that one should use objective methods for establishing knowledge

---

8. T. H. Huxley, op. cit.

claims as far as possible and that one should only accept beliefs if they have been properly justified by reason and evidence. Beliefs that do not come up to this standard can be doubted. This criterion means that our beliefs should be based on the best available evidence and that the grounds for them should be adequate. In regard to belief in God, for example, an agnostic could consistently doubt or deny its claim because it does not meet the demands of objectivity or adequacy.

Huxley himself was led to this position. He said that he "invented . . . the title of *agnostic*. It came into my head as suggestively antithetic to the 'gnostic' of church history, who professed to know so very much."[9] And Huxley was straightforward in his rejection of Christianity:

> I verily believe that the great good which has been effected . . . by Christianity has been largely counteracted by the pestilent doctrine . . . that honest disbelief in their more or less astonishing creeds is a moral offense, indeed a sin of the deepest dye.[10]

Summary. This latter form of agnosticism as properly interpreted and atheism thus overlap; namely, we ought not to believe in the statement that "God exists" unless we have adequate grounds to do so (atheism), and since the case in favor of theism does not satisfy the demands of objectivity (agnosticism) we have a right to be skeptical of belief in God and remain doubtful of it (agnosticism). Indeed, it is very unlikely that such a being exists (atheism). Both of these positions are consistent with igtheism, which finds the belief in a metaphysical, transcendent being basically incoherent and unintelligible. I therefore conclude that the case for the existence of God has not been demonstrated, and that a constructive skeptic can with good reason maintain that it is highly improbable that such a being exists.

---

9. See "agnostic" in *Webster's New International Dictionary*, 2nd ed., unabridged, or *Random House Dictionary of the English Language*, 2nd ed. (1989).

10. T. H. Huxley, "Agnosticism and Christianity," op. cit.; see Lionel W. Hepburn's article "Agnosticism," in the *Encyclopedia of Philosophy*, ed. by Paul Edwards (New York: Macmillan, 1967).

Religion as a Way of Life

An entirely different apologetic tactic has been adopted by religionists, especially since Kant and James, attempting to demonstrate that belief in God is nonetheless still not unreasonable. Even
if there are no demonstrable proofs or a sufficient range of experience to which we can refer in order to validate the existence
of God, the *belief* itself that God exists is justifiable on pragmatic
grounds. This brings in a set of utilitarian arguments that I will
summarize. These are not unlike the conclusions drawn by the
ancient skeptics, who, reaching an impasse in regard to epistemological claims, ended up by following the ways of custom.

The Pyrrhonist skeptics illustrate this paradoxical choice. They
claim neither to affirm nor deny the existence of Gods, but to
suspend judgment. They are attempting to be neutral about all
claims to knowledge, including those of religion. In practical life,
however, Sextus Empiricus states, the Pyrrhonists "conform to
the ordinary view" in that they "affirm undogmatically the existence
of Gods, reverence Gods, and affirm that they are possessed of
foreknowledge."[11] The practical implications that are drawn from
this skeptical stance are most perplexing; for unable to resolve
the question of the existence or nonexistence of the Gods, Pyrrhonist
skeptics revert to their ancestral customs. Sextus thus states, "the
Gods do exist," and he performs "everything that conduces to
their worship and veneration."[12]

Similar sentiments, as we have seen, were expressed by some
modern skeptics, who, mired in utter epistemological uncertainties
concerning the truths of the metaphysical God, nonetheless behaved
religiously. Were these skeptics dissembling because of fear of social
disapproval, or were they genuine in their choice? We do know
that atheism and agnosticism have had rough going in that unbelievers have often been persecuted. The history of religious per-
secution for dissent from the reigning orthodoxies was extensive,

---

11. Philip P. Hallie, ed., *Skepticism, Man and God: Selections from the
Major Writing of Sextus Empiricus* (Middleton, Conn.: Wesleyan University
Press, 1964), Chapter 3, p. 16.

12. Ibid., p. 188.

from Socrates to Spinoza, Hobbes, Hume, and Shelley down to the present. True martyrdom is a fate that few mortals are willing to bear. Perhaps the model being followed was dictated by prudence, not genuine conviction. Here the criteria for adopting a religion does not depend on whether it is true or false, but upon extraneous practical considerations in the social and political climate.

Ancillary with these considerations is the effort by religionists who believe in God, and do not doubt that he exists, to make a positive case for theism over and beyond the counsels of epistemological doubt offered by skeptics; and that is the argument that it is not unreasonable to believe in God on pragmatic grounds. Again I am here referring not necessarily to the truth content of the belief in God so much as the practical consequences of the *belief* itself as it spills out into action.

It is important that we recognize a gradation in scale concerning the strength of beliefs and their role in life. (1) There are beliefs that may or may not be true and are held without deep commitment. (2) There are true beliefs justified on adequate grounds that are considered part of the body of knowledge. But over and beyond these (3) there are convictions, based on intellectual and passionate grounds, that one's beliefs are true and important. Such beliefs have a powerful hold upon one's conduct and behavior. Religious beliefs, whether or not they are true or have been adequately justified, can have a powerful impact upon people's actions, and their beliefs can determine how they live. Beliefs become embedded in behavioral patterns as a way of life, and they are institutionalized and reinforced by social customs. Such traditional modes of behavior structure the ways of life that have been adopted. They are enduring elements in a cultural fabric of linguistic habits, rituals, ceremonies, and morality, and they are defended because of that. The religion people have, like their race, defines their ethnicity and gives them their identity. To be Christians or Jews or Hindus thus provides a structure to their very being. This cultural framework has deep historical roots. The major classical religions are among the oldest institutions in human history. They have a life of their own, as it were, and exert an enormous influence on human conduct, even transcending national frontiers. They are transmitted from generation to generation, from parent and grandparent to children and their progeny. Religion is deemed so important that even when emigrants leave their native shores for new frontiers, their religious customs are transported with them and are immediately given root in the new soil in which they are transplanted.

In one sense, what religion a person has is arbitrary, a product of chance or fate. Religions develop haphazardly, without plan or design; they become ingrained with other social institutions and are deeply entrenched. Where a religion is an old one in a defined geographical area, it may be so indelibly interfused with the way that the people live that it becomes essential to the entire functioning of the society. How people are first received into the world (if they are baptized or circumcised), how they are nurtured and educated by their parents and teachers, how they are married, how they deal with tragedies, and how they are buried, are all defined by the traditional religious code. More essentially, the moral principles and values that are cherished are imbibed from the religious environment. Each person is washed by the waves of faith in the surrounding waters and is molded by the socio-cultural context.

However, the traditional role of religion is being altered in our rapidly changing world; for the religious hegemony of earlier eras is giving way to a plurality of competing sects. Thus there are numerous options for choice—of conversion and deconversion—in the modern world. Moreover, secularism has undermined the authority of religions in many societies, and alternative secular institutions have developed to perform the functions of the heretofore exclusive domain of religion.

Nevertheless, religious institutions do not simply seek to provide us with true beliefs or instruct us in knowledge; for they remain as the repositories of ancient metaphysical conceptions of the universe long since shown to be untrue. Distinctively, they are vehicles for *praxis* or action. For religious institutions provide conventional structures by means of which individuals can transact in a cultural framework; they prescribe basic rules deemed vital in governing behavior.

In those societies in which a particular religion has a monopoly of power and influence (as in modern-day Islamic countries), it is difficult or impossible to shed the institutional-cultural network

223

on skeptical grounds and choose to live independently outside of it. If one grows up in China, one cannot easily abandon the Chinese language and the system of characters used in reading and writing. Religion is akin to the language we use, the clothing we wear, the manners of civilized life we follow. We cannot very well begin afresh. Similarly, the priests have a vested role in society, and their temples and churches remain as convenient places to carry out a number of secular tasks. One surely cannot invent a private language, adopt idiosyncratic clothing, a bizarre style of life, or an entirely new moral framework, and hope to be easily accepted by others. This would mean a radical rupture with the existing cultural context. To assume the role of the dissenter or nonconformist is to risk one's very being: infidels are in constant danger of being ostracized or expelled by the guardians of manners, morals, and traditions. One can thus appreciate the apprehensions of skeptics, who reject the reigning dogmas, yet are unable to abandon the practices of their ancestors. Religions, according to their proponents, seem to serve convenient, even necessary, functions in society. And this line of argument leads to a pragmatic justification for religious beliefs. Let us evaluate the functions of traditional theistic religion.

The Moral Case for Religion

First, religions have moral functions that according to their proponents justify our continued commitment to them. Kant attempted to provide a philosophical justification for this approach. He did not think that we could prove the existence or nonexistence of God, for the speculative idea transcends the categories of experience. Unlike others who used this argument, however, he thought that morality was autonomous, and that we could, by moral reasoning, discover our duties and determine what is right or wrong. Nonetheless, given the antimonies between virtue and happiness, duty and pleasure, he felt that morally righteous persons may have to sacrifice their happiness. He thus introduced the unprovable postulates of God, freedom, and immortality to overcome any disparities between them. Presumably any injustices in this world would be settled at Judgment Day in the next.

This kind of argument is popular today. Without religion, we are admonished, people would behave indecently. Religion thus provides an incentive for us to fulfill our duties and obligations. It provides the moral bond in a community of people. Where the law is not able to intervene, religion can sanctify certain forms of conduct, reward those that are virtuous, and prohibit those that are wicked. The Decalogue, the Torah, the New Testament, and the moral authority of the Roman Catholic church, for example, all lay down a finely woven set of commandments that we cannot break without dire consequences. Those who disobey God's will (as interpreted by clergy) will suffer punishment for their sins; and those who abide by them will be rewarded.

Some skeptics have rationalized that, even if a religion is false, it may be efficacious and that the social order needs some sacred authority to instill and enforce the principles of morality. They believe that if religion were to collapse, chaos would reign. Without the fear of divine punishment hanging over their heads, people would steal, cheat, rape, and murder.

Thus, whether or not religious beliefs are true or false, people act as if they were because of the pragmatic effect of these beliefs upon their conduct. The fallacious character of this argument should be apparent, and for the following reasons. First, there is no guarantee that belief in the fatherhood of God or the threat of Judgment Day will ensure moral devotion. Religious piety is no guarantee of moral virtue. Belief in God does not automatically lead to purity of motive or rectitude of deed. Many heinous crimes have been committed in the name of God, from the bloody Inquisition to the Islamic Holy Jihad. Second, religious systems often differ about the moral code. Some favor capital punishment, others oppose it. Some prohibit abortion, others permit freedom of choice. Some allow divorce, others deny it. There are diverse dietary laws and prohibitions and differing views of proper and improper sexual conduct. Thus there are contradictory moral commandments between different religious creeds. Are they all worthwhile, or only some? If we argue for the former, we have a relativistic morality; if the latter, then we need to transcend religious morality in favor of ethical principles established on the basis of their rationality.

Third, many persons, without a belief in God, have led exemplary lives of nobility and excellence, based on independent ethical grounds. One can think of Aristotle and Spinoza and John Dewey, for example. The development of moral character, the exercise of self-respect and self-discipline, and the beneficent regard for the needs of others can spring from nonreligious ethical motives. Moreover, to say that the fear of eternal damnation or the promise of everlasting reward is an essential motive for moral behavior is really immoral, for it is based on a concern for one's own long-range well-being and self-interest; and unless the determination to do good is rooted in a genuinely experienced internalized, autonomous moral conscience, rather than in obedience to God, then a person is not truly moral. Thus moral rules need not be founded on a theistic source to be effective. What is at issue here is the conflict between philosophical ethics based on rational grounds and religious morality rooted in habit, tradition, and faith. But the skeptic asks, Is there any rational or objective basis for ethics or, in the last analysis, does it depend upon arbitrary postulation, cultural relativity, or subjective caprice? This is a serious charge, and I will defer consideration of ethical skepticism and responses to it to Chapter 9, where we will ask: Is there such a thing as ethical knowledge, and is it possible to be objective about moral choices?

Nonetheless, the moral case in favor of religious practices does have some merit. For in one sense, moral rules and principles have their locus in an historical context. It is very difficult, perhaps even impossible, for individuals to decide every moral question on their own, to invent or design their own moral compasses. The principles of moral conduct, in a sense, express the collective wisdom of the culture, handed down from generation to generation, and what we are left with are the residues of moral truths discovered by our forebears. Accordingly, it is an enormous hurdle to simply throw them aside and start afresh. We are born in the midst of a moral framework, and this is so intermeshed with our religious heritage that it cannot be easily unglued or dislodged without the entire scaffolding crashing down. Thus it is not, I submit, unreasonable to adhere to the existing moral-religious framework of practices based on the principle that *some* rules of behavior are better than none and that, although we may not agree with everything handed down, what has endured at the very least provides regulative norms, as it were, with which we can work.

A good illustration of this is a conversation that I had with a highly intelligent, well-educated couple at dinner in San Francisco one evening. Both had careers, he a prominent attorney, and she a teacher. Both were Mormons, but both rejected the literal truths of the Mormon faith. Nonetheless, they attended the Mormon Church, sent their children to Mormon Sunday school, and participated in the various community functions of the church. The institution provided them with a nexus for their moral and social lives, and this had value for them. (This leads to a second justification of religiosity, its sociological function, which we shall consider shortly.) The problem with this argument is that it doesn't work very well in many social contexts, where there may be competing religious denominations and where there are alternative, secular opportunities available. Thus one is not forcibly condemned to accept the faith of one's forebears without question, and it is possible to break from the fold. Widespread intermarriage in modern society often brews diverse religious influences within the family. In many Western societies one might have a Scotch-Irish Presbyterian father and an Italian Roman Catholic mother, or a Japanese Buddhist mother and an African-American Protestant father. How does one resolve these competing loyalties that strain traditional familial bonds? How does one cope with different views on sin and virtue; or real differences about abortion, birth control, and divorce; or how to bring up one's children. These all concern practical questions of prudential choice. But the actual religious background of the participants may be in conflict and may not provide a basis for easy resolution of disagreements. Can such disagreements be overcome by objective methods of inquiry? Or should we throw up our hands and say that there is no solution to fundamental disputes in value and morality and that one way of life is as good as the next? Is it only a question of emotive choice and cultural relativity, or can we say what is right or wrong? We will address these issues in Part 4. Suffice it to say now that religion does not always help to resolve moral dilemmas.

The Sociological Case: Cultural Relativity and Ethnic Loyalty

Closely tied to the moral case is a second kind of argument in favor of a religious system often adduced, and this concerns the broader sociological functions that a religion may have. Religion not only structures our moral behavior and provides us with precepts to instill in our children, but it expresses a deeper set of social practices and traditions; for religion and ethnicity, nationality and identity, are intertwined. And religion is not simply identified with a set of beliefs and practices that a person may or may not actively espouse, but at its very core it defines what a person is. One is brought up as an Episcopalian or a Baptist, Greek Orthodox or Jew, Roman Catholic or Hindu, and this becomes essential to that person's identity. There is a heritage that many or most parents and grandparents transmit to children from the beginning, whether consciously or unconsciously. To stray from the fold is to break the bonds that cement the individual to his or her family and community. These ties are strengthened and reinforced by kinship relationships. People are most often bred to a religion, not converted to its creed or doctrine. It is not the proofs of theologians or philosophers that cements one to a religious faith, but consanguinity. Religions are thus rooted in the reproductive cycle of the common stock. To question one's religion is to throw into doubt one's genetic inheritance.

A good illustration of this occurred when a colleague of mine agreed to write an article for *Free Inquiry* magazine critical of the Jehovah's Witnesses. This article provided a powerful indictment of a rather literalist-dogmatic sect. But to my surprise the author insisted that the article appear under a pseudonym. When I asked him why, he said that he did not wish to hurt his parents' feelings. They were devout Jehovah's Witnesses and would feel terrible if they learned that their own son had publicly disavowed their religion. He did not wish to betray their devotion to him and his affection for them.

In another case, a young Jewish man told his Rabbi that he did not believe in God. The Rabbi responded that this was all right as long as he remained a Jew. A religion thus performs a sociological function, not the least of which is the fact that it serves as a transmission belt and sustaining force for the ethnic group. Many Jews will continue to observe dietary habits, forgo work on the Sabbath, and marry within the faith, because not to do so would break their parents' hearts and betray their traditions. Religions must demand loyalty and fidelity to sustain them. And they exert an enormous influence on the individual to conform. Spinoza rejected the religion of the Old Testament, but the Jews of Amsterdam, fearful of Gentile reactions to irreligion, bade him to return to the fold and to be silent. He refused to do so, and so was excommunicated. This was extremely painful for him; he was a pariah within his own community, alienated and alone.

A skeptic might conclude that caution is the better part of valor, and that one ought to conform to the demands of the religious culture, at least outwardly, so as to avoid the risk of charges of heresy and betrayal. Better to close one's eyes than to be plucked from the social fabric of which one is a part. The sociological pressures are very strong, for the entire way of life, not simply its moral commandments, may be at stake. Manners and customs, language and literature, standards of marriage and achievement, norms of permissible sexual conduct, expectations and recrimination, reward and punishment, are all interfused in the social-religious fabric. It is difficult or impossible for most individuals to shatter, destroy, or abandon the sociological womb.

The argument above perhaps makes some sense in a stable and/or isolated society where traditions limit choices. In a dynamic, rapidly changing, and pluralistic world, where fixed social structures are being transformed, the individual has many options. One can pick up and emigrate to another country, learn another language, convert to another religion, or live as a free and independent person. Thus prudential choice is not limited in its option to believe or not believe one religion. Moreover, we have the power to consciously modify the social systems in which we live by restructuring them. We can legislate and reform our society. If we cannot live outside of it, we can at least attempt to remake it along more rational grounds. Here we are brought to the arena of politics, where we seek to determine social policies. But are political policies and plans themselves subjective and beyond rational control, simply a question of power and coercion, or are they amenable to objective criticisms? These questions we will treat in Chapter 10. Suffice it to state now that politics is not simply a question of taste or power, but involves some room for rational criticism.

The Aesthetic Case

Related to the moral and sociological arguments is the appeal to aesthetic value. Many people find that religious traditions, even if false and outmoded, have a kind of beauty of their own and that they inspire profound aesthetic experiences. The majesty and splendor of the great cathedrals, mosques, and temples evoke a sense of awe and reverence. They are, if nothing else, testaments to the faiths of our ancestors; and they can arouse intense feelings. Religion dramatizes the human condition, as human beings face death and tragedy and contemplate the finitude of mortal existence. Religion, like music, art, and literature, thus evokes a passionate sense of beauty, and as such it has intrinsic worth for many people. The paintings of the great masters of the Louvre, the choral compositions of Bach, and the rose-colored stained glass of the Reims Cathedral are creative expressions of the human imagination and are cherished as such.

Similarly, the aesthetic sensibility finds beauty in tradition, in the pomp and majesty of the Communion rite, the prayers during Ramadan, or in the process of meditation of a Buddhist monk bedecked in saffron robes. Aside from whether or not its doctrines are true, people can participate in a rich religious cultural tradition, and this ought to be preserved, or so the advocates of religion based on the aesthetic argument maintain.

All of this no doubt has some merit. But I wish to point out again that we are dealing with artistic appreciation, and the sensibilities of skeptics or nonbelievers may not be as equally stimulated as those of the believers. I remember attending a service at a Russian Orthodox church in Zagorsk, near Moscow. I was deeply impressed by the ornate interior, the splendid works of art, and the chanting intonations of the choir of women whose heads were covered by babushkas, even the commanding figure that the priest displayed in the ceremony. These experiences are not unlike those evoked by attending a Wagnerian opera with all of its pomp, majesty, drama, music, and choral power. Neither the opera nor the religious spectacle are true, yet both express powerful symbolism and metaphor that can move people deeply. The true believer no doubt approaches the scene in a cathedral in a frame of mind different from that of the skeptic. For the drama renders the believer certain "truths" that the skeptic cannot accept—that God in some mysterious way, working through the priest, is present during the service and hears the prayers of the devout. None of these symbols, which believers accept, are true. In fact, part of the charade appears offensive, even ugly, to the skeptic, not beautiful.

Nonetheless, the aesthetic argument holds that there is a richness to one's heritage and that the eloquent expressions of traditional culture ought to be preserved. The skeptic can appreciate all forms of art, secular and religious, none of which he is willing to endow with any mystical significance or ontological sanctification. The central question for the skeptic concerns the relationship of the truth value of a symbol to its aesthetic function. Will a system of beliefs and practices continue to have powerful influence if all of their claims to truth are disavowed? If a system of belief is taken as mythological and understood as such, does it nonetheless continue to satisfy a person's religious needs? It is one thing to take a work of art as art and appreciate its aesthetic effect; it is another to try to transform it into a kind of truth. It is this latter claim that the skeptic would deny. Thus, although religious metaphors have poetic functions, this in no sense renders them true; nor is it a justification for the claim that they communicate a special kind of knowledge, if this is what believers wish to infer.

The Existential-Psychological Case: The Placebo Effect

This leads to the fourth argument that is often appealed to in order to justify a religious commitment. It is an argument offered by thinkers as diverse as Kierkegaard and James. It concerns the question of the meaning of life, especially as it relates to the solitary individual. Even if one cannot prove the existence of God or make an adequate case for the truths of the Resurrection, for example, to *believe* that God in His Divine Majesty rules the universe and/

231

or that Jesus will redeem our suffering souls, still provides some lonely people with enormous psychic satisfaction and security.

For theists, a secular universe devoid of eternal purpose is painful to contemplate. Their lives would be meaningless if this were the case. Why should they strive to achieve their goals, why strain so hard to fulfill their ends, if in the last analysis they're all for naught? How reconcile their being in the world now with the ultimate state of nonbeing or death? How can they bear the thought that those whom they cherish and love the most will someday die and never be seen again? The idea of an empty universe for many individuals is an unbearable source of existential torment and anguish, fear and trembling. The only solution for them is to accept as reality that God exists and that Christ's message is authentic (or Moses' or Mohammed's, and so on). Even if paradoxical, contradictory, incoherent, and unintelligible, and even if not fully supported by evidence or reason, still one can have the will-to-believe. I have a *right* to believe if I wish, the believer says. For the very act of believing and acting upon these beliefs will soothe an aching heart and help heal the pains of an otherwise tragic existence. Belief in God, though irrational to the skeptic, thus may provide a powerful remedy: It has a *placebo* effect. Just as sugar-coated pills given to a patient with no discernible organic disease, if he believes they are curative, may be a potent therapeutic remedy. Religion is thus a palliative for many people who claim to need it. Why remove the last illusion, asks the functionalist, if it will make them whole, and if it will enable them to overcome the metaphysical *weltschmerz* of living?

William James's famous will-to-believe argument thus seeks to justify belief on pragmatic grounds. A universe where God is present, he maintains, provides some basis for optimism and inspires the will to live. If God is restored to the universe, and if all the furniture of heaven is back in place—in spite of the scornful doubts of the skeptics—or at least if a person *believes* that, then he can go about the business of living, confident, buoyant, hopeful about a future world, perhaps, beyond the grave. Thus if the truth of the belief has not been verified, the consequences of the belief may have value to the individual and provide some basis for psychological stability. It provides a stimulus for high motivation and it enables a person to function in a world that might otherwise be difficult or impossible to endure. Is this an unreasonable justification for religious belief, and does it provide some basis for rational conduct? Can a person derive any benefit from beliefs, if, when critically examined, they collapse under the weight of error? Will we be better persons, will our lives be richer and more significant, if we accept the response of the agnostic and suspend judgment, or the position of the igtheist and atheist and reject all belief? What role does fantasy play in life? Can we live entirely without illusions? It is to these questions that we must now turn.

Chapter 8

Fantasy and Illusion

The Psychology of Belief

Undoubtedly there is a strong propensity in human beings to use critical intelligence to understand nature and to cope with problems encountered within it. It is clear that we need to be in some cognitive touch with the real world if we are to function and survive. But the rational mode of response is not the only one that we are capable of, and there are other impulses, interests, and needs in human nature often contradictory to our cognitive capacities. These may tempt us so strongly that we are willing to abandon the reality principle and imbibe that which is patently false. There are passionate demands urging us at different moments in life not only to accept the incredible as true, but even to sanctify and worship it. The skeptical mode of inquiry is important in the life of a reflective person, and it is an essential source of reliable knowledge of the world, which all human beings need to come to terms with if they are to go about the business of living. Nonetheless, very few people are able to consistently abide by the skeptical frame. There is often insufficient time to test every truth claim or to carefully weigh its consequences. There may even be an aversion in many people to skeptical inquiry, especially insofar as it may undermine their core beliefs and values, or threaten their religious outlook. Perhaps only a tiny minority within a

235

minority is able to live consistently the life of reason. Perhaps it is an elusive unobtainable ideal. The standards of objective inquiry recommended by W. K. Clifford, Bertrand Russell, and T. H. Huxley—to suspend judgment about those beliefs for which there is insufficient evidence, and to accept only those for which there is no doubt—is too radical for most people. Instead, credulity and faith all too often dominate human affairs.

Socrates represents the historic partisan of skeptical inquiry, for he sought to question and define ideas in order to arrive closer to the truth. Yet he was sacrificed by the Athenians for challenging their sacred cows. Jesus was also crucified. But there is a significant difference. For Jesus had an incredible tale to tell, so unbelievable that after his death powerful religious institutions were erected in his honor, and he was worshipped as a deity. If Jesus truly thought that he was the son of God, then he was out of touch with reality. His claim is certifiably false under skeptical scrutiny. Yet human culture has preferred the message of Jesus to that of Socrates. Few temples have been built to honor Socrates— his devotees remain cloistered in philosophy and classics departments in the universities, and his influence on history pales in comparison with that of Jesus. It is the promise of eternal salvation that has tempted people to subvert their critical intelligence. Why is credulity preferable to reflective skepticism? This question has puzzled skeptical inquirers. The solution, in my judgment, lies in human nature. We need to untangle the intricate strands that intertwine in our loins, rather than in our cerebral cortexes, if we are to understand who we are. The human primate has evolved on this planet over millions of years. In the long history of humankind, superstition and credulity were rampant; only recently have people developed the capacity for skeptical inquiry.

The objective method is an ideal. When used, it has had a powerful effect; yet most of us are reluctant to generalize its application. It is viewed as threatening insofar as it does not allow us to bask in our romantic reveries and accept them as true. The history of culture vividly demonstrates the often irreconcilable tensions between skeptics and believers, mathematicians and mystics, logicians and poets, doers and dreamers, those who proclaim the ideal of skeptical reason and those who seek to restrict its hegemony.

The skeptical critic of the official doctrine is often sacrificed at the altar of duplicity and hypocrisy. That the heretic is outlawed by most societies vividly dramatizes the deep cleavage in human civilization between reason and faith, the desire to be cautious and the impulse to throw caution to the winds. The pagan cultures of Greece and Rome—in which reason was defended—were followed by the ascendancy of Christianity, Judaism, and Islam during the Middle Ages, when faith prevailed. The Renaissance, the Enlightenment, and modernism were rejected by the romantic reaction, theological fundamentalism, and postmodernism. The lesson is clear: human beings have a capacity for both rationality *and* emotion, neither one of which by itself can determine how we shall live. Much as we may glorify reason, powerful forces deep within us surge up to overwhelm or restrain its influence.

The key to understanding why men and women are tempted by illusions and fantasies lies within ourselves. The belief that the key to the universe is intimately related to human destiny is a form of presumptive self-deception rooted in our bio-psycho-sociological nature. Instead of asking whether God, reincarnation, immortality, or other paranormal phenomena exist, we should ask *why* there is such a strong propensity to believe in them. My detailed study of the cults of unreason that prevail in the contemporary world has led me to a number of surprising conclusions: I have elsewhere postulated the "transcendental temptation" to explain the persistence and power of paranormal and religious myths. But this is closely related to other puzzling characteristics about human psychology.

The first surprising fact about human beings is that *a belief does not have to be true in order to be believed by them.* Indeed, most of the belief systems that generations of humans have heralded, lived by, and died for are in fact patently false. Yet they were held with deep conviction and fervor. This does not mean that the believers were aware that they were false. They undoubtedly thought them to be true, but their truth value had not been warranted by the evidence. The fads and fallacies, delusions and fantasies that people have believed in are so numerous in human history that they constitute, as it were, the very fabric of our cultural existence. The list of erroneous belief systems is endless: Judaism,

Christianity, Islam, Hinduism, and Mormonism; astrology, phrenology, UFOlogy, and spiritualism; Marxism, fascism, and laissez-
faire libertarianism; medical quackery and charlatanism; South Sea
bubbles and speculative fervor; the Crusades and wars to end all
wars. Human culture is comprised of the castles in the sand that
we have constructed out of creative work and play. These are
the products of our fertile imaginations and especially of our
yearnings for other worlds. The web of human civilization contains
both the ingenious ways that humans have developed for understanding and dealing with the world with clarity and precision
and the extraordinary palliatives and smoke screens that they have
laid down to deceive themselves.

The salient point is that our beliefs are not simply cognitive
states of consciousness, nor are they based on carefully tested truth
claims. The hunger for clear beacons by which to live far outstrips
the deliberate patience and cautious procedure necessary to test
them. Objectivity is readily abandoned by the demands of our
passionate concerns. Beliefs, as forms of behavior, are interfused
with feelings, desires, fears, and longings. A belief system, however
false, may integrate and define a way of life. Once codified and
institutionalized it becomes a form of socio-cultural control, per-
sisting long after the demise of its original proponents. It becomes
so deeply embedded in habit and custom that it takes on a life
of its own. We are all trapped in the net of our cultural heritages.
The foundations of entrenched systems of human belief are usually
questionable, although the superstructures built upon them, the
literature and the practices that follow from them, may have a
ring of authenticity in their applications. Yet at the same time
they are false or even fraudulent in their basic premises. They
are seen and interpreted only through biased lenses, which distort
the real world in terms of human desires.

Such belief systems are not devoid of smatterings of truth;
they dip in and out of reality; and they at times touch the empirical
world. But they are more often than not *projections* of human
desires and interests spilling out into the world. What we believe
about the world is often merely a rendition of our own soliloquies.
Our views of reality thus are fixations lodged in the eye of the
beholder. Although this analysis of human belief may be accused

of negative skepticism, I think that it applies to a great extent to most of the major institutions of human culture, to our systems of religion, politics, ethics and law. These institutions delimit normative behavior, and they prescribe both belief and conduct. The beliefs we live by are not descriptive accounts of the world of nature independent of the culture in which we live, the linguistic modes by which we express ourselves, our aesthetic metaphors, or the values that we cherish. In the realm of normative cultural beliefs, we are not talking simply about descriptive truths per se, but about how we should live; and these beliefs at root express affirmations of human striving. The truth claims of the major systems of religion and the paranormal are mistaken about what they attribute to the universe. They are simply human constructions. It is here that they find their true significance and relevance. One may ask, Are there any objective modes of reference by which we may test normative claims, or are we led to complete skepticism? Is it possible to develop a reasonable way of life? I want to make it clear that there is no such thing as pure science. Science is itself a normative mode of behavior, committed to certain ways of inquiring and acting. I am going to defer consideration of normative beliefs until Part 4 of this book.

What I will focus on in this chapter is an examination of beliefs about the world that explicitly claim to be true. Although these claims are continuous with other forms of our behavior, they rest at least on some factual foundations. Here I think we have, as I have already argued, a basis for reliable knowledge, tested experimentally by reference to the real world. All other competitors to the methods of science on a scale of comparison are unreliable.

Humans are predisposed to ignore negative evidence adduced against their cherished belief systems. Two illustrations of this tendency are appropriate: Both astrology and Christianity are highly questionable in their basic premises, i.e., for astrology, that our personalities and future destinies are correlated or determined by the positions of the heavenly bodies at the time and place of birth; and for Christianity, that Jesus is the son of God, and that only through faith in him can we hope to attain eternal salvation. Although both assumptions are, as nearly as I can tell, false, countless billions of people have lived by their precepts as if they were true. What are we to make of this puzzling phenomenon? Why are such beliefs held with such tenacious fervor in spite of ample scientific refutation of their claims? The proponents of astrology and Christianity would say that they are believed in because they are basically true.

Let us focus on astrology. There are probably more believers in astrology than in almost any other system of belief, even though the alternative systems of astrology (Western, Chinese, and Indian) are internally contradictory, and the premises of astrology have been amply refuted by astronomy, biology, and psychology. Astrological beliefs can be traced back thousands of years to ancient Babylon and Egypt. In the Western world, astrology was first codified in the second century by Ptolemy in the *Tetrabiblos,* and it has remained essentially the same in spite of the Copernican revolution and the developments of modern astronomy. The classical systems postulated the Earth as the center of the universe, which the planets, sun, and moon traverse. A horoscope cast by an astrologer based on a person's time and place of birth gives us a picture of the position of the heavenly bodies. The astrologer is allegedly able to say something about the cosmic weather and thus interpret a person's psychological and physical characteristics and future destiny.

I will not here enter into a detailed scientific critique of astrology. I only wish to point out that the most exhaustive testing of its hypotheses demonstrate that they are untrue.[1] Astrologers are not able accurately to characterize personality traits, nor are they able to predict what actions will be favorable or unfavorable. At one time astrologers played a powerful role in the courts of rulers and emperors, claiming to interpret omens and signs, predict propitious times for battle, and guide policies of states. This is no longer the case. Yet they still exert a strong influence on the public consciousness. There is a vast popular literature promoting

---

1. For some writings critical of astrology, see Geoffrey Dean, "Does Astrology Need to be True?" Parts I and II, *Skeptical Inquirer,* Winter 1986-87 and Spring 1987. See also Roger Culver and Philip A. Ianna, *Astrology: True or False?* (Buffalo, N.Y.: Prometheus Books, 1988).

astrology. It is a sad commentary on this scientific-technological age that there are more astrologers in the world than astronomers. Unfortunately, some astrological claims are nonfalsifiable. Where they can be tested they are invariably shown to be false. The efforts by skeptical scientists to debunk astrology have met with hostility, not only from astrologers but from some scientists who claim that skeptics are "closed minded" and "dogmatic." Persistent attempts to confirm sun-sign astrology and horoscope readings nevertheless continue to lead to negative results. In spite of this scientific criticism, large sectors of the public continue to find astrology fascinating, and to accept its major unexamined claims.

One reason for this is the operation of a second principle in human behavior, namely, *the truth of astrology and other paranormal phenomena is found in the eye of the beholder*—that is, it is subjectively validated by a person's preconceptions, preferences, prejudices, and interpretations, rather than by objective reference to the external world. I have sometimes called this the "stretched-sock principle." One can today buy a pair of socks that can be stretched to fit virtually any and every size. Similarly, astrological readings are self-validated and made to be true by the person who hears them. Something similar applies to "psychic readings."

Professor Ray Hyman, a psychologist at the University of Oregon, has provided an astute analysis of "cold reading."[2] He has demonstrated that certain psychological factors may predispose people to accept a psychic's reading as true. He has devised "stock readings," which he says anyone can learn to do. Hyman worked his way through college reading palms. He was impressed by the positive responses he evinced from those people whose palms he read. A friendly critic who was skeptical suggested that Hyman revise his readings, contradicting the traditional rules of interpretation used by palmists. When he did so, Hyman was surprised to discover that he received equally positive expressions of approval from the individuals he read! He thus was able to demonstrate the power of a cold reading, especially when it is done with an aura of authority.

---

2. Ray Hyman, " 'Cold Reading': How to Convince Strangers That You Know All About Them," *Zetetic* (*Skeptical Inquirer*), Spring/Summer 1977.

A cold reading is different from a "hot reading," i.e., a reading that is based on prior knowledge of the person, which the reader has obtained through surreptitious inquiries. The use of such knowledge in such a situation would be a clear case of deceit. A cold reading, on the contrary, is extemporaneous. The person is completely unknown to the reader. Yet it often works extremely well, because when doing a cold reading, the reader makes statements so general that they may be applied to almost anyone. For example, many or most people may concede that the following stock reading applies to them:

> You mean well but are often misunderstood by others. You would like to make real friends, but it is sometimes difficult to find someone you can fully confide in. Although you often do people a favor, you are not fully appreciated.

Similarly, a shrewd cold reader can make general predictions about a person's future, some of which may eventually come true, given the probabilities of human behavior. Often readers observe behavior, facial expressions, and other visual cues in the process of reading to help their probings:

> I see a hospital visit in the coming year, either concerning you or a friend or a relative. (Chances are 50-50 for this.)

> You are grieving for a loved one. (If a woman comes dressed in black, you may surmise a death in the family.)

If not, a cold reader can make a calculated guess:

> Someone you know will die in the coming year. (Alas, it happens to almost everyone.)

Or the reader can say:

> You have financial problems. (Who doesn't?)

> I see some stress and turmoil related to your job. (Most people do.)

I see a new romantic attachment on the horizon. (Hopefully the person will look for a likely prospect, if otherwise unattached, and make the prediction come true.)

One particularly effective ploy is the following reading:

I see the letter M. Do you know who that might be? Perhaps Michael or Margaret or Mary? ("My Mom!" someone once exclaimed to me, in response to a cold reading I was giving.)

From the predictions above, the subject tries to select some features in the reading that he believes the astrologer or psychic reader has accurately characterized. Or there may be a kind of self-fulfilling prophecy where the very idea of the prediction will help to validate it, and the wish becomes father to the fact. Thus, although those who give such readings do not have any special psychic powers, there is a tendency after the fact to attribute such abilities to them. This kind of rationalization applies especially to persons predisposed to believe in astrology or psychic phenomena, and they strive to justify their unexamined faith-systems. The fact that astrology has a complex system of houses and planetary configurations only adds to the mystery and the willingness of clients to authenticate the prognostications for themselves.

Another illustration of this principle is the desire to validate a pre-existing belief system by selective confirmation. If you are a racist and believe that a hated minority has certain egregious faults, then any instance of such a fault is appealed to in order to reinforce your prejudice. If you are a Marxist-Leninist and believe in the inevitable collapse of capitalism and the triumph of the proletarian revolution, then any negative economic facts about capitalist countries are cited in order to point to the inevitability of the prediction. In other words, if you have a coherent system of belief, ad-hoc appeals are made to validate the system by ignoring contrary evidence and emphasizing positive data. The system is true because you believe it, and you tend to select those instances of fact to support it, thus bolstering your faith; and, conversely, you conveniently ignore those that might undermine it.

The reason for this is that belief systems are psychological stabilizers, giving some meaning, direction, and structure to life. Everything encountered must be filtered through and find a place within the system. Contrary evidence must be discounted, or else there will be instability and disorder. Thus the standards of critical evidence are ignored in order to preserve the framework. Unless there is a new system to replace the old, to undermine the existing one is to wreak havoc with one's sanity. Old systems do collapse of dead weight at some point in history; but new ones succeed in replacing them. Belief systems thus provide the individual or the culture with a coherent and meaningful structure. If they are not true per se, they are accepted *because they give us order rather than disorder, and there is an apparent psychological function for that.*

The astrological belief system thus provides some comfort for countless human beings who believe that their destinies are tied up with the cosmos and that their time and place of birth is related to the astral and planetary configurations. There is a kind of solace in this magical idea.

A third illustration of the will-to-believe is the fact that under certain conditions *people will ignore or discount any contrary evidence, even the falsification of specific prophecies* essential to the core beliefs that might undermine these convictions. In their book *When Prophecy Fails,*[3] Festinger, Riecken, and Schachter have studied modern-day groups of people who believed that Armageddon would engulf mankind and that the world would soon end. This prophecy was biblically based. When the predicted event did not occur, thus falsifying their faith, instead of undermining their belief, it strengthened their convictions. Paradoxically, as time went on, the true believers made an allowance for the falsification by an ad-hoc rationalization. Is this behavior anomalous, a curious oddity of a disoriented group? No. For there have been many other such instances in history. After all, Jesus predicted the end of the world in his own time, and apocalyptic and messianic leaders have reiterated this for future generations. A good illus-

3. Leon Festinger, Henry W. Riecken, and Stanley Schachter, *When Prophecy Fails: A Social and Psychological Study of Modern Groups That Predict the Destruction of the World* (New York: Harper and Row, 1956).

tration of this is the Millerites, a religious cult that in 1844 expressed the same doomsday prediction. Miller predicted the end of the world. When it did not come he "corrected" his original date. When the end of the world again did not occur, he became personally disillusioned. Many predictions are very general. In this case they were specific and could be easily disconfirmed after the event did not happen. Yet, paradoxically, his followers emerged unscathed, and this gave rise to a new movement, known as the Seventh-Day Adventists, which grew in spite of the scoffings of unbelievers.

What Festinger, Riecken, and Schachter found is that many individuals emerge from such a disconfirmatory experience unbroken in their convictions. This especially occurs, they say, when a belief is held with "deep conviction" and has some "relevance to action." For this psychological state to prevail, the person holding the belief must have committed himself to it; and for the sake of the belief, he must have undertaken some important action. But what is essential is the *social support* that the believer has, enabling him to withstand the disconfirmatory evidence and the derisive criticisms of doubters. Interestingly, the negative evidence seems to give the belief a new lease on life. Individuals will even move to a new locality and re-dedicate themselves to a Second Coming, now put off to some new time in the future.

This phenomenon has repeated itself time and again. The crucifixion of Jesus did not end Christianity. Nor did the murder of Joseph Smith and his brother and their exposure as polygamists end Mormonism. Similarly, for a long time the apparent failure of Marxist-Leninist societies to deliver the goods to their people did not dissuade true believers from the conviction that their cause was righteous and would be vindicated by history. It only intensified their commitment. The point is that if there are other powerful urges and needs in the human breast, evidence is ignored and there is a redoubling of the commitment to the belief. The tenacious clinging to patently false beliefs is irrational, say skeptics, yet it so often occurs in human history that we may ask why.

There is a fourth psychological propensity in human behavior that invites our attention. I am here referring to the role of *suggestibility in the formation of attitudes, opinions, beliefs, and prac-*

tices. Certain individuals are no doubt more prone to suggestion than others. Yet certain charismatic individuals can exert an inordinate and dramatic influence, such that many people will willingly accept what they say as true and follow their commandments and even lay down their lives. This is especially evident in religion and politics, where messianic leaders have emerged to entrance and enthrall millions. They seem to cast a hypnotic spell on their disciples; they have such an electrifying magnetism that credulous people will swallow whatever they are fed. Thomas Hobbes has observed that if people would but chew carefully the miracles fed them, they might spit them out, but if they swallow them whole, they have no chance to analyze them. Yet it is not simply a question of naive gullibility, because this phenomenon is too pervasive. In one sense, the human animal is a suggestible species. Much of human communication and interaction depends upon suggestion, but there are undoubtedly degrees of suggestibility.

The ease with which suggestion works can be demonstrated in the laboratory. As I pointed out in Chapter 6, in the discussion of hypnosis, individuals probably do not go into a special "trance state," yet there is a tendency for them to be swayed not only by the so-called hypnotist but also by the ideological or religious prophet. Suggestibility is a pervasive aspect of human behavior; it defines our cultural and social existence; and it provides the cement, as it were, that binds us together. The term *suggestibility* may be defined as a person's propensity to respond to suggestive communication. The response involves a change in attitude, opinion, belief, or behavior, and it is done without critical response. Boris Sidis, in a classic work on suggestion, defines it as "the intrusion into the mind of an idea; met with more or less opposition by the person; accepted uncritically at last; and realized reflectively almost automatically. By *suggestibility* is meant that peculiar state of mind which is favorable to suggestion."[4]

Some have maintained that there is an inherent psychological and biological basis for suggestibility. John F. Schumaker has postulated that it may have some adaptive value in survival advan-

---

4. Boris Sidis, *The Psychology of Suggestion,* first published in 1898, reprinted by Arno Press in 1973.

tages for the species.[5] Suggestion allows people to transcend reality and themselves, to discharge their emotions, to escape from tradition, and to maintain social cohesion and control. Schumaker shows that suggestibility is ubiquitous in human behavior and that, along with religiosity, it is nigh universal. He even maintains that it is found in all cultures and that without it there would be social conflict and chaos.

From the standpoint of the rational skeptic, suggestibility provides a special problem, for it indicates how widespread irrational behavior is: the fact that people will accept beliefs uncritically and automatically, and that beliefs can be communicated without adequate logical or evidential grounds, places skepticism in a quandary. The reality principle, which demands evidence for a claim, is readily abandoned, especially in regard to basic faith commitments. Is there a deep need for order and harmony in fulfilling our ultimate concern about who we are and where we will end up? And does this explain the willingness to believe? *Fear* is a great equalizer. It enables many people to subvert rationality in favor of passionate needs and the quest for consolation and hope. Where this psychological propensity prevails, the requirements for cognitive caution can be overwhelmed.

A fifth factor that emerges demonstrates vividly each of the above-described characteristics of human behavior: if a passionate interest in strong enough, people will do almost anything to satisfy this interest. I am here referring to a *rationalization principle, where when evidence fails, the belief-state may be intensified.*

Our critical thinking seems to be "disengaged" during the process of suggestion. Suggestion thus is not a result of cognition or rationality. People are persuaded to accept or act on something independent of rational considerations. Individuals will inhibit their logical and critical faculties when they so behave. Thus the judgmental process gives way. Schumaker interprets this as a "dissociative response." Reality is distorted; either there is mispercep-

---

5. See John F. Schumaker, ed., *Human Suggestibility: Advances in Theory, Research, and Application* (New York and London: Routledge, 1991). See especially Chapter 5; see also John F. Schumaker, *The Wings of Illusion* (Buffalo, N.Y.: Prometheus Books, 1990).

tion, or a highly selective process of interpretation is at work. Rather than maintaining that subverting our cognitive faculties is an abnormal process, he says that it is an essential aspect of culture and of community and that it operates in subtle ways. The authority figure guides and directs belief and practice, but so does the entire culture use rewards and taboos to maintain and reinforce its cherished symbols, metaphors, values, and beliefs. Suggestion is thus the mechanism by which myths are acculturated, transmitted to future generations, constantly conditioned and strengthened.

In this regard charismatic leaders may play a crucial role: they may consciously believe in the reigning orthodoxies and, like others, be deceived as to their truth. In other cases, however, they may be the purveyors of false promises; they may consciously tell lies, use trickery, be consummate and skilled practitioners of deception. On the one extreme are the fraudulent hoaxers who seek power, fame, and fortune, and who will use any devious methods to achieve their aims. They wear masks and only take them off in private before their immediate circle of co-conspirators, or in their own bedrooms. But most often there is a mixture of deception and self-deception, where they come to believe their own oratory and infallibility. They are able to use rhetoric and the art of persuasion, and they not only succeed in convincing the larger public and perhaps their own immediate circle, but themselves as well. This is seen in the builders of great empires, dynasties, and vast fortunes—self-made men and women who become heroes to their worshipping public, but who are megalomaniacal about their own power. It is seen most vividly in the area of religion, where great prophets are transformed into Gods, apotheosized, sanctified, and worshipped by their grateful followers.

For suggestion to work on a grand scale a passive acquiescent audience is essential. It also requires a dramatic actor who can assume the role of the charismatic leader for others to follow: Alexander, Elizabeth I, Napoleon, Lincoln, Hitler, or Stalin. In some cases they inspire believers only after their death, so to speak, when movements develop to honor their legacy: Moses, Jesus, Mohammed, and Marx. I have witnessed suggestion, gullibility, deception, and self-deception on a less magnificent scale in the marketplace where paranormal beliefs contend. Here both conscious and unconscious deception is at work. A fraudulent con man is able to dupe a gullible public, which passively submits to his importunities.

But these are extreme instances of the role of suggestion in human culture; for as I have indicated, suggestibility is a *pervasive* feature of the human condition. It applies to a student spellbound by a professor, a person sold an insurance policy by a salesman, a client of an astrologer or psychic doing a reading, the lover entranced by the beloved, a jury being swayed by a lawyer, and the ordinary person influenced and persuaded by friends and neighbors.

Dispositions, Tendencies, and Desires

I have touched on only some of the psychological processes at work in human behavior, tempting or entrancing us to abandon or avoid our cognitive relationship to reality. We can approach the problem from still another angle, however, and that is from the standpoint of dispositions, tendencies, and wants. There are powerful drives in the human species that often lead human beings to subvert their senses and reason and to accept popular delusions. These tendencies are rather general, and they may be invariant in all cultures. If so, this would explain the ready willingness to override perception and cognition and to abandon truth in a frenzied quest for the Holy Grail.

The Desire to Know the Future

The desire to know the future touches the heart of every person. There are two extremes: There is, on the one hand, the fear of the unknown and the corroding pessimism of despair—the enemy is at our borders, ready to pounce and overrun us; or the enemy is within as a conspirator, prepared to subvert our values and destroy us. We may be worried about economic decline or collapse, disease or death, earthquakes or drought. When frightened, we desperately want to know what tomorrow portends. Conversely, there is the hope for a better tomorrow to realize our bountiful goals, expand our horizons, and fulfill the projects of our imagination. We hope for economic prosperity, the extension of our political power; there are new frontiers to forge and challenges to overcome. There is thus the persistent human hunger to peer into the future and know it in advance, and this has a powerful pull on human curiosity. We are always at the crossroads. Given the swings of mood between optimism and pessimism, there is a desire to plumb unchartered waters yet to be crossed. Human consciousness is thus focused on the future, which it strives to know, to prepare for, and, if possible, to mold.

The lover asks: "Will she love me in return if I confess my love to her, or will it go unrequited?"

The farmer wonders: "Will there be a bumper crop again this year?" Or, "How long will the drought last?"

The investor calculates: "Will the stockmarket rise or fall next year? How high or low will interest rates be?"

The general is in a quandary: "Will the enemy's armies strike or fall back in retreat?"

The mother asks: "Will my daughter pass her bar exam or will she have to wait to try again?"

The gambler betting on a horse race wonders: "Who will come in first?"

Such predictions have to be made on a day-to-day basis. We need to know the future if we are to live and survive in the world. If prudent, our prognostications are based on the best available evidence. We make generalizations from the past and we make inferences about the future. The most reliable way is by understanding the causes at work. Here our hypotheses are probabilistic. Our actions presuppose reliable knowledge. Often we are unable to make wise judgments because there is insufficient information. In such cases the prudent person will suspend judgment.

But the human psyche is not content with this state of affairs. We have an intense desire to know the future. Hence we make guesses. Often they are wild. We may operate on intuition, or act upon a hunch. Sometimes this can be extremely successful. A person buys a lottery ticket and picks a number, hoping to hit it big, and he does. He makes a leap of faith against insuperable odds that at the next roll of the dice his number will come up, and it does. Lady luck is on his side. The improbable occurs.

There are vast legions of soothsayers and prophets catering to the desire of people to plumb the future. Today as in the past, fortune tellers, astrologers, psychics, necromancers, sorcerers, and geomancers all claim to be able to peer into the future by magical means. They deal in charms, amulets, philters, crystals. They use entrails, palmistry, horoscopes, crystal balls, tea leaves, and tarot cards. An entire army of quacks and charlatans prey on the unsuspecting and the gullible.

One such prophet was Nostradamus, born in 1503 in France. A physician and astrologer, when he was about 50 years old, he published a book of rhymed prophecies titled *Centuries*. Although they were most likely meant to be applied to his own time, they were read in subsequent centuries and still are today. His forecasts are so general and vague, however, that they can be applied to every age. The following quatrain illustrates the point. In Century I, verse 60, we read:

> An Emperor shall be born near Italy
> who shall be sold to the Empire at high price.
> They shall say, from the people he associates with,
> that he is less a prince than a butcher.

Does this quatrain apply to Napoleon (born in Corsica, near Italy), Hitler (born in Vienna, near Italy), or Ferdinand II (a Holy Roman Emperor), or Tito (born in Yugoslavia)? The stretched-sock principle applies all too well to all four rulers. It all depends on how far you wish to stretch the reading beyond the times in which Nostradamus lived and wrote.[6]

Similarly, Bible prophecies are quoted as having foretold the birth of Jesus as the Messiah. The authors of the New Testament

---

6. For a critical examination of the claims of this prophet, see James Randi, *The Mask of Nostradamus* (New York: St. Martin's Press, 1990); and James Randi, "Nostradamus: The Prophet for All Seasons," *Skeptical Inquirer*, Fall 1984.

knew the prophecies of the Old Testament (especially Isaiah) and based their writings on them. In Isaiah (7-14), we read, "Therefore the Lord himself shall give you a sign: Behold a virgin shall conceive and bear a son, and shall call his name Immanuel." In the first place, it is highly unlikely that the author of Isaiah was prophesying something that was supposed to occur seven centuries later. It is likely that the passages cited were referring to the eighth century B.C.E., when they were probably written. The New Testament authors knew the Old Testament writings and so stretched them after the fact to predict the virgin birth of Jesus unto Mary. One problem with this use of gospel fictions was a mistranslation of *almah* in the original Hebrew, which meant "young, unmarried female," but which they read as *bethulah,* or "virgin." This might explain the misinterpretation of the passages by Luke (who was most likely a Greek), but perhaps Matthew (a Hebrew) should have known better, though he also read the Greek translation of the Old Testament. (The original Matthew, now lost, was written in Hebrew and was called Levi. The extant gospel, now called Matthew, was written in Greek.) The Bible today is often used to foretell a host of climactic events—the Apocalypse, the Second Coming, and the Rapture. None of these ancient texts can be reliably used to prophesy the future; although many believers continue to do so and base their lives upon such questionable prophecies.

Today the ancient soothsayers and prophets have been replaced by economists and financial advisors who claim to be able to forecast economic trends. Here the self-fulfilling and suicidal prophecies are self-confirmatory. If people believe that the stockmarket will rise, they will rush to buy, which sends it soaring. Conversely, if they believe there will be a collapse, their panic feeds a fall in the market as they dump stocks with a frenzy. If a sufficient number of people are contrarians, however, these events will not occur. Psychological factors are crucial in all economic decision-making. Knowledge of the future is invaluable to the investor. The tale is told of how the Rothschild bankers in London were able to learn about Napoleon's defeat at Waterloo before anyone else. They hired rapid couriers to relay such news to them first, and so they were able to corner the London stockmarket before the public could act, and thus they reaped a handsome profit.

Political analysts create the very conditions they fear most by writing about possible catastrophes in domestic politics or on the international scene, and this encourages their fulfillment. I am surely not claiming that we cannot make prudent predictions about the future. We often do, and the whole of science presupposes that we can. The point is that wish often outstrips reality, and people will leap in and buy or sell on any kind of advice in the hope of outsmarting their fellow human beings. Here skepticism is thwarted by the wings of fancy; it is difficult to restrain the soaring imagination as it attempts to fathom the future.

The Desire for Health

There are a number of other strong desires pulsating within the human heart that can lead a person to abandon rationality. The desire for health is surely a powerful motivation. Medical science has been a great boon to humankind, extending our lifespans, curing our illnesses, and alleviating our pain. Yet people often look elsewhere for cures and nostrums. Why do so many flock to faith healers and charlatans? One answer is that when people are seriously ill and cannot be cured by scientific medicine, they may be willing to try *anything* to get relief; and in such cases they may be prey to every medicine man or guru hawking magical wares. When all other therapies have failed, the sick and dying become desperate. They will seek out any quack or try any therapy, no matter how untested; there is always a scintilla of hope that it may help lead to recovery. Sometimes the psychological factor is powerful, and a placebo effect may work to produce "miraculous" cures.

A graphic illustration from history makes the point all too well. The Prince of the House of Orange, during the siege of Breda in 1625, allegedly cured his soldiers of scurvy.[7] The Prince sent his physicians two or three small vials containing a harmless concoction of wormwood, camomile, and camphor, pretending that

---

7. Charles Mackay, *Extraordinary Popular Delusions and the Madness of Crowds* (London, 1852).

it had powerful medicinal powers and had been received from the East. It was so potent, he claimed, that only two or three drops to a gallon of water would heal. The medicine was worthless, yet the soldiers believed in their commander, and, after taking the medicine, allegedly rapidly recovered. Placebos may or may not always be effective. Nevertheless, men and women will often throw caution to the wind and seek out any claim to miraculous healing. The *belief* in a cure, however far-fetched, at times may be therapeutic; that is, if a disease is psychosomatic in origin. But this is unlikely to occur if the disease is physical and organic. We have seen the dangers of faith healing in Chapter 6.

Human history is full of examples of wonder cures being desperately sought after—from visits to shrines and faith healers to the use of sorcery, witchcraft, magic, and magnetism. They include secret potions and herbal medicines, chiropractors and psychic surgeons, acupuncture and iridology, Dianetics and wonder vitamins, peach pits and laetrile, the orgone box and camphor packs, hot baths and chicken soup. Some of these nostrums may very well have some effect, but most of them will not. Still when life and limb are at stake, many suffering souls will abandon all canons of objectivity.

The saga of alchemy perhaps best illustrates the quest for secret magical powers. Alchemy was an art that was pursued for over a thousand years. The goal was to discover the "philosopher's stone," which would be able to dissolve all of the baser metals, such as iron, lead, and copper, and transmute them into gold. Men and women of all ranks and character were involved in this pursuit, including the greatest philosophers and scientists of the day. The philosopher's stone, it was believed, would also cure diseases and prolong life indefinitely. It was a prize to be sought after because it would bestow upon us both health and wealth. As we know, the intensive efforts of the alchemists failed. This quest had a positive side effect, however, for it eventually gave way to chemistry, which had far less ambitious goals, but whose formulae could be tested empirically.

The Desire for Sexual Gratification

The passion for sex is a powerful drive in all animals, including *Homo sapiens*. The male peacock will rustle his brilliant ocelot-spotted plume and display it with pride. His iridescent golden and green colors are used to attract females. He will strut, pose, and show himself vaingloriously. Similarly for humans, who expend enormous energy in attracting sexual partners. In this continuing quest for gratification, we are often overwhelmed by passion. Reason gives way to glandular throbs and hormonal rushes. The sheer amount of energy poured into winning the object of one's affections is expressed in sonnets, poems, and letters. The competition for sexual partners, the rivalry for sexual pleasure, and the intense reproductive urge goads and feeds human motivation. Cognition is often vanquished by the id and the unconscious quest for libido gratification. Freudians have perhaps exaggerated in making sexual desires, whether conscious or unconscious, the ultimate arbiter of human motivation. Nevertheless, many humans will do almost anything in order to satisfy their desires for sexual pleasure. Sex is a deep wellspring directing our conduct and coloring our beliefs and attitudes. We may be pessimistic or optimistic, happy or sad, depending in part on whether we are sexually repressed or satisfied. Our cognitive beliefs are often a function of the state of our sexual lives. Knowing whether someone is sexually frustrated, has enjoyed romance, or is overwhelmed by phobias will tell us a good deal about that person's outlook and whether he is given to skepticism or reverie.

The Quest for Youth

Another powerful human impulse is the desire to remain young. Men and women fear the process of growing old. Historically they sought the secret elixir that would restore their long-lost youth. Faust made a pact with Mephistopheles in order to captivate Marguerite, and he was willing to barter his soul in order to fulfill his longing. Today there is a vast industry promising to stem the ravages of aging and catering to the vain desire to look and feel younger. Cosmetics, face-lifting, hair transplants, special diets, and other medicines are marketed to a youth-conscious culture. People seek out those who promise them a youthful figure, vigor, and sexual potency. There is much we can do to maintain health and fitness: exercise, diet, the minimization of stress. Yet the quest for eternal youth is an illusion, although one that is difficult to resist.

The Lust for Wealth

Perhaps an arena where the most notorious scams have occurred is in the desire for money, property, and wealth. Undoubtedly the strength of this desire varies from culture to culture. In some societies financial advisors, bankers, corporate managers, lawyers, real-estate agents, and stockbrokers are legion; all compete within the system to reap their fortune. There are suckers born every day to help them succeed.

A graphic illustration of this is the famous South Sea bubble of 1711. The South Sea Company was created by Robert Harley, first Earl of Oxford. A monopoly of trade on the South American coast was granted to this company by the British government. Everyone who heard of the vast riches of that part of the world wished to invest in this and other stock companies. Speculative frenzy began to build. Caution was thrown to the wind, as people devoted all their funds to this get-rich-quick venture. Alas, when these riches did not immediately accrue, people sold their stock in panic, and the bubble burst. A similar speculative frenzy occurred in the Netherlands in the seventeenth century; it went by the name of "tulipomania." Tulips were introduced into Europe in the mid-seventeenth century. In a short period of time, these lovely, colorful flowers were sought by most of the wealthy of Amsterdam. As demand built up, higher and higher prices were charged. Eventually, the market became saturated, the prices tumbled, and people lost fortunes. The same kind of speculative frenzy and subsequent economic collapse has been repeated time and again as greed overcomes caution and people act on ill-advised tips and invest their money to reap a fortune. In America the great stockmarket crash of 1929, the Florida real-estate collapse of the 1920s, and the speculative take-over bids in the 1980s vividly illustrate the human temptation to make a killing and the dangers of losing it all. It illustrates how reason can be supplanted by greed, and how the lust for wealth can make and break fortunes.

Is the quest for possessions universal, or is it only present in capitalist, monarchical, feudal, or other such acquisitive societies? Utopian socialists and Marxist communists dreamt of a future society in which private property would disappear and all would share in the common pot. Marx thought that ownership, particularly of land in feudal societies and of the means of production in capitalist societies, was the source of injustice. It was based on class conflict and on the exploitation of peasants and working people. Labor, he said, was the only real source of value. Thus Marxists attempted to transform the economic structure of society, hoping thus to substitute a caring and sharing society for one based on the acquisition of wealth, private property, and personal gain. Marx thought that the evils of oppression were rooted in the relationships of property. Production was social: If we could truly recognize this and destroy classes, we might re-create the conditions for justice. But were the communists merely utopian dreamers, and was their scheme contrary to human nature?

Humans have often prized gold, diamonds, and other precious metals and stones, not simply because of their beauty, but because of their "intrinsic value." But value is a function of social interaction, demand, and availability. Prices are determined by what people are prepared to pay for commodities or services, and by their scarcity and the relativity of demand. Economists have long debated the nature of economic value. Is it a result primarily of market forces, or does it depend on the amount of labor invested in it (as Marx thought), or is there some qualitative intrinsic worth? Water to a thirsty person on a desert island may be of inestimable value, worth more than all of the treasures of China; to someone in rainy Seattle it is of little value. I surely do not expect to resolve this question here. Economists have postulated the rational investor, producer, and consumer making decisions on the basis of calculative self-interest. Their ideal models enable them to explain and predict economic behavior in the marketplace. Alas, passions run deep in human beings; the lust for possessions and wealth and the desire for conspicuous consumption may override any rational assessment of genuine needs and dominate all other considerations.

The Desire for Power, Fame, and Glory

The quest for power, fame, or glory has stimulated great human endeavors, but it also has allowed men and women to subvert their critical faculties. Generals and statesmen, titans of industry and finance, scientists and scholars, poets and novelists, thespians and singers, have all worshipped at the altar of the "Bitch Goddess Success." And they will often do anything to advance their careers and/or their notoriety. Reason beats a hasty retreat in disarray in the face of an all-consuming ambition to achieve. No doubt this and other motives vary from individual to individual.

Some people are uninterested in amassing wealth; they would rather settle for the quiet pleasures and to live abstemious lives. Similarly, many individuals are not interested in controlling others. They may be passive, willing to follow the dictates of a leader. They do not wish to hold the reins of power. Perhaps only a minority of persons are turned on by the lust for power and are willing to do anything to achieve it. Power-hungry despots strain every fiber to build armies, conquer and create empires, whether large or small. For some it is not the reality but the symbols of power that they crave.

Some men and women do not seek power over others, but only fame or glory. They want other people to appreciate them, know who they are, and admire their talents and achievements. There are many sources of fame and glory. For some, it is the desire to be loved, perhaps sexually, or to be approved of and valued; for others, it is to be glorified as a creative genius or deified as a god. Interestingly, the mad quest for celebrity status is never satisfied, and a hunger for flattery needs continuously to be fed. Their hearts beat more rapidly if there is adulation and praise. For some, social approval is not the end, only recognition. They would rather be notorious or even condemned rather than be unknown. Their only demand is that their name be spelled correctly.

The converse of the quest for power is resentment against achievement by those who lack it and/or are unable to achieve great things. This has been derogated as the "herd mentality" by Nietzsche, who indicted both Christianity and socialism for heralding the virtues of submission and acquiescence. The weak will fear and oppose the strong and they will huddle with others to protect themselves from them. Resentment is tied to envy and jealousy of the possessions and attainments of the achievers, even of their beauty or magnificence. This passion may subvert all bounds of reason. It may consume individuals in prejudice and hatred. They may either cower in submissive acquiescence and adulation, particularly if they are suggestible and if their leader has magnetism, or they may seek to destroy success for others if they cannot realize it for themselves.[8]

The obverse of this is *pride,* a quality related to power, ambition, fame, and achievement. Here some individuals will refuse to believe anything that goes contrary to or violates their pride. There is an eternal war between power and acquiescence, glory and diffidence, pride and resentment. Promethean individuals strive mightily to reach new heights, and their creative juices catapult them forward; mystics retreat into the womb of passive acquiescence, suspending their aggressive desires in an intense desire for peace and quiet. Prometheans break new ground, mystics build protective shields. Prometheans challenge the gods, mystics worship them in fear and trembling. They either willingly submit to their Promethean leaders or turn against them in resentment, loathing, and wrath.

The Tendency for Aggressive Behavior

Another powerful impulse in human behavior is *aggression.* Some writers, such as Konrad Lorenz, believe that aggressive behavior is so preponderant in human history because it is a biological instinct. It has a genetic basis, he maintains, playing a vital role in the evolutionary process. Moreover, this instinct is shared by other animals.[9] The startling thing about aggression is that it is not expressed simply against other species in the battle between predator and prey and in the struggle for survival, but toward members of the same species. The instinct to fight, and even to

---

8. See Robert Sheaffer, *Resentment Against Achievement* (Buffalo, N.Y.: Prometheus Books, 1988).

9. Konrad Lorenz, *On Aggression* (New York: Harcourt, 1966).

259

kill, displays itself most directly in the rivalry between the males of a species for the sexual favor of the females. Bulls will battle ferociously until the dominant one expels the other contenders from the herd, and he is then able to attract the female and her young to his control. The same phenomenon is repeated by countless other species, from goldfish to gorillas. Lorenz speculates that this enables the species to preserve itself and to pass down only the strongest adaptive genes; and it also applies to the human species, where rivalry is not simply between individuals, but between tribes or nation-states.

Lorenz believes that this explains the tendency of human societies to go to war with others, and to fight to the death. We are naked apes, he observes, with our tendencies rooted in the primal struggle to survive. The instinct for aggression, he believes, spills out in many ways: the competition for power, political and economic, but also the quest for fame, glory, and riches. A healthy outlet for these otherwise destructive forces, he says, is competitive sports. Here we do not wish to destroy our opponent physically, only win the game. Victories are symbolic, not real. It is not only the participants who thrive in the battle, but the spectators who identify with the home team. The bloodthirsty adulation of conquering armies slaughtering the barbarians is played out in a contest of endurance between sports champions. Is Lorenz correct? Or is violent aggression and the desire for competitive advantage only a product of human culture, and can it be conquered by rational restraints? Whether it can be overcome surely depends on social conditions and the level of ethical control that can prevail.

Is there a single explanation for the quest for wealth and power, pride and resentment, sexual dominance and acquiescence? Does the key lie in the instinct for aggression, or in our own sexual libido, as Freud thought? Many have been attracted by reductionist interpretations, but it is clear, whatever the roots, that there is a plurality of human passions and interests that stir human motivation—and it is difficult to locate one underlying motive for a wide range of emotions. All of them, nevertheless, contribute to the subversion of rationality.

Bonding: Kinship Relationships

Closely related to aggressive behavior is our natural propensity to protect the members of our own brood. There is the love of husband and wife, parents and children, brothers and sisters for each other, and the affinity for members of the same family or tribe. We have a moral obligation to bond with those of the inner circle, and this relationship may be so powerful that it will dominate all others. It is not our own personal wealth, power, health, or sexual gratification that we seek, but the preservation of our offspring and our family. This spills over on a grand scale into the building of dynasties and kingdoms. But it involves every man and every woman in an intimate sense. Reason can be resisted if it challenges love and devotion in the family, filial piety, sibling affection, or avuncular duty.

Ethnic Loyalty and Racial Chauvinism

The group loyalty impulse is extended beyond intimate personal relationships to members of the same tribe, nation, or race, particularly when aliens threaten at the gates. Here I am talking about ethnic, racial, or nationalistic loyalties. There seems to be a deep-seated affinity for people to congregate and associate with their own kind. This tendency can lead to cooperative behavior, shared values, and mutual undertakings among those within the same group. But it can also be divisive. Separatism has its roots in language and culture as well as in blood ties and inbreeding. If given free vent it may lead to hatred of the strangers in our midst, and to oppression, brutal violence, and bloodshed toward those who differ from us in color, ethnicity, belief, language, or custom. As isolated breeding pockets are gradually inundated on the planet Earth and there is widespread intermingling and intermarriage of races and ethnicities, will prejudice disappear and will we be able to overlook our superficial differences? Ideological and political programs often feed on ethnic and racial difference, and they can arouse irrational hatred, as occurred in Nazi Germany and separatist South Africa. Stoking the coals of anti-Semitism or racism awakens ugly animosities. Is it because of the instinctive desire to cling to one's own kind and to detest or fear that which is unfamiliar or strange? Can it be overcome?

Facing Death

The final powerful temptation for us to consider, invariant among all members of the species, is the fear of death. Human beings seem to be the only animals, as far as we can tell, who are aware of their own impending death, although most individuals find this reality hard to accept. Indeed, the fear of death is the originative source of most of the powerful religions of the world, and its perennial presence explains the staying power of these irrational mythic belief-systems. Human beings are so overwhelmed by the dread of death—of themselves, their loved ones, their friends or revered leaders—that they will spin out tales of consolation in the hope to deny it. How is a person to cope with the defeat of all of one's ideals and aspirations by the impersonal onslaught of death and by its often cruel and haphazard occurrence? Death not only strikes the old and decrepit, who have lived full lives, but the young and the beautiful, seemingly without rhyme or reason. It is this existential awareness of human finitude that leads men and women to invent desperate solutions. By denying death they seek to be rescued from the fear of the unknown, the raging of the blackness of the night. They invent God, the Father or Mother protector, to save them from falling into the abyss. This has the double function of saving those whom we love from the terror of nonbeing and of fulfilling our personal desires and dreams in orgiastic mystical reunion or eternal bliss.

How explain the persistent attraction of Christian or Muslim doctrines of heaven or of Buddhist and Hindu doctrines of reincarnation and rebirth? Isn't it unlikely that God would become human and kill his only son to make a point to us? Christianity is saturated with myth and metaphor, blood sacrifice, and redemption, which enables human beings to overcome suffering and death and achieve resplendent new dimensions of immortality. Similarly for Islam, the afterlife can be obtained by obeying Allah's commandments and performing the required rituals. The Hindus and Buddhists advise the suspension of desire and seek a release to

Nirvana. Although none of these tales of salvation or Karma can be seriously taken as true, they do not have to be true to be fervently believed. It is what they promise that is important, in spite of the objections that skeptics raise about their veracity.

The transcendental temptation is thus a powerful impulse in the human breast, constantly predisposing us to accept the incredible because it is a soothing palliative that enables us to go on. It is the skeptic, or the iconoclast, that is the enemy, because he or she is unable to swallow the tale spun out by our cultural history to resolve the problem of death. It is the unbeliever who needs to be silenced, for to point out that the emperor has no clothes or that God does not exist is a great sacrilege. For many believers atheism is the most pernicious sin imaginable, for it would deny us the comfort of God and his minions. It would leave us bereft of consolation, naked in the wind, unable to cope with tragedy and the torment of death and dying. Life would have no meaning if the only tale to be told of one's existence is that it is a brief flicker between two oblivions. People thus refuse to accept the reality of death; they yearn for a transcendent reality over and beyond the grave. And the creative imagination feeds this passion with symbols and metaphors that breathe a life of their own and are believed in no matter what the grounds. Skeptics demand objective truths. Believers mock them, for it is not truth but comfort that they themselves crave, and this enables them to subvert their rationality by contrived rationalizations: The question of the meaning of life is resolved by rejecting death and immortalizing who and what we are.

Science, philosophy, and skeptical doubt thus are no match for the psychological-existential demand for something more. Whether or not they exist is not the point. Some people need occult or paranormal beliefs no matter what. It is the need, temptation, and desire for them that makes them true.

Can We Live Without Myths?

Is the reality principle so strong in human consciousness that we have to invent lies in order to function in the world? Is some degree of deception, even "insanity," necessary if we are to survive? Do we need at times to be out of touch with the real world, and in cognitive dissonance with it? Are illusions or fantasies essential in healthy psychological functioning and in maintaining our sanity?

These are difficult questions to resolve, and there are no easy answers. But the history of human civilization strongly suggests that few can live entirely without some myths, and that these have a functional role in human behavior. One paradoxical implication of this is that without illusions many humans would go mad. I say this only reluctantly, having been puzzled by the dogged persistence of human irrationality. As a skeptical inquirer often deeply mired in the bogs of paranormal, cultist, and religious belief, perhaps I have a distorted view of the general state of human beliefs. On the other hand, I have found that irrational beliefs are not necessarily deviant aberrations but perhaps the norm, inasmuch as they are so widely held. The use of scientific methods of inquiry pales in comparison with the reign of superstitious nonsense. This may explain in part why otherwise rational or highly intelligent beings constantly deceive themselves, and why they are willing to abandon the confrontation with truth for other beguiling mistresses or masters.

Let us define our terms more precisely by distinguishing various forms of self-deception: hallucinations, delusions, illusions, fantasies, and myths.

Many people suffer from hallucinations. They are unable to function in the world. Their behavior is psychotic. A *hallucination* is a subjective experience, not shared by others. Hallucinatory persons claim to perceive stimuli that they believe really exist, but they are only imaginary. Independent observers are unable to detect any such stimuli. Hallucinatory thoughts or experiences are completely subjective and figments of the imagination. The hallucinatory person is disoriented and out of touch with social and natural reality. A good illustration of this might be a person who thinks that he or she is Frederick the Great or Marie Antoinette and acts accordingly, or one who suffers from schizophrenia or the mood swings of manic depression. Such individuals are often unable to function, being grossly out of touch with reality. This behavior is characterized by psychiatrists as "psychotic."

An *illusion,* on the contrary, has some origin in the empirical world, and this triggers a response. The stimulus is misperceived, however. An illusion is such that the person perceives a stimulus and believes that it really exists and is not imaginary. Here independent observers are able to detect the stimulus, but they are also able to show that it is misinterpreted or misperceived. An illustration of this is the interpreting of the dark spots on the moon as a face (the Man in the Moon), sunlight in a bush as an angel, a dark shadow as a ghost, or a particular person as a greater hero than he or she is. It is something like a mirage, where an oasis is perceived just ahead in the desert.

A *delusion* is midway between a hallucination and an illusion. Delusions occur not only to individuals but also to groups of individuals; an entire society or culture may share a delusion. Delusions are false beliefs, errors of perception, or customary misconceptions. However, there is a strong conviction that the belief is true. Delusions in psychiatric terms are also common in paranoia, such as delusions of grandeur. According to the dictionary, *delusion* is a much stronger word than *illusion,* for it implies that one is consciously deceived or is misled. Delusion also connotes properties attributed to things in themselves, which are regarded as real when they are not. Personal delusions may be highly idiosyncratic and may completely lack social validation. Delusions may be held with extraordinary conviction and are firmly sustained in spite of what almost everyone else may believe. The delusion may be due to a cognitive deficit, such as a failure of logical reasoning or an error in information processing. If excessively overweening in the life of the individual, it may (like a hallucination) interfere with social functioning, doing one's job, or interaction with others. A personal delusion is rejected by others because the claim is incredible. It is thus implausible, yet the person seems preoccupied with it.[10]

Unlike hallucinations, which involve some physiological or mental disorder of the individual, popular delusions can be widely

10. See Thomas F. Octmanns and Vrendan A. Mather, eds., *Delusional Beliefs* (New York: John Wiley, 1988).

shared by crowds of people who are not misperceiving what is present but only misinterpreting what they see and grounding their beliefs on it. No one else shares the hallucinatory experience, but delusional belief systems have been widely shared by cultures and societies throughout history. Indeed, the commitment to a belief system can become as obsessive for a society as for an individual, especially if an entire society focuses on it. A good illustration of this is the belief during the Middle Ages that there were witches. So strong was this belief system that countless innocent women were considered diabolical and burned at the stake. A similar delusional system was the Nazi belief that the Jews controlled the world. This was grounded in theories of racial superiority and inferiority. The same thing can be said for many systems of religious dogma that have been held with intensity and fanaticism. Delusional beliefs need not be negative. For example, an entire culture may believe in pacifism as a civic virtue and maintain it against all odds in spite of evidence that it is out of touch with the tendency for aggression. Fundamentalist beliefs, also out of touch with the real world, have the characteristics of delusional systems. There is a conspiratorial psychology that pits the entire group against the surrounding world. Those who reject the delusional system are treated as pariahs or satanic sinners. Similarly, for the speculative binges or war fever that may possess a nation at certain times in history.

Illusions are weaker and show fewer symptoms of psychiatric disorder. They may be entirely personal or social in character. A strong case can be made that both hallucinatory and delusional systems of belief are out of touch with the world as publicly confronted, and they are basically dysfunctional, especially when individuals and societies clash. There is, however, some evidence that no one can live entirely without some illusions, even though the beliefs based on them may far outstrip the evidence.

Is it possible to live as a skeptic, examining each claim in the light of the evidence, suspending judgment where there are insufficient grounds for a belief, and accepting only those that pass the tests of reliable knowledge? The answer is that this is an ideal criterion that we should be prepared to extend wherever possible, though it is difficult to fully generalize it to all of life.

Indeed, some illusions may be therapeutic and may be essential for healthy functioning. In other words, it is not necessarily always wise to break every illusion that a person holds; for to do so may undermine conviction, commitment, and the motivation for living.

Thus a man may believe that his wife is the most beautiful woman in the world. He is deeply in love with her, and their relationship is normative. For you to try to convince him that his wife is homely would surely be inadvisable. If beauty is in the eye of the beholder, is it always wise to rub one's eyes to see clearly? Yes, says the demanding skeptic, but should skepticism always give way to truth, or are there other interests in life—such as the need for compatibility? Some areas in life are not as vital, and you may decide that a white lie is preferable. If a woman friend spends all day preparing a special dessert for you, say a French soufflé, and you taste it and think it is terrible, do you tell her outright, "I hate it, Ugh!" Or do you try to save her some self-respect and allow her to continue to believe that she is a fine French chef with culinary skills? Suppose this friend has suffered a divorce (her husband left her because she was homely, short, and plump). She had been in a state of despair and hopelessness until she took up cooking in evening school. She now has developed a new interest and a hobby: French cuisine. Should she not be encouraged to continue her new-found outlet for creative activity? You might buffer your criticism in the context of qualifying terms, such as, "Well, it is good, but perhaps too sweet." Or, "I really admire what you have created, but I am not a big fan of soufflé," hoping that she will continue to believe she is a good chef and continue her interests but will serve something else next time. In any case, the unvarnished truth can be devastating. If you tell her that the soufflé is awful, she might be reduced to tears: "I am no good, no good!" she may cry and give up her newly developed interest in cooking.

A similar problem arises with the appraisal of students. They hunger for approval by their professors; and their interest and motivation depends on their grades. Do you say to a student: "You are stupid," or "You are mediocre," or "You have no abilities at all. I think you should drop out of college and become a garbage collector"? You ask pointedly, what is the role of illusion in a person's life, where a belief in oneself and one's own ability is father to the fact? In this case, one might make an argument that some illusions about oneself and one's own powers and abilities are necessary for life. If people truly believe that they have no talents, they may think they are worthless and give up the battle. Life is a struggle to overcome obstacles, and the conviction that one can achieve one's goals is a key ingredient need to do so. To believe that some people are incompetent may make them so, for they may give up before they start, thinking the battle is hopeless.

In a similar way, a brutally realistic appraisal of the social climate in which some people live and breathe may convince them that it will be an uphill struggle all the way to achieve their goals and that it is very unlikely that they will succeed. Do they allow the reality principle to get to them and do they thereby abandon any further efforts because they are likely to be hopeless? Life is full of dreams and aspirations, many of them vain and illusory. Many are never possible to achieve. To allow the real to overwhelm people's ideals may mean that they will never achieve them. Life is full of insuperable dreams, some of them may come true, but if they become true it is because of a person's persistent and dogged determination to make them true. If people shatter all of their dreams and illusions and thus undermine their self-confidence and zest for living, what will be left for them but to live out their lonely days in quiet desperation until the bitter end, or possibly to bathe their sorrow with alcohol?

Many illustrations of self-deception are seen every day: for example, that of the first woman to go to medical school to become a doctor although the male-dominated world opposed her admission and graduation. A realistic appraisal might have discouraged her from her determined action. Or Stephen Hawkings, the physicist who was able to make his mark in the world in spite of a debilitating disease. Or the person who believed that he would become a great novelist and devoted his life to it, though he only wrote pedestrian works. Perhaps he should not have written at all, but not to have tried is to have lost the lust for life.

Accordingly are not *some* illusions, at least about oneself, justified? The total debunking of illusions may mean a collapse of meaning and effort in life. On the other hand one must have some realistic appraisal of one's potentialities and powers, or else one will, like Don Quixote, be forever tilting at windmills.

Similarly, there are some illusions and ideals that may stir a nation to greatness—Plato's "noble lie." For example, the belief that Washington, Jefferson, Madison, and Franklin were giants, heroes, and men of sterling virtues may be believed by successive generations of Americans, and this may contribute to a commitment to the civic virtues of democracy, although an exhaustive and historical study might reveal their many personal faults and defects of character. "Still," you may say, "why deify the Founding Fathers?" To which others may respond that "some pride in our democratic heritage is essential if we are to cement the bonds of civic patriotism and continued commitment to democratic values." "Ah," says the skeptic, "but you are only purveying falsehoods. What is the difference between theistic religious nonsense and secular myths? Are they not all false? Should they not all be committed to the flames as mere metaphysical quackery?" Good questions. Do we need illusions and myths to live by? Can we be free of any taint of falsehood?

Let us distinguish two other categories: Fantasies and myths. A *fantasy* is clearly a concoction of the creative imagination, like the fairy tales we read to our children. The story of Little Red Riding Hood is not literally true, in particular that the wolf swallowed Grandmother whole, that he was caught and killed by the hunter who saved Grandmother by opening the wolf's belly. Although the story is factually false, there is a moral to it that is true: Little Red Riding Hood should beware of the Big Bad Wolf. Wolves have suffered a bad press. They are not as mendacious as depicted. The story of the Three Little Pigs dramatizes another point: Only the third, the prudent pig who built his house of brick rather than straw or twigs, was able to withstand the wolf's blows at the door, and he made a pot of boiling water to catch the wolf as he came down the chimney. So there is some educative value in telling and retelling these stories. Some educators believe we should rid the world of all fairy tales and carefully instruct our children with facts that are true. Santa Claus is a fairy tale and one should label it as such. To teach our children to believe in the incredible only releases the wings of fantasy and uproots children from reality.

So at some point we need to tell our children, "No, Santa does not exist, Virginia, nor did he come down the chimney. It was Mother and I who put the presents in the stocking hanging by the chimney, not Santa Claus." Fairy tales are meant to be enjoyed, not believed in literally. They are literary metaphors and parables, not true stories. Walt Disney's fantasy world of animal characters amuse and delight young and old—if they are taken as fantasy. If they are taken as real, then there are genuine problems with a person's interpretation of reality.

Unfortunately, some individuals are apparently fantasy-prone and they live believing in many untruths. If this tendency dominates their lives, they are very likely pathological. But if they are selective, they may otherwise function normally. I am not here defending fantasies, merely pointing out that it is one thing to enjoy tales of fiction and know that they are fantasies, and another thing to believe in them. Or again, sexual fantasies may have a useful role in stimulating the imagination. The problem arises when people are unable to distinguish fiction from reality and the edges between the real and unreal world are ragged and blurry. And this is particularly true when the fantasy world spills out into religion and when the belief in a fantasy, which now has become a myth, becomes the most important thing in a person's life. The skeptic has a right here to protest duplicity and self-deception.

But what about myths? A *myth* (derived from the Greek term *mythos*) is a fable or legend, the historical origins of which have been forgotten. Myths were especially concerned with tales about God-like creatures or deities with supernatural powers. They clearly apply to Hellenistic polytheistic religion, whose vague origins began in the Homeric literature. Mythological belief systems are associated with mystery and paradox and they often inspire fear and awe. Myths apply equally well to the other great supernatural and monotheistic religions that have prevailed. Do they have a function? Can we live without them? Surely, when taken literally, they are false; like fairy tales, they disseminate lies and deception. Should they be taken poetically and metaphorically? Joseph Campbell, himself an agnostic, believed that myths can exert a powerful aesthetic, moral, and existential influence in human life.[11] As such, they have metaphorical and symbolic meanings, depicting the human condition and expressing our longings to overcome it. A functionalist interpretation of religious symbols discovers some value in such myths of human culture. For example, the Resurrection myth, though not literally true, dramatizes the reality of human finitude, the importance of sacrifice, and the power of religious belief in creating another dimension to human existence.

I must say that I fail to see how such myths can have power if they are no longer taken as factually true. The parables of Jesus, we are told by functionalists, should be read as a way to provide moral edification; they are not to be taken as divine ideas for all eternity. I am not unmindful of the aesthetic and moral qualities that myths and parables may render for some. Though personally I find the Resurrection myth ugly, the fact that a father would kill his son morally reprehensible, and the promise of eternal salvation delusional.

Thus I submit that there are different kinds of myths. Some forms of poetic metaphor are more eloquent than others. Here the myth as myth is interesting and provocative, but it is not in any sense true. The religionist wants it both ways: to believe in the universal power of myth, to luxuriate in the fable, and also to imply that it is true "in some transcendent and ineffable sense." I can enjoy reading about a myth in a literary mood, but not if it is taken as any more than that.

What about secular myths? Are they necessary? Marxism is a good illustration of a utopian vision based on the dialectic that was eventually shattered because its promises about this world were not fulfilled. Eternal and eschatological myths, which are to be fulfilled in the next life, defy easy disconfirmation, for they are always put off to some future state for their realization. Such myths prey on the morbid fear of death and the illusory hope for a transcendental universe that cannot be discovered in this life; thus they are essentially nonfalsifiable.

---

11. Joseph Campbell, with Bill Moyers, *The Power of Myth* (New York: Doubleday, 1988).

Can the skeptical person live without myths about the ultimate end of life? What immediately comes to mind, as a test case, is the Promethean myth, because it has inspired countless generations of atheists and unbelievers who reject God and aspire to reach incomparable heights. What is the Promethean myth? What does it mean? Is it nothing but an illusion? Prometheus stole fire from the gods and challenged them in their abode, and he gave fire and the arts and sciences to humankind. This myth encourages humans who wish to follow his example, to challenge the gods in their own abode, to strive mightily, to live vigorously, and to endure by using one's powers of intelligence and courage. It has led to an emphasis on the heroic virtues, confidence in science, belief in human progress, and the conviction that there are some things that are within our control. Prometheus allegedly endowed humans with divinelike powers and he admonishes against retreat into cowering fear or dependence. In the second part of the Prometheus legend, pessimism takes over. For Prometheus is bound to a rock by Zeus, and a vulture devours his liver.

In a third part of the myth, Prometheus is unchained by Zeus in gratitude for foretelling his future. Prometheus thus emerges from his ordeal unbound and victorious. Many existential religious believers maintain that the ultimate fate of humankind, in the last analysis, is to be bound, for all of our strivings will fail in the end. It is Prometheus soaring and unbound and the optimistic potentialities implicit in this tale provide the humanistic model. Is this, too, all vain illusion; for are we not all conquered in the end by death, and will not all of our plans and projects from the standpoint of eternity disappear? Is the unbeliever thus in no better a situation than the believer in his desire to express with conviction and gusto human aspirations? "Vanity, O Vanity," will the ideals of Prometheus unbound likewise sink into the quicksand, and in the end are we not all immersed in a quagmire of doubt and indecision? Are we not left with the eternal question, How live? And does not this raise the further query, Why live? In the last analysis, is there no answer to this ultimate quest for meaning, and are we led to the pit of utter skepticism?

By recounting the powerful tendencies in human nature to defy skepticism, I do not wish to be overly pessimistic. The issue is not simply the role of doubt, but the role of effective critical intelligence, for both go hand in hand; and I do believe that we need to use doubt along with reason in life—the question is simply how much and when.

Surely, skeptics cannot consciously accept illusions, delusions, fantasies, or myths without any critical dissent. They need ideals by which to live, as individuals and in society, but presumably they should have some realistic footing in empirical probabilities; we do not wish to deceive ourselves about their ultimate viability. Thus skeptical inquiry needs to go on. It need not be negative, nihilistic, destructive. The new skepticism can be useful and constructive. Some skeptical inquiry is thus a necessary ingredient in any life that is lived well. Truth is still a value that we cannot denigrate on the scale of values. It has a vital role to play in formulating judgments of practice by which we live.

This leads us to the final section of this book, an examination of the ethical life and of the foundations of human choice. Is it possible to develop some rational, reliable, and realistic foundation for ethics, and, if so, what direction will this take. It is important that we begin first with an examination of skepticism in ethics and politics, and second with an attempt to resolve the challenge and to see whether or not, and to what extent, an authentic eupraxophy can be developed.

Part Four

The Judgments of Practice

Chapter 9

Skepticism and Ethical Inquiry

We have analyzed in Parts 1 and 2 the role of skepticism in developing true beliefs about the world. But as we have seen, men and women do not live by knowledge alone, nor do they always seek truth for its own sake. On the contrary, knowledge is desired for the ends that it will enable us to achieve: whether fame or fortune, power or love, happiness or God. Which ends ought we to seek? Can we say what is ultimately good? Can we develop normative knowledge? Does it make any sense to talk meaningfully about "good," "bad," "right," "wrong," "justice," and "responsibility"? Is there such a thing as "ethical truth"?

There is a long historical tradition, from Protagoras and the Sophists down to Hume and the emotivists, that denies the possibility of a rational or a scientific ethics, and that reduces ethical judgments to subjective sentiment. These skeptics deny that values are amenable to cognitive criticism, or that standards of objectivity can be discovered. I think that they are profoundly mistaken and that a modified naturalistic and situational theory can provide some basis for rationality and objectivity in ethics.

In what follows, I wish to review the key arguments brought by classical skepticism against the possibility of ethical knowledge, and my responses to them. We may distinguish three types of ethical skepticism, corresponding to the three types of epistemological skepticism that we outlined in Chapter 1.

Ethical Nihilism

The first kind of skepticism is that of *ethical nihilism,* i.e., total, negative skepticism. This is the claim that it is not possible to test ethical judgments empirically or by an appeal to reason. This argument assumes various forms. Let us begin with the critique of ontological value. Ethical skeptics, I submit, correctly observe that it is impossible to discover any framework for morality in the universe at large, independent of human experience. The converse is more likely the case; namely, human beings are disposed to read into nature their fondest hopes and to attribute moral qualities to the universe, but these represent the expression of their own yearnings to find an eternal place for their values in the scheme of things.

The most common illustration of fallacious moral extrapolation is the postulation of a divine being (or beings) and the attribution to him or her (or them) of the highest good. For Aristotle, the unmoved movers were engaged in *nous,* or pure thought; they were thinking about thinking. This was considered the noblest form of excellence that Man could attain, and it was what Aristotle himself prized as the highest good. The Old Testament had Man created in the image of God, though in reality God is fashioned out of the human imagination and assumes human form, possessed of all of the qualities that we cherish, but in extended form: power, omniscience, immortality. Yahweh is prone to anger and is vindictive and unremitting in his demands for obedience to the moral rules. He is a lawgiver, who issues commandments (through his emissaries, the priests and prophets) that men and women are required to submit to if they are to escape punishment; but these rules in actuality reflect the social structure of the times. The New Testament continues the same kind of moral deception, for it deifies certain moral imperatives found desirable: for example, to love one another as God loves us. In the case of Jesus, this divine form of morality is embodied in human flesh at some point in history. Mohammed has given the Muslim moral code endurance and strength by claiming that it was Allah who defined and proclaimed the code.

Thus theistic creeds that attempt to ground the moral life in ultimate theological truths simply mask the tendencies of humans to attribute their own moral purposes to the universe at large, and to use this postulation to insist that those divine commandments ought to be obeyed. Skeptics have identified the implicit self-deception intrinsic to theological foundationalism. They have pointed out that mutually contradictory injunctions have been derived from the same deity. God has been used to defend both slavery and freedom, monogamy and polygamy, abortion and laws against abortion, war and peace, depending on the religious tradition and the social context in which it was revealed or interpreted. The divine commandments are made to fulfill eminently practical purposes, and the universe is endowed with moral qualities. These ultimately have their source in existential despair, which is transferred into hope by means of religious faith. God is invoked to enable people to endure death and tragedy, to provide some consolation and resolution of the human condition and to guarantee a future existence *in saecula, saeculorum*.

Skeptics have rightly demonstrated that all human values and ethical principles are intrinsically related to the human condition. "Man is the measure of all things, of things that are that they are, and of things that are not that they are not," observed Protagoras, the great Sophist who denied the reality of moral ideas independent of human existence. Theological moral systems do not depart from this, for their moral beliefs and Gods are drenched in human significance and relative to human concerns, although believers may deny that this is the case. Indeed, theism holds that God is a person much like a human being, which only emphasizes the anthropomorphic basis of theistic morality.

A similar indictment can be brought against any kind of Platonic moral realism, i.e., the notion that eternal moral ideas are implicit in a realm of being, and that the task of human reason is to discover and apply these essences to life. Socrates attempted to define "justice" and "the good," hoping that his definitions of absolute ideas would provide a beacon for both the individual soul and the *polis*. For Plato, nature is interpreted as the basis for "the good" over and beyond convention. Skeptics have rightly rejected this theory as pure postulate, without reasonable justification or proof. The reification of essences makes an unwarranted epistemological leap. According to Protagoras, ethics has a relativistic basis: "Whatever is seen just to a city is just for that city so long as it seems so."

A similar critique has been brought against naturalistic theories, that is, any effort to find an ultimate ground for ethics in "human nature," "natural law," "the march of history," or "evolutionary progress." Surely these naturalistic forces are not without human content, for they are related to human institutions. Accordingly, relativism would seem to be necessary as a starting point for any conception of value.

An important distinction must be made, however, between relativism and subjectivism, for to say that morality is related to human beings does not necessarily mean that it is irreducibly subjective. Relativism and subjectivism are not the same, and the former does not imply the latter. One can be a relativist and an objectivist. Total negative skeptics argue that there are no objective standards that can be used to appraise what the individual or city deems to be just or good. They maintain that to say that something is good or right means simply that we feel this to be the case, and that our sentiments are disposed either to like or dislike it. Some forms of subjectivism reduce to nihilism. For if moral beliefs in the last analysis are nothing but an expression of tastes, feelings, and sentiments—*de gustibus non disputandem est*—then we cannot really demonstrate the moral excellence of one belief over another. If, from the standpoint of the state, whatever is just is relative to convention, custom, or power, then there are no normative criteria for adjudicating differences. "Justice is the interest of the stronger," affirmed the nihilist Thrasymachus in the *Republic;* therefore "might makes right." It is the strongest faction of society that defines moral rectitude and lays down laws to adjudicate conflicting interests. Ethics is nothing more or nothing less that that.

The emotive theory, introduced in the twentieth century by the logical positivists, also expresses a strong form of ethical skepticism. The emotivists distinguish between three kinds of sentences: (1) descriptive statements, which they said could be verified directly or indirectly by factual observations or experiment; (2) analytic statements, which are tautological and established as formally true by deductive inferences; and (3) emotive utterances, which have no cognitive or literal significance, but are expressive and imperative in force. To say that "rape is wrong," for the emotivists, merely means that I (or we) are repulsed by it, and that I (or we) condemn it and command others to do so as well. These sentences cannot be verified in any objective manner, for they violate the principles of verifiability and analyticity.

Extreme subjectivity thus leads us to an impasse, because we need to get on with the business of living with others in the community. Nihilism is a posture that we can hardly afford to adopt in practical life. There is therefore a serious question as to whether or not the reduction of ethics to subjectivity is true to our ethical experiences. For to maintain that there are no cognitive criteria that can be brought to bear in ethical questions, and that in the last analysis it is simply a question of feeling or force, seems to impose a tremendous strain on credulity. For example, if there are no objective standards of ethical value, is the statement that "the policies of Hitler and Stalin were evil" without any basis other than that I or we do not like them? Is the ethical principle "Mothers ought not to torture their children" similarly without any merit? If so, subjectivity reduces human morality either to the toleration of barbarism, for there is no meaningful ground to oppose it, or utter absurdity, in which anything is as good as anything else, and right and wrong have no signification. Under this theory, monsters may be equivalent to martyrs, sinners to saints, egoists to altruists. But if no ethical distinctions are allowed, social life would become impossible. Why doesn't a person steal, murder, torture, or rape? Is it simply a question of sentiment or the fear that one will be punished by the police (or God)? This position is contradicted by the evidence of the ethical life: We *do* make ethical judgments, and some are considered warranted. We criticize moral monsters and tyrants and applaud altruists and humanitarians, and with some justification. Ethical nihilism is infantile, and those who vehemently proclaim it in all ethical situations have not fully developed their moral sensibilities. They are concealing their own moral ignorance, and by their total negative skepticism reveal that they have not achieved mature moral growth.

To argue the position of the ethical neutralist—that is, that one must be "morally neutral" about *all* moral questions—is similarly mistaken. I would agree that *some* moral quandaries are difficult to resolve, particularly where there are conflicts between rights and goods, both of which we cannot have, or the choice between the lesser of two evils, one of which we must choose. To urge the *universal* suspension of ethical judgment, as the ethical nihilist advocates, however, does not follow. If a skeptic cannot decide between two sides of *any* moral issue, and thereby refuses to choose or to act, is he or she not confessing a similar blind spot concerning the phenomenological character of moral experience and reflection? Or, if one does act, but only from feeling, or because one thinks that following conventional custom is the safest course, is one not insensitive to the deeper nuances of the moral life? Such a position, if consistently defended, reduces to a perverse kind of moral dogmatism.

Agnostic skepticism is not without some redeeming virtues, however. For in opposing moral absolutism or fanaticism, and in seeing through the sham of self-righteous claims that one's moral theories are the ultimate truth, skepticism may be a useful antidote for paternalistic or authoritarian claptrap. Moral absolutists assume that their views are intrinsic to reality, and they all too readily are prepared to suppress those who dissent. Some will seek to apply Reason or Progress or Virtue or God to impose views that simply mask their own preferences. As such, they have substituted dogmatism for inquiry. On the other hand, the persistent denial that there are *any* moral truths at all, if it is consistently asserted, belies its own form of moral intransigence, based largely upon epistemological error; for to deny that there is any kind of moral truth or reliable knowledge is to flout the considerable body of reliable ethical knowledge that we have as a product of the collective wisdom of the race.

Mitigated Ethical Skepticism

A second kind of skeptical theory is less extreme than the first. This we may call *mitigated ethical skepticism*. It assumes various forms. In particular, it states that although sentiment is at the root of all human values, this still leaves some room for rational criticism and control.

One can see this position again first presented by the Sophists. Glaucon, in the *Republic,* outlines the social contract theory, which is later elaborated by modern political philosophers like Thomas Hobbes: All men seek to satisfy their own desires, and self-interest dominates their choices. But they soon see that if individuals had carte blanche to do whatever they wished, there would be "a war of all against all," in which case life would become "solitary, poor, nasty, brutish, and short." Rational persons thus are willing to restrain their passions and enter into a social contract, agree to limit their liberties, and abide by the rule of law. Here the criterion is the social good, and this is justified because it is to the self-interest of every person to establish a framework of peace, law, and order, in which common guarantees and protections are provided by the civil society and the state. One variation of this is the utilitarian theory; namely, we agree to adhere to the moral rules of society because they provide the conditions of happiness for all. This theory does not attempt to ground justice in God, the Absolute, or Nature writ large. Ethical principles are related to human interests, and they have a conventional basis. But they also provide a consequential and experimental test. Although they are relative to the individual, it is not subjectivity alone that rules, for ethical judgments are still open to rational criticism and may be justified in terms of their instrumental effectiveness.

Hume was critical of certain assumptions implicit in classical ethical theory; for he argued that a moral judgment intrinsically involves feelings: When we judge an act or trait of character as good or bad, we are saying that we approve or disapprove; and we do so because we have sentiments of pleasure or displeasure, and/or we consider it to be useful or harmful. Hume argued that there were basic differences between judgments of fact and judgments of value. Judgments of fact can be ascertained to be true or false. Judgments of morality, on the contrary, like judgments of taste, cannot. Hume inferred from this that reason by itself cannot decide moral judgments, nor can it alone make moral distinctions or resolve moral quandaries. It is "moral sentiment" that is the wellspring of action, not rationality. What we consider good or bad is dependent on whether moral sentiment is attached to it, and by this he meant the feeling that something is pleasant or useful. Hume was thus a skeptic in ethics, for he held that reason by itself cannot resolve moral questions. His statement that "Reason is, and ought to be, the slave of passions," is both provocative and controversial. The point that he wished to make was that moral judgments are neither like factual statements, tested by observation, nor like logical inferences, concerned with the relationships of ideas.

In his *Treatise on Human Nature,*[1] Hume observed that in all "systems of morality" that have been enunciated, the proponent would begin with "ordinary ways of reasoning." For example, he might attempt to prove that God exists, or he might describe human society; but at one point he makes a leap, going from what "is" or "is not" the case, to suddenly introducing what "ought" or "ought not" to be the case. Here something not contained in the premise is suddenly introduced into the conclusion. There is an unwarranted gap in the argument. The "ought" is not deduced from the "is," but is arrived at by the surreptitious introduction of the author's sentiment or feeling. The conclusion that Hume drew from his analysis is that we cannot deduce the "ought" from the "is" and that any effort to do so is fallacious. Interestingly, given his skepticism, Hume ended up a conservative; for if there are no ultimate guides or moral truths, then we ought to abide by the customary rules of conduct.

In the twentieth century, a great deal of effort has been expended by philosophers, from G. E. Moore to the emotivists, to analyze moral language. Moore used the term *naturalistic fallacy* to describe all efforts to define "the good." The naturalistic fallacy is similar to Hume's theory of the "is-ought" dualism.[2] Moore

---

1. David Hume, *Treatise on Human Nature* (1739), Book III, Part I, Section I.
2. G. E. Moore, *Principia Ethica* (Cambridge, 1903).

thought that any definition of "good" was vulnerable to the open question argument and that it applied to theological as well as naturalistic ethical systems, to John Stuart Mill as well as Thomas Aquinas. He asked, "*Why* should we accept your definition of good'?" and he ended up doubtful of any and all attempts to define "good." Moore's own epistemological theory assumed a form of Platonic realism. "Good" was an "indefinable, non-natural property" by definition, and that was why it could not be defined.

Other twentieth century neo-Kantians (H. A. Prichard, Henry Sidgwick, and W. D. Ross) agreed that ethical predicates could not be derived from nonethical ones.[3] They thought that the basic ethical terms were deontological ("right," "wrong," "obligation," and "duty"), not teleological ("good" and "bad," "value" and "disvalue"), and that these were indefinable because they contained an implicit *obligatoriness*. Even though they could not define ethical terms, neither Moore nor the intuitionists considered themselves to be ethical skeptics. Prichard thought that classical ethical inquiry rested on a mistake, for it attempted to prove its first principles, whereas one's moral obligations could be known intuitively and directly within moral situations.

It was the emotivists, whom we have already referred to, especially Charles L. Stevenson, who were ethical skeptics, though some were mitigated.[4] They maintained that the reason *why* we could not define ethical terms was that they were not descriptive, like "hard" or "brittle," but emotive in character. Ethical words were expressive or evocative, much like "ugh" or "whew," and imperative, such as "drop dead" or "kiss me." These terms give vent to our emotional attitudes and they express our desires that other people agree with us and/or do our bidding. Efforts to define such terms are at best "persuasive definitions," they said, for they simply express our own moral sentiments.

Of special significance is the belief of the emotivists that

---

3. H. A. Prichard,"Does Moral Philosophy Rest on a Mistake?' *Mind,* 21, 1921; Henry Sidgwick, *The Methods of Ethics,* 6th ed. (New York: Macmillan, 1901); W. D. Ross, *The Right and the Good* (Oxford, 1930).

4. A. J. Ayer, *Language, Truth and Logic* (Oxford, 1936); Charles L. Stevenson, *Ethics and Language* (New Haven: Yale University Press 1943).

disagreements in the moral domain often degenerate into disputes between contending parties that could not, even in principle, be resolved. This was due to the fact that the disagreements were "disagreements in attitude," as distinct from "disagreements in belief." As mitigated ethical skeptics, they said that the latter disagreements could be resolved by empirical, rational methods, where two or more parties to a dispute differed about factual claims. These controversies at least in principle could be overcome—that is, if the moral dispute was based upon the facts. In some cases, the disputes may be purely analytical and concern the meaning of a term, and these could be clarified by definition and again be overcome. For example, C maintains that a fetus weighs 8 ounces, and D claims that it weighs 6. Presumably they could weigh the fetus and decide the factual issue. Or again, if C and D disagree about the definition of "euthanasia" and whether or not it is voluntary or involuntary, then presumably by clearly defining what they mean, they can possibly overcome some forms of disagreement. However, if the dispute is distinctively *moral,* according to Stevenson, then it is attitudinal, and we may not be able to resolve the differences. For example, if D says that "abortion is *wrong*" because the fetus is a person, and and E declares that "abortion is *right*" because it is based upon the principle of freedom of choice for women, then we may not be able to resolve the dispute; for the disagreement is not purely factual, but an attitudinal difference about which principle to accept. Hence, an impasse may be reached.

Such moral disputes may not in principle be resolvable. F may think that euthanasia is wrong, because we ought never to take the life of another, and suffering is not necessarily evil; and G may think that euthanasia is right if it is voluntary, because unnecessary pain and suffering in terminal cases is evil. Unless both parties can agree in their basic attitudes about suffering and pain, or voluntary and involuntary death, then they may never be able to resolve their moral controversy.

This second form of ethical skepticism is *mitigated,* because in spite of the ultimate subjective differences in sentiment, feeling, or emotion, the moral life is not entirely bereft of rational considerations, and some moral disagreement may be grounded in belief, not attitude. If, for example, H says that she is in favor of capital punishment because it is a deterrent to future murders, since that belief is contingent on the deterrence issue presumably we can do a factual study to resolve the disagreement. Similarly, if J is against the death penalty because she doesn't think that it deters murder, we could again perhaps resolve this by doing a sociological study, examining murder rates in those states or countries that have the death penalty and those that do not, to see if there is any statistical difference. Similarly, we can study those states or countries before and after the imposition or repeal of the death penalty to see whether there is any significant difference. If these moral judgments pro or con were truly a function of the facts, then if they were mistaken about the factual truth, the persons involved might change their beliefs regarding the death penalty.

There are other arguments that mitigated skeptics can introduce in disagreements in an effort to persuade other persons to modify their judgments. They can appeal to the *consistency* criterion. If some persons hold a particular moral principle, and yet make exceptions to it, they are contradicting themselves. For example, they may say they believe in democracy as the best form of government, yet they may exclude one portion of society from exercising the franchise. Presumably, if we show them that they have disenfranchised blacks, we would have an argument against apartheid in South Africa; or if they disenfranchise women, we could make the case for universal suffrage. And if our moralists believe in consistency, they will change their views, for they would want to order their values in some coherent form.

The same considerations apply to the test of *consequences;* that is, persons who hold a principle, even with intensity, may not appreciate all of the consequences that may ensue from it. They may, for example, be committed to equal legal rights for all adults above the age of eighteen, the age at which an individual can vote or be conscripted into the armed services. Yet they might be willing to make an exception to this general principle and prohibit the serving of alcohol in bars to individuals under the age of twenty-one. They may have changed their views because the dangerous consequences—in the form of high rates of fatal automobile accidents—have been pointed out to them. Here consistency may give way to considerations of consequences, and in weighing the latter they may be willing to override the former.

Therefore, even though values may at root be attitudinal, they may be restructured by rational considerations. We have to live and function in the world and to modify our attitudes in the light of these considerations.

The subjectivistic skeptical rejoinder to this, however, is that the reason that some individuals believe in deterrence is that they find murder emotionally repulsive. The reason they find drunk driving abhorrent is that accidental death due to negligence is likewise repugnant to their feelings. Likewise, they believe that universal suffrage is right because they approve of it attitudinally. Even the mitigated skeptic agrees that rational criticisms are accepted ultimately only because they rest on nonrational grounds. These moral postulates, they insist, are without any cognitive justification beyond our sentiment.

Aware of the epistemological pitfalls inherent in morality, some skeptics have urged a return to custom, and they have adopted a conservative bias. If no sentiment is ultimately better than any other, we had best choose those that are less dangerous to society and/or those that do not impede individual liberty. Even this stance is mitigated in its justification. Other skeptics, in agreeing that there are *no* rational foundations for ethics or politics, may choose to be liberals or radicals. But this stance, in the final analysis, say the skeptics, is likewise based on taste, and no rational proof is possible.

Ethical Inquiry

This leads to our third form of skepticism, that which is related to inquiry. This position involves a skeptical component that is never fully abandoned: cognition in the course of skeptical inquiry. Our search for ethical judgments is thus continuous with our quest for reliable knowledge in all fields of human endeavor. At the very least, our choices are based upon our knowledge of the world and ourselves. The relationship between knowledge and value is central to the concept of *ethical inquiry.*

If we say that ethical choices may be related to rationality, the question that is immediately raised is whether there are any *ultimate* principles that are foundational to our ethical decisions and to which we must be committed if we are able to make sense of ethical rationality. I must confess an extreme reluctance to assert that there are; at least all such efforts heretofore to find such first principles a priori seem to me to have failed.

The salient point is that ethics is relative to life as lived by specific person or societies, and it is rooted in historical-social conditions and concrete behavior. Ethical principles are thus in the mid-range; they are proximate, not ultimate. We do not reason about the moral life *in abstracto* and hope to make sense of it; we always begin *here* and *now,* with *this* individual in *this* society faced with *these* choices. The basic subject matter of ethics is action and conduct. It is not concerned essentially with *propositions* about practice, as some analytic philosophers thought, but with *praxis* itself. The knowledge that we seek is practical: what to choose, how to act, and how to evaluate the courses of action that confront us. We are interested in formulating wise, prudential, effective judgments of practice. This does not deny that we can generalize about human practice, and indeed formulate rules of conduct applicable to similar situations or values that have a wider appeal. Still, the contents of our judgments have concrete referents.

Rarely when we engage in ethical inquiry do we begin at the beginning—except perhaps in crisis/existential situations where we are forced to examine our root values. Rather, we find ourselves in the midst of practical demands and conflicts, trying to make sense of the web of decisions and behavior in which we are entangled. And included in our nexus is the considerable fund of normative data that we bring with us: the things we cherish or esteem, or conversely detest or reject, and the principles to which we are committed. Ethical inquiry is initiated when there is some puzzle about what we should do or some conflict between competing values and norms. It is here that skeptical inquiry is vital: for it is the open mind in operation that is willing to examine our values and principles, and to select those that seem approximate. The ethical inquirer in the best sense is committed to the use of reflective intelligence, in which he is able to define and clarify his values and principles and to search for alternative courses of action that seem most fitting within the context of inquiry.

The ethical inquirer, like the scientist, seeks knowledge, but he does not simply describe what is factually the case or explain events by means of causal theories. Nor is he interested primarily in arriving at analytic or formal truths. His goal is eminently practical: to choose something that will guide behavior and affect the world. This knowledge is similar to the kinds of knowledge sought in the applied practical sciences and arts. It is similar in one sense to the use of technological know-how in such fields as medicine, pedagogy, engineering, and architecture, where we are concerned with doing something, changing events, or creating, making, or manufacturing things. These require some skill and expertise, the prudential adaptation of means to ends. The doctor, lawyer, or teacher wishes to achieve certain goals: to cure patients, protect clients' rights, or educate students. And there are reliable procedures by means of which these purposes can be achieved. An engineer wishes to build a bridge or construct a space station. There is a considerable body of technological knowledge to guide him or her in doing so. Ancient Greece and Rome had not developed the technological arts to the extent that they have been developed since; if they had, they would have recognized their tremendous impact, and the skeptical schools of philosophy would perhaps have made less headway. Nihilistic and neutralistic skepticism about technological knowledge makes no sense today, since technology presupposes causal theories about how nature operates, and its principles are tested experimentally. However, all such technological fields, replies the ethical skeptic, presuppose their ends—for example, the desire to improve health, to achieve rapid travel, and so on. Where do we get our ends from, if not sentiment? asks the ethical skeptic.

Valuational Base

My answer is that cognition has a role in formulating our ends. But we begin again *in the middle;* there is already a body of ethical principles that we possess concerning our ends. The evaluation of ends in each case is a function of tested procedures. In any context of ethical inquiry, it is best to consider ethical beliefs— including those inherited from the past—as *hypotheses.* They should be tested each time by reference to the relevant facts, the *valuational base.* What do I mean by this?

Common Moral Decencies

First, there is a set of what I have called the common moral decencies, that is, the ethical wisdom that we have inherited from human civilization. I am here drawing on the abundant evidence that humans, no matter what their culture, have similar needs and face similar problems—such as the need to survive, maintain health, and find adequate food and shelter; to engage in sexual intercourse and reproduction; to nurture, protect, and educate children; and so on. In spite of cultural relativity, there are similar responses to life's problems. In order to satisfy human needs and guide human interactions, a set of common moral decencies is developed. In my book *Forbidden Fruit: The Ethics of Humanism,*[5] I list the basic moral decencies as follows: (1) *Integrity:* truthfulness, promise-keeping, sincerity, honesty. (2) *Trustworthiness:* fidelity and dependability. (3) *Benevolence:* good will, nonmalfeasance, sexual consent, and beneficence. (4) *Fairness:* gratitude, accountability, justice, tolerance, and cooperation.

To illustrate: The principles that we ought to tell the truth and that we ought to keep our promises are prima facie rules that in general apply to all civilized societies, notwithstanding that in some situations there may be conflicts between them and that exceptions may be made. Our *actual* duties in practical situations are not the same as our prima facie general duties. These principles, I submit, are transcultural, and they are as meaningful to the Christian and the Hindu as to the Confucian and the Muslim, the atheist and the unbeliever. Those who violate the common moral decencies challenge the basic body of ethical truths governing moral conduct that has been transmitted to us as the collective

---

5. Paul Kurtz, *Forbidden Fruit: The Ethics of Humanism* (Prometheus Books, Buffalo, N.Y., 1988).

learned wisdom of humanity. I recognize that there is still considerable cultural diversity, and that not all societies recognize all of these principles. Moreover, there are many disputes about values and principles that are virtually irreconcilable. But I submit that humankind has reached the stage where the fundamental moral decencies are now generally accepted by the reflective person, and they are even endowed by some with "sacred" significance or given legal sanction and support. The term *civilized* is virtually identical to the recognition of the common moral decencies; and *uncivilized* or barbarous behavior means that they have been grossly violated.

Basic Human Needs

Similarly, we discover a set of basic and invariant human needs that are essential to all members of the species. These require some satisfaction if human beings are to survive and function in a meaningful way. In my books *Decision and the Condition of Man* and *The Fullness of Life,* I list what these needs are.[6,7]

First are the *biogenic needs:* (1) *Survival needs:* the need to be protected from dangers or death from natural disasters, wild animals, or threatening human beings. (2) *Homeostatic needs:* sufficient food, clothing, and shelter. The organism needs to maintain some equilibrium against threats to its health and, when it is disturbed, to restore homeostasis. (3) *Growth needs:* the normal patterns of growth and development of the infant, child, and adult, including standing, walking, talking, reading, sexual development, and maturation. These are intrinsic to the biology of the species and have some genetic basis, though they also have a sociocultural dimension.

Second are the *psycho-sociogenic needs:* (4) *Love needs:* the ability to relate to others intimately and to achieve orgasmic satisfaction. Love entails affectionate regard for other persons on many different levels, not only the ability to receive love, but to bestow it upon other persons. This implies not simply sexual love but

---

6. Paul Kurtz, *Decision and the Condition of Man* (Seattle, Wash.: University of Washington, Press, 1965).

7. Paul Kurtz, *The Fullness of Life* (New York: Horizon Press, 1974).

parenting care and other forms of tender attachment to the well-being of others. (5) *Belonging to some community:* the ability to identify on a face-to-face basis with others, both in friendship and collegiality, and this involves a relationship of charity and some altruistic concern. (6) *Self-respect:* some self-confidence in one's own abilities is essential for normal growth and development. Self-love may be in part a reflection of how a society evaluates a person, but it also depends on a person's own self-validation. (7) *Autonomy:* the capacity to make choices, to be self-determined and self-directed; the ability to think or act by oneself without following the dictates of others or conforming to the crowd. (8) *Creative actualization:* the ability to work creatively, to develop novel goals, to re-organize the varieties of materials in the world, and to introduce changes in the environment. (9) *Cognition:* the capacity to reason and think; the development of a wide range of intellectual skills, including the ability to make practical judgments.

Related to these needs are a concomitant set of excellences, or virtues. There are comparative standards by which we may evaluate whether or not a person has achieved health and vitality, has developed the capacity to love, to belong to a community, to have self-respect, to be autonomous and creative, and to respond intelligently. They are normative criteria that we may use to appraise moral excellence. These are qualitative standards of nobility that apply to moral character and behavior.

Now I realize that a skeptical challenge may be brought against elements within the valuational base as outlined above. Someone may ask: Why accept the common moral decencies? Why have integrity or be trustworthy, benevolent, or fair? To which I respond that some reflective inquiry can be made about the application of each of these principles to a given situation. These are only prima-facie, general rules that provide us with some general guidelines, not absolute norms. Yet a nihilist may seek to deny them all. "Why not kill or rape if I want to?" he asks.

A skeptical critic may raise similar doubts about the concept of "basic human needs" I refer to above. "Why actualize my potentialities, or seek to grow, or be intelligent?" A drug addict or alcoholic may throw caution to the winds and abandon health for the sake of pleasure. "Can you prove or demonstrate *why*

I cannot overthrow all of these norms?" he may plead. My response is that there are processes of growth intrinsic to the ethical person and that we are potentially moral beings, both in relation to others and to ourselves. Individuals, however, need to go through the stages of development in order to appreciate the authentic ring of ethical excellence. I am thus presupposing a level of ethical awareness, or conscience, that individuals at certain periods of life need to understand and realize. Human beings have some means of freedom, and they may choose to abandon the call of the ethical life in a mad quest for power or pleasure. Or they may wish to tempt fate by a determined effort to think the unthinkable and perform the grotesque or bestial. There are moral monsters who will lie, steal, cheat, torture, and maim others for the hell of it, or because they are self-destructive. What are we to say of them?

I submit that such individuals are grossly underdeveloped; they are moral cripples. Their ethical understanding has been thwarted or is impaired; they are impervious to ethical truths and unsuited for ethical conduct. Some individuals are unable to do mathematical computations; some lack technological know-how or musical proficiency; some are unable to change a fuse or fix a flat tire. Ethical actions likewise depend upon some degree of ethical knowledge, and some individuals may be sadly deficient in this regard. They may need ethical education in order to develop general habits of responsibility, to have an authentic regard or a loving concern for another person. They may lack self-discipline and self-restraint, temperance, moderation, prudence, or practical ethical wisdom. I am prepared, of course, to admit that some individuals may be psychopaths (such as serial killers), though this may be due to some genetic defect and some distortion in their psycho-sexual development. They may have lacked proper moral training as youngsters, such that they never developed a mature ethical appreciation. But this says more about their personal disorientation than it does about the existence or nonexistence of a body of ethical truths as the repository of civilized conduct.

Pluralism in Values

Now I have referred to the "common moral decencies" and "basic human needs" as data within the valuational base to which we may appeal. But this no doubt is too general to tell us what to do in specific cases. Moreover, human wants and needs, values and principles, are infinitely multifarious. They differ as human personalities differ, and they change as society changes. There is a wide range of tastes in food, wine, sports, art, dress, and mannerisms, and there is pluralistic diversity in cultural values. Many different kinds of idiosyncratic wants become virtual needs and are linked with our basic biogenic and psycho-sociogenic needs. Ethical choices are always functions of the unique, deeply private tastes and desires, wishes and preferences, of each person. The choices we make are also relative to the concrete socio-cultural-historical framework in which we live, and this includes the particular laws and social customs of our society. Life in ancient Egypt, Israel, Greece, or Mesopotamia, differs from that lived in medieval China, modern Japan, the Middle East, Western Europe, or the Americas.

All these differences must be packed into the valuational base, and they influence the choices we make. The decision whether something is good or bad, right or wrong, is accordingly a function of the actual de facto prizings and valuations, customs and mores, laws and institutional demands of the times in which we live. What was a wise choice for Pericles in ancient Athens may not be the same for the Roman statesman Seneca, or for Abelard's Heloise, or for Sir Walter Raleigh, Mary Wollstonecraft, or Admiral Peary. Hence, there is an intrinsic *relativity* and *contextuality* of all choice, for it is always related to specific individuals and cultures. Yet, although the relativity of choice is *endemic* to the ethical life, there are still ethical qualities that are generalizable to the human condition. This is why we can empathize with a Hamlet or an Othello or a Lady Macbeth as they wrestle with their moral dilemmas. They have a kind of universal message, and can speak to each and every one of us.

The point that I am making is that there is a phenomenological structure to ethical experience, and some objective considerations are relevant to choices. Our individual values and principles may be tested on a *comparative* scale, in terms of the alternatives and options facing us. They may be *evaluated* by their *effectiveness*. They may be appraised by their *consistency* with the norms that we hold. In judging, we can estimate the real *consequences* of our decisions in the world, the effects upon us and others within the range of interaction. Insofar as we take into account these factors, then a reflective component has intervened in the process of judgment. John Dewey has distinguished between a *prizing,* where we value something and an element of immediacy, feeling, and pleasure is involved, and an *appraisal,* where a cognitive element intervenes.[8] It is the difference, he says, between a de facto acceptance of the given and a de jure warrant that it is fitting within the situation. The difference between prizing and appraisal is that the latter involves a *transformative* aspect; that is, in the process of inquiry the reflective judgment can become constituent of the valuation and may modify the prizing.

For example, I may be in the market for a new car. The infantile approach would be to buy the automobile with the most appealing lines and color. An adolescent's response would be to purchase the sports model simply because he *likes* it. But an adult would say that he needs to appraise the value of the automobile. In a process of valuation, the adult weighs merit on a comparative scale: "Can I afford this car?" "How much will I receive for my trade-in?" "Does it get good mileage?" "How safe is it?" "How does it compare with other models of other manufacturers?" In the process, this person may end up by purchasing a different model after having calculated the comparative costs, effectiveness, and consequences. Although one's feelings are relevant in the valuing process, the final decision is also related to one's cognitive beliefs. An estimate of the value of the car is a function of the objective qualities of the object. One's prizings are dependent upon one's appraisals. Ralph Barton Perry defined a value as "the object of any interest."[9] I would modify this definition as follows: "A

8. John Dewey, *The Theory of Valuation* (Chicago, 1939); *The Quest for Certainty* (New York: Minton, Balch, 1929), Chapter 10.

9. Ralph Barton Perry, *General Theory of Value* (Cambridge, Mass.: Harvard University Press, 1926, 1954).

value is an interest in an object in which I have both prized and appraised its worth."

A normative belief is not the same as a descriptive belief. The first entails an evaluation and prescription of a course of conduct, the second describes or explains a factual state of affairs. Formulating a normative belief is not dissimilar, however, to testing a descriptive belief. In both cases we seek to justify our belief as true or normative. In questions of valuation, we appeal to reason to justify our choice. We consider evidence, we take into account consistency and consequences, and there is a body of previously tested ethical principles upon which we draw. I know that if I have a headache, and I take two aspirin tablets, I may alleviate my pain. This is a prescriptive recommendation that has been verified empirically. Similarly, I learn that, if I were to lie to another person, I wouldn't be trusted, and that if another person were to lie to me, our relationship would be jeopardized. Thus, I learn that telling the truth is the most prudential policy to adopt, and as a mature adult I come to feel *strongly* about this common moral decency on both cognitive and attitudinal grounds.

What I have been describing is the constitutive role that deliberation can have in the process of decision-making. Thought becomes essential to the very fabric of the ethical life, and we thus have some role in developing our own ethical sensibilities. We are able to resolve moral questions without necessarily deriving what we ought to do from fixed or ultimate principles. The "ought" cannot be easily deduced from the "is," yet in any process of intelligent deliberation it can be a function of a process of valuational inquiry. What I decide to do is relative to the facts of the case, the circumstances before me, the various alternatives I face, a consideration of the means at my disposal, and the likely consequences of my acts. Intrinsic to the valuational base in terms of which I make my choices are value-laden data: my previous prizings and appraisals, the common moral decencies, the ethical principles of my society, considerations of human needs, and my own unique wants and desires. We need not deduce our duties from absolute universal rules. Moral reasoning is not the application of simple recipes, nor is the process one of drawing inductive generalizations from the past. Ethical reasoning involves a process of what I have called act-duction.[10] By this I mean that we infer the actions that are most appropriate—we act-duce—given the valuation base at hand. On the basis of this, some choices may thus be said to be more reasonable in the situation than others.

Ethical Fallibilism

Ethical knowledge has a degree of probabilism and fallibilism attached to it. We need to recognize that there are alternative lifestyles and a wide variety of human values and norms. This presupposes some comprehension of the fragility of the human condition and some skepticism about our ultimate perfectability. Thus, ethical wisdom recognizes that life is full of uncertainties. In one sense, it is permeated by indeterminacies. We can very rarely, if ever, be absolutely certain of anything. There are few finalities that we can grasp onto. There are always new challenges, new problems and conflicts, new discoveries and opportunities that confront us. The pervasive character of human existence is the fact that we are forever confronted by ambiguities. No one knows for sure what will happen tomorrow, or next year, or during the next century. We can make predictions and forecasts, and these may or may not come true. We note regularities and trends, and we find some order in nature and society (in the sciences and ordinary life), on the basis of which we can make wise choices. Alas, life is full of surprises: An unexpected accident upsets our best-laid plans; a freak storm fells a tree and it lands on our house; the bizarre suddenly intrudes into our life-world. There are sudden breaks or chance contingencies. Anomalies beset us, like a typhoon suddenly blowing in on us, or a hailstorm in the summertime. Thus one can never rely entirely on one's past experiences or achievements. There is always something new to contend with. We encounter paradoxes, dilemmas, and puzzles. And we may be faced with insuperable odds or excruciating choices. Our options may be awesome and terrible. We may suffer great financial losses

---

10. For a discussion of "act-duction," see Paul Kurtz, *Philosophical Essays in Pragmatic Naturalism* (Buffalo, N.Y.: Prometheus Books, 1990), Part II.

and be close to bankruptcy. Or we may have an overwhelming victory in politics or war, although we cannot sustain heroic efforts indefinitely without becoming exhausted. Other persons or societies may emerge to challenge our hegemony, and this may lead to conflicts. Polarities are ever-present. The virtuous may become corrupt; the corrupt may be reformed; the good turns out to be bad; our grand successes may be followed by ignominious defeats. For every move we make there is a counter-move by someone else. Life is replete with sorrow and tears, but also with laughter and joy.

Given these indelible generic factors about the human condition, we cannot escape from making choices, however painful or exciting they may be. And what we ought to do depends on the situation. Often the dilemmas we face have no solution. We sometimes have to make a choice between two unmitigated evils, or between two goods, both of which we cherish but cannot have. The skeptic or the cynic or the pessimist is wont to point out that any effort to achieve utopia, ultimate perfection, or nirvana is an illusion and bound to fail. Yet some optimism is warranted. We may be inspired by the steady progress and achievements of the human species in history. This may be attributed to the humanist virtues of courage and endurance, the will-to-become in spite of obstacles, the use of critical intelligence (mingled with compassion) to solve our problems, and the determination to lead the good life as best we can. This ethical position may be described as *melioristic*. It does not hope to attain the unattainable, whether in this life or in the next, but it does believe that we can improve the human condition and that we can achieve the better, on a comparative scale, if not attain the absolute good. But to succeed in life requires the constant use of ethical rationality. We do the best we can, given the limitations and the opportunities discovered within the situations of life. In making choices, we can draw upon our knowledge of the common moral decencies, our moral heritage, and the fund of human wisdom. But ethical inquirers must be prepared to modify their beliefs in the light of altered circumstances.

There is thus a revisionary character endemic to morality, for new principles are constantly being discovered and introduced.

It took a long time in human history to finally eliminate slavery and to begin to liberate women from male domination. It is only relatively recently that the ethical principle that "all persons are entitled to equality of consideration" has been recognized. In the field of medical ethics, the principles of "informed consent," "voluntary choice," and "autonomy of adult patients" now provide guidelines for medical practice. A whole new constellation of "human rights" is now being recognized worldwide. Thus there is a continual revision in our ethical values and principles as we learn from experience and make new discoveries in the sciences. Yet we are constantly confronted by moral absolutists—conservatives or reactionaries, on the one hand, or radical innovators, on the other—who wish to substitute moral fanaticism for ethical inquiry.

Some degree of skepticism is thus a necessary antidote to all forms of moral dogmatism. We are continually surrounded by self-righteous moralists who claim that they have the Absolute Truth or Moral Virtue or Piety or know the secret path to Progress, and they wish to impose their convictions on all others. They are puffed up with an inflated sense of their own rectitude and they rail against unbenighted immoral sinners who lack their moral faith. These moral zealots are willing to repress or sacrifice anyone who stands in their way. They have unleashed conquering armies in the name of God or the Dialectic or Racial Superiority or Posterity or Imperial Design. Skepticism needs to be applied not only to religious and paranormal fantasies, but to other forms of moral and political illusions. These dogmas become especially dangerous when they are appealed to in order to legislate morality and are used by powerful social institutions, such as the state or church or corporation, to enforce a particular brand of moral virtue. Hell hath no fury like the self-righteous moral fanatic scorned.

The best antidote for this is some skepticism and a willingness to engage in ethical inquiry, not only about *their* moral zeal, but about *our own,* especially if we are tempted to translate the results of our own ethical inquiries into commandments. The epistemological theory presented here, the methodological principles of skeptical inquiry, has important moral implications. For in recognizing our own fallibility we thereby can learn to *tolerate* other human beings and to appreciate their diversity and the plurality of lifestyles. If we are prepared to engage in cooperative ethical inquiry, then perhaps we are better prepared to allow other individuals and groups some measure of liberty to pursue their own preferred lifestyles. If we are able to live and let live, then this can best be achieved in a free and open democratic society. Where we differ, we should try to negotiate our divergent views and perhaps reach common ground; and if this is impractical, we should at least attempt to compromise for the sake of our common interests. The method of ethical inquiry requires some intelligent and informed examination of our own values, as well as the values of others. Here we can attempt to modify attitudes by an appeal to cognitive beliefs and to reconstruct them by an examination of the relevant evidence. Such a give-and-take of constructive criticism is essential for a harmonious society. In learning to appreciate different conceptions of the good life, we are able to expand our own dimensions of moral awareness; and this is more apt to lead to a peaceful world.

By this I do not mean to imply that anything and everything can or should be tolerated and/or that one thing is as good as the next. We should be prepared to criticize moral nonsense parading as virtue. We should not tolerate the intolerable. We have a right to strongly object, if need be, to those values or practices that we think are based on miscalculation, misconception, or are patently false or harmful. Nonetheless, we might live in a better world if *inquiry* were to replace faith; *deliberation,* passionate commitment; and *education and persuasion,* force and war. We would be aware of the powers of intelligent behavior, but also the limitations of the human animal and of the need to mitigate the cold and indifferent intellect with the compassionate and empathic heart. Thus I conclude that within the ethical life we are capable of developing a body of melioristic principles and values and a method of coping with problems intelligently. There is a form of *eupraxia,* or good practice, that we can learn to appreciate and live by, and this can be infused with *sophia,* or wisdom. When our ethical judgments are based on ethical inquiry, they are more apt to express the highest reaches of excellence and nobility, and of civilized human conduct.

Chapter 10

Politics and Skeptical Inquiry

Three Kinds of Skepticism in Politics

It is apparent that the ethical choices of individuals cannot be dealt with separately from the political and social institutions that regulate their conduct and in terms of which they live and function. Many ethical issues can only be resolved within the public square; yet it is forever rife with controversy. If ever there was an arena that needed skeptical inquiry, it is in the political domain. For in the modern world, political ideology has served as the chief moral inspiration for large sectors of humankind. It is not God or the afterlife, but the building of the just society that has moved men and women to dedication and devotion. Historically more individuals have benefited from or been abused by the state than perhaps by any other social institution. The emergence of the city-state, the empire, and the nation-state, has brought great good, but it also has inflicted great harm. First, because it is the state or government that has the power to make, interpret, and apply the law; and, second, because the state generally possesses a preponderance of coercive military and police force. It alone has the supreme authority to tax, regulate, and control the lives of its citizens and, if it so wishes, to enforce its decrees and compel obedience to them. It has been primarily the national state that has waged ferocious wars of mass genocide and destruction.

Although many positive programs have been enacted to fulfill human needs, protect the health, safety, welfare, and property of its citizens, often the opposite has occurred. Political ideologies have both inspired unquestioning commitment and engendered skeptical disenchantment. Indeed, political philosophers compete with theologians in spinning out theories of mystification. No wonder that a downright distrust of all ideological programs and politicians has emerged for large sectors of public opinion.

There are three forms of political skepticism that correspond to the three kinds of epistemological and ethical skepticism that we have already outlined. The first is *political nihilism, total negative skepticism and subjectivism.* This position claims that there are no objective standards of judgment by which we may evaluate the policies of statecraft. For this viewpoint, justice, in the last analysis, is simply based upon sentiment, convention, or power, nothing more and nothing less.

If we were to accept this extreme interpretation of political decision-making, one form of political rule would be as good as the next. There would be no ground for criticizing tyrannical laws other than that a person or group finds them emotionally repugnant. Any opposition to or support of fascism or Stalinism, for example, would simply be a question of taste or caprice. Such nihilism in politics, as in ethics, is contradicted by experience; for we constantly formulate political and ethical judgments, and we attempt to justify them by argument and evidence. To deny that any objective considerations are present is to reduce politics to irrational feelings or brute force.

The second is *mitigated skepticism,* which recognizes that, in spite of the relativity of political power and the rule of sentiment and self-interest, we need to live and work together, and hence some principles of justice need to be developed. Here some rational standards are introduced to justify social polity. This marks a decided advance over political nihilism. Are the criteria to which the mitigated skeptic defers—such as an appeal to the greatest-happiness principle or the common good—based solely upon sentiment, and are these standards without any further justification? In the last analysis, does everything reduce to subjectivity? I submit that this is not the case, for the mitigated skeptics at the very least recognize that there are principles of prudential rationality and of pragmatic effectiveness that they appeal to in order to guide policy; and these are not based solely upon taste or sentiment.

The third is the full application of *skeptical inquiry* to the political domain. Here the method of critical intelligence is relevant to the affairs of state and to the formulation of judgments of practice in all social institutions. Nonetheless, skeptical inquiry is based upon a healthy mistrust of leadership and possible abuses of power. Yet it is still possible to work out wise decisions, not only on prudential grounds, but even concerning our ends and goals, which are not *simply* a matter of sentiment and can be modified in the light of reason and practice.

Political Abstractions

Skeptical inquirers are critical of the use of unexamined political abstractions, ideological fictions, illusions, and fantasies, to justify practice. They are dubious of the appeal to "First Principles" as an ultimate ground for political action. There are many illustrations of this kind of abstract reasoning in politics. Plato's Idea of Justice was supposed to serve as a beacon for the *polis.* The philosopher kings were supposed to create a utopian society that would realize the Absolute Good. Implicit in this line of reasoning is the moral sanctification of the totalitarian state. If any group believes that it possesses a monopoly of truth or virtue, then it can impose its vision upon the rest of humanity with or without their consent.

In Plato's *Republic,* everyone fulfilled a function and thus fit harmoniously into the whole. When Socrates is asked by Glaucon whether the people under such conditions were unhappy, he responded, "That is not important, for the principle of Justice is being applied." The skeptic questions the authority of any elite to know the best interests of everyone and to rule in their name— especially where there is no room for dissent, where the citizens have had no say in enacting the laws, and where they are nevertheless required to submit to the edicts of the state. The most heinous forms of tyranny have been justified in the name of abstract reason. This was the case during the French Revolution, when Robespierre sought to vindicate the tyranny of the guillotine. This totalitarian logic often devours the leaders of the revolution. Thus, if your end is considered ultimately right, you may feel justified in using any means, however extreme, because you see your duty as being to the higher ideal.

There are many infamous illustrations of this logic. Two horrible gulags of the twentieth century are still fresh in our memory: Communism and Nazism. In the case of the Leninist-Stalinist state, the Bolsheviks believed in the proletarian-communist utopian society. Therefore, the old Czarist order had to be destroyed; and once they seized power, any threats to the revolution were dealt with decisively. This was all based on their commitment to an abstract dialectical interpretation of history, which put justice on their side. It also enabled them to engage in class warfare with impunity and to use any tactic, however despicable, to realize their ends. Even Trotsky, who was an early critic of Stalin and was condemned by him for having betrayed the revolution, was willing to justify the use of state terror if it led eventually to the greater good. The psychology of the mass murderer intent on achieving utopia is such that once he commits murder and gets away with it, there is no end to his mendacity. There is confusion between the interest of the people, which he claims to represent, and his own self-interest. For those who possess a monopoly of power, any opposition to their rule must be dealt with summarily. Those who control the reigns of power in time become corrupted, for the taste of power is intoxicating. Absolute power feeds on itself, especially if it is mixed with glory and sweetened by the sycophantic praise of those who fawn in the presence of the tyrant. Megalomania demands more and more of its victims' blood. It enabled Stalin to murder Bukharin, Kamenev, and Zinoviev, and most of the other original Bolsheviks, in order to consolidate his rule. An estimated 20 million victims in the Soviet Union eventually suffered at the hands of this totalitarian mentality, and the brutal police system dominated everyone's lives.

The same pathological syndrome was seen in Nazi Germany. Although the fascists lacked a coherent philosophical position, they invoked the will to power to achieve their confused abstract ideals.

Their theories of racial superiority, on the basis of which they resorted to brutal terror, were a hodgepodge of bad history, bad biology, bad science, and the metaphysics of "sturm und drang." Nonetheless, fervent belief in the Third Reich and the destiny of the German people led a nation to madness, and it explained the willingness of legions of otherwise sane and decent people to follow Hitler and the SS to the bitter end. Here political ideology was infused with pure passion. It drew upon primitive emotions: dedication to the Fuehrer and the German nation, and hatred for the Jews and other "inferior" races. This led to the slaughter of millions of innocent people in World War II, genocide, and the Holocaust, and the eventual twilight of the "Aryan Gods."

There is a continuous thread in political ideology, from Plato to the present, that maintains that if a party or group has a special path to truth or glory, it is justified in seizing power and imposing it not only on one's own people but on others as well. This had been the case from Alexander to Caesar, from Napoleon to Hitler and Mao. Thus the concept of nation, nationality, empire, class, or race—all ideological abstractions—can command allegiance and sacrifice from its subjects. We need skeptical critiques of the inflated claims made by political leaders intent on carrying out their missions—whether of the Roman legions, the Ottoman Empire, the Mongol invaders, or even Pax Britannica and Pax Americana. Regretfully, nationalistic and chauvinistic slogans have been used everywhere in history to arouse blind allegiance. The young men have usually gone off to be slaughtered in war, while the old men who command them in the name of some national abstraction die quietly in bed. The blood of millions has been sacrificed at the altar of political ideologies that have inflamed countless nations. The patriotic cause has too often been embodied in a leader who represents national aspirations—whether Cromwell or Elizabeth I, Louis XIV or Bismarck, Washington or Churchill, Emperor Hirohito or Joseph of Hapsburg. Wars of national liberation and self-defense, of revolution and civil war, have turned countries into turmoil, and have been waged by leaders who were lionized as heroes—Lincoln and Wilson, Franco and Ho Chi Minh, Lenin and Tito.

Whether or not Konrad Lorenz's "instinct for aggression" has some basis in human nature, history surely testifies to the prevalence of bloody conflicts, ethnic rivalries, and nationalistic wars. Competition between national groups have been fed by the impulse of fear and the lure of plunder, and justification for this aggression has often been made in the name of some abstract ideal.

The skeptical inquirer, as I said, is able to see through the deceptive use of the language and symbols of national pride, and the hoax of the bugle call or drumbeat beckoning armies to serve as cannon fodder for the cause. The defense of the fatherland or the motherland, the old order or the new order, the utopian ideal or the vision of the great society, has each in its turn goaded men and women to kill each other. Patriotism has lured both scoundrels and idealists to be vanquished or victorious on the ramparts of human folly.

An especially pernicious form of political deception is the use of abstract religious symbols to inspire sacrifice. Mohammed used the sword to conquer the whole of Arabia in the name of Allah. This was followed in subsequent centuries by the fall of North Africa and the Middle East, and it led Islam eventually to the very gates of Constantinople and Seville. The Koran was the holy justification for Muslim hegemony. The infamous Crusades and the wars between Catholics and Protestants, Hindus and Sikhs, Jews and Christians, Christians and Muslims, are all testaments to the efforts by religious prophets to employ the state to impose the Faith, to wrap the Bible or the Koran in the flag, or to demand allegiance by the threat of damnation. The Inquisition was carried out by monarchs in alliance with the Church to compel belief in the Faith, and dissenters were broken on the rack by religious fanaticism. The union between religion and politics is a double-edged sword, for it inflicts the power of both the church and the state on unbelievers in order to compel obedience. The blind devotion of the true believer willing to die not simply for country but for God only evinces cynicism on the part of clear-headed skeptics who can see through the charade. Unfortunately, some forms of skepticism are highly selective. Some skeptics are willing to use skepticism in the sciences, or in evaluating paranormal claims; some fearless skeptics are even willing to apply freethought to religion. But all too few are courageous enough to use the skeptical eye in unmasking political slogans. Fearful of being called "unpatriotic," most skeptics dare not intrude into the archways of chauvinism, nor to challenge wars fought in the name of national pride or for aggrandizement.

Mass Movements

Alas, humanity has a proclivity for uncritically being swept up by mass movements. At times, waves of reform, revolution, or reaction overcome large sectors of humankind, including otherwise sophisticated individuals. Extremist movements promise redemption or salvation, an ultimate remedy for all the ills of society. They inspire crusades and revolutions, wars of aggression and civil wars. They demand a united front, preach a fervent message of hope, generate within the flock enthusiasm for the cause. This is true of major religious movements, such as militant Christianity or Islam, or political ideological movements, such as fascism or communism, the "white man's burden," or laissez-faire capitalism, and to a lesser extent to cults, such as Scientology and Mormonism. During their periods of rapid growth, leaders demand allegiance, even blind faith, and fanatic devotion to the righteousness of the beloved cause. True believers willingly renounce their individuality for the movement; they become submerged by it, yet their lives take on meaning because of their identity with it. The cause is powerful, not because it appeals to rationality, but because it appeals to passion and will. Often the message is so nonsensical that it is hard to see how anyone can swallow it; and the bigger the lie, the more fanciful or outrageous the myth, the greater the intensity of commitment. The movement appeals to deep psychological needs, and it employs symbols of drama and poetry, pomp and ritual. Skeptical inquirers are unwilling or unable to be swept up by the madness of the times; they stand aside murmuring dissent; their criticisms often fall on deaf ears, and they may be ostracized or subject to retaliation. True believers condemn them as subversives or sinners: "If you are not with us," they scream, "you are against us." They rail against indifference or neutrality. Where the movement captures state power, it turns with vindictive fury and hatred against the opposition: The Gestapo and the KGB murdered dissenters; Christians burned heretics at the stake; and Muslims execute apostates.

I know of many poignant cases in recent years of innocent people who were duped by fundamentalist and evangelical preachers into joining a church. They went through a process of conversion, in which there was a strong dose of passionate feeling, perhaps a smattering of intellectual questioning, and finally, total acceptance of the message. They were welcomed at first with loving care by their new circle of like-minded friends. However, some were fortunate and soon discovered that the continuing demands made upon them were overpowering. To be a true Christian was not a nominal relationship, but a full-time commitment. Only with difficulty could such a person break away from the pressures of the movement, but not without painful difficulty and guilt.

The processes of conversion and deconversion are similar, whether in religion or ideology. Many devout communists joined the party in their youth out of disenchantment with the unjust world. They had the idealistic conviction that, if the existing system were destroyed, a new order could be brought into being. And so they became members of a cell, and willingly agreed to submit to party discipline. The party dominated their whole lives, and they were all too ready to sacrifice their autonomy as they followed the party line—all for the greater good that they believed someday would be brought into being. Arthur Koestler describes the moral dilemma of dedicated Bolsheviks who were purged and then devoured by terror, yet accepted their fate as inevitable, still dedicated to the ideal.[1] Such ideological movements, like systems of religious dogma, provide the believer with a coherent world-view, a unification of thought and action, and they seemingly provide easy solutions to all the major problems of life. A distinction is made between *us, our* side, *our* movement, which is allied with the angels and the righteous, and *them,* the enemy, sinners, capitalists, Jews, blacks, the undeserving rich, or the lazy poor. If only they could destroy the corruption that exists, seize power, and take control, believers are convinced, a better world would result. In time, those who are perceptive may see that the prophet or leader has no

---

1. Arthur Koestler, *Darkness at Noon* (New York: Macmillan, 1941).

clothing, that the flock is being misled, that new forms of corruption—as bad as the old, or even more terrible—may be committed by the new order, and that the revolution is being betrayed.

Sometimes these movements begin at the bottom, not by converting the highly educated classes, but by enlisting the youth and the lumpen proletariat, the unemployed, the poor, and the outcasts and misfits of society, those who lack purpose, are bored, or find life without meaning. The movement defines them and gives them a mission in life. In time the movement may swell in numbers, and it eventually may garner recruits from all levels of society. As it grows in influence, others are swept up by the fervor or madness of the times. The movement may seek to discredit the entire status quo or only certain aspects of society, or it may seek to return to "the old ways." It can infect men and women regardless of their leanings—whether of the right or of the left, theists or nontheists, radicals or reactionaries. It has ready-made answers and simple nostrums. Action replaces words; coercion replaces persuasion. Essential to the power of the appeal is the emergence of charismatic personalities who promise the millennium and whose pronouncements, revelations, or commandments are gladly accepted and followed. His or her personality is so powerful that people are prepared to sacrifice everything for them. A set of sacred books and texts emerge containing the Absolute Truth; unanalyzed, every word and sentence is taken as Holy Writ.

There are other kinds of *political abstractions* quite independent of extremist movements and less destructive, but equally specious. Such political abstractions have the power to move all manner of men and women and all strata of society, and they have appeared throughout history. They have affected the intellectual classes as well as ordinary men and women. Indeed, political leaders have often turned to their philosophers, poets, and scientists to invoke the cherished abstractions and sing praises to them.

Natural Law

For example, natural-law theories have been appealed to in order to provide a theoretical rationale for political practice. Aristotle criticized Plato's realm of forms; he was skeptical of the attempt to base a just society on the idea of the Good. Form is connected to matter, and hence political decisions must deal with concrete choices in the real world. Nonetheless, he found a basis for natural law implicit in a common human nature and common human needs. This doctrine in time was further elaborated by natural-law theorists and provided a set of abstract concepts delimiting ethical behavior and serving as a basis for political policies. Thomists, particularly in the contemporary world, have appealed to the natural law. They resort to it to oppose birth control. Contraception, they maintain, interferes with the "natural function" of intercourse, which is procreation, not pleasurable satisfaction. Natural law is also used to defend the position of the Roman Catholic church against divorce (monogamy allegedly fulfills the natural law) and abortion (it is illicit to interrupt fetal development, for the human soul is implanted at the moment of conception). The difficulty with such abstract doctrines is that they are interpreted in the light of prevailing church doctrine. The church is a political institution dominated by a celibate priesthood. In fact, one could argue that voluntary celibacy is unnatural—only sick animals forgo their sexual functions. Human beings consistently intervene in natural processes; indeed, this is the primary role of medicine, which seeks to improve or impede so-called natural functions. Any effort to prohibit reproductive freedom (contraception, abortion, sterilization, *in vitro* fertilization, *in vivo* fertilization) is arbitrary. Similarly for the church's aversion to voluntary active euthanasia—where terminal patients are dying and wish to mitigate their suffering by hastening the process and ending their lives. Here abstract doctrines in opposition can be repressive. Homosexuality is also condemned as a violation of the natural law. But who is to say what is "normal" or "natural"? There is considerable evidence that a person's sexual orientation has a genetic basis and is not a matter of free choice. Yet many natural-law theorists have sought to prohibit by legislation the private sexual proclivities of adults. Skeptics have pointed out that Roman Catholic theologians have subtly moved from the natural to the "Divine Law," as interpreted by Papal doctrine, to determine what is right or wrong. The natural law is a pretext used to justify one's own bias.

Natural Rights

In the modern era, one form of the natural-law doctrine was converted into the theory of inalienable natural rights: "Life, liberty, and the pursuit of happiness." Theorists on all sides of the political spectrum have appealed to natural rights to restrain arbitrary power, or to justify the revolution against the state, as did John Locke and the leaders of the American Revolution. Many deem this a progressive doctrine, a necessary postulate of the democratic society. Many skeptics, however, have pointed out that the epistemological basis for the doctrine is questionable. Such rights are not "self-evident," for it is not the case that everyone recognizes them as intuitively certain. Moreover, they are framed in such general abstract terms that how they should be interpreted is often open to dispute. Natural rights were invoked by abolitionists in the nineteenth century in order to oppose slavery, but those who believed in natural rights were unwilling to extend them to women. Interestingly, natural-law doctrine was also appealed to (by Aristotle, John C. Calhoun, and others) in order to justify slavery. Postulating natural inequalities in humankind, they argued that some people were "superior" and ought to rule over "inferior" slaves. Historically, others have interpreted the right to own property as a natural right, and they have used the doctrine to oppose *any* effort by the government to tax citizens or regulate commerce. The clash of the right to liberty with the principle of equality is likewise a source of continuing controversy. Which should rank higher as a normative standard, liberty or equality? The problem becomes all the more complicated when the principle of equality is taken as self-evidently true. The doctrine of natural rights thus should not be interpreted in abstract terms. By raising these skeptical queries, I am not denying the importance of a doctrine of *human* rights, but its epistemological justification does rest on doubtful ontological grounds. If human rights are to be justified, they must be tested empirically by reference to their consequences.

The Theology of Laissez Faire

Related to our discussion of abstract concepts is the prominence of laissez-faire economic doctrines in capitalist societies. These theories draw upon the philosophy of libertarians like Adam Smith.[2] They point to the fact that free-market economies have contributed enormously to economic expansion, particularly in comparison with bureaucratic, highly regulated, and centralized economies. Unfortunately, a kind of "*theology* of laissez faire" has developed, which takes on a quasi-religious character. Its adherents express the truth of the theory with great fervor. They insist that all individuals are self-interested economic decision-makers. As such, they should be allowed to engage in production, distribution, commerce, and the consumption of goods and services freely, and supply and demand should set prices and policies. It is the discipline of the marketplace, they say, that should determine economic investment and exploitation. Those enterprises that do not show a profit will become marginal and in time disappear; those that survive and prosper are most efficient and are satsifying consumer wants. Free competition in the marketplace should prevail, they argue, without government regulation, for it is the most productive method of ensuring prosperity, expanding wealth, and fulfilling the common good.

This theory was introduced in the eighteenth century, when the market was composed of individual entrepreneurs, land-owners, renters, and small-scale enterprises. With the emergence of the Industrial Revolution and in time the technological, information, and service society, the nature of the marketplace has been drastically altered. Large corporations and multinational conglomerates now dominate much of manufacturing, agriculture, trade, and finance. Moreover, large-scale unions have emerged in some industries to engage in collective bargaining to determine working conditions and wages. To continue to believe that the "hidden hand" of the marketplace will in the last analysis work beneficially is largely conjecture. Prices are sometimes set by monopolistic practices. Moreover there are many social needs that are best

---

2. Adam Smith, *The Wealth of Nations* (1776).

fulfilled by philanthropic activities or nonprofit voluntary organizations, and/or require public investment and regulation by the government. Here the state can play a role, for it is concerned with ensuring the health, education, and welfare of its citizens, the maintenance of the police, fire protection, and national defense, the equitable regulation of transportation and communication, the preservation of the environment; and other basic needs. Some intelligent justification for governmental intervention thus makes sense. This does not deny that the free market is essential for economic prosperity, yet extreme laissez-faire libertarians resist any effort of governments on the national or international level to regulate by lawful means for the common good. The realm of pure ideological abstraction too often dominates policy decisions. My criticisms here only apply to absolutist forms of economic libertarianism, not to libertarianism in the political sphere, where the defense of civil liberties is essential; nor to moral libertarianism, which defends the right to privacy.

Marxism

As we have seen, abstract theories have also been appealed to by Marxists to defend the opposite of economic libertarianism. The world has emerged from a period of intoxication with communist ideology. Marx claimed that he was a scientist. He attempted to formulate his theories by means of rational analyses and reference to historical evidence. According to Engels, Marx made two basic scientific discoveries.[3] The first was "the law of development of human history." This was his concept that "the production of the immediate material means of subsistence, and consequently the degree of economic development attained by a given people or . . . a given epoch [are the] foundation upon which the state, legal institutions, art, religion, and everything else, have evolved and must be explained." This was sometimes known as the economic interpretation of history. The second contribution of Marx

3. Friedrich Engels,"Speech at the Grave Site of Karl Marx," March 17, 1883, in *The Marx-Engels Reader,* ed. by Robert C. Tucker (New York: W. W. Norton, 1972), pp. 603–604.

was that he discovered the special laws governing the "capitalist mode of production." This was rooted in Marx's "theory of surplus values." For Marx it is not our consciousness that determines our existence, but our social existence that determines our consciousness. At a certain stage in history the material forces of production come into conflict with the relationships of production (i.e., property relations). They become the fetters of change. This leads to a social revolution in which the entire superstructure is transformed. The "contradictions" of material life, and the "conflict between the social forces of production and the relations of production, make the social revolution possible."[4] In capitalist societies, the class antagonisms between the bourgeoisie and the proletariat will be resolved by the emergence of a new communist society.

Marx's general theory was applied to human history to interpret what was causative. It was supposed to enable us to make predictions of future economic and social development. Central to Marx's analysis was the use of Hegelian concepts, in particular Marx's view that history manifested a dialectical process in which theses were negated and contradictions overcome. Marx supplemented the dialectical laws by giving them materialistic content; hence his theory is known as "dialectical materialism." For this reason, the Polish philosopher Leszek Kolakowski considers Marx primarily a philosopher, not a social scientist.[5] For Marx, the dynamic causes of historical development were related to the mode of production prevailing in an epoch. These include the contradictions between the forces of production (technology, material resources, etc.), and the relationships of production (primarily the class structure). He believed that certain economic class relationships served economic development in a period of history, whether agricultural or feudal, where landlord and serf are the two major classes. Capitalism, he said, involves the development of a bourgeois social class, dominated by the quest for profit, and a laboring proletariat class who sold its labor to the capital-

---

4. Ibid.

5. Leszek Kolakowski, *Main Currents of Marxism* (Oxford: Clarendon Press, 1978).

ists. Accordingly, capital is only the "surplus value" extracted from labor by means of profit, rent, or interest. Capitalism has its dynamics of growth, but it has internal contradictions that will lead to its inevitable collapse—in particular the steady deterioration of the lot of the workers. Workers are not paid sufficient wages above and beyond the subsistence level; and therefore at some point the capitalists will be unable to sell their goods, and an economic crisis will occur, which will eventually destroy the entire system. And it is out of this crisis that a new society will emerge. This is based on new relationships of production, rooted in the collectivization of the means of production. The proletariat will seize power and wrest control of its destiny from its oppressors.

Marx succinctly summarized his theory as follows: "What I did that was new was to prove: (1) that *the existence of classes* is bound up with *particular historical phases in the development of production,* (2) that the class struggle necessarily leads to the *dictatorship of the proletariat,* and (3) that this dictatorship itself constitutes only the transition to the *abolition of all classes and to a classless society.*"[6]

In the century following the death of Marx in 1883, his theories were heralded as the key to human progress and vast revolutionary movements sprang up to undertake the struggle to realize his dreams and fulfill his prophecies. Marx surely cannot be identified with the so-called Marxists who claimed to follow him. Whether the Stalinist-Leninist interpretation of Marx's thought is accurate is extremely doubtful. Was Marx a democrat, or did he believe in the dictatorship of the proletariat? The democratic socialists, who thought that socialism could come into being by democratic means, differed with the Leninists, who claimed that only revolutionary violence and a party- and state-dictatorship could bring about socialism.

Surely the father cannot be held responsible for the sins of his offspring. A persuasive case has been made by Sidney Hook that Marx would have been among the first to have rebelled against

---

6. See "Letter to Joseph Weydemeyer" (March 5, 1852), in Lewis Feuer, *Marx and Engels' Basic Writings in Politics and Philosophy* (Garden City, N.Y.: Doubleday, 1954), pp. 456–57.

the dictatorships imposed by the Bolsheviks in his name. Claiming to represent his theories and ideals, they became the chief executioners of them. For Marx was a fighter for human freedom and democracy, and he wished to liberate humans from oppression and allow them to actualize their creative freedoms. There is much of Marxist analysis that is useful. Marx had powerful insights into historical development; he emphasized the economic and material factors that had been overlooked or neglected by previous writers who thought that history was simply a result of different ideas, or a clash of political forces. Sidney Hook argues that the "dialectic" can or should be used as a tool of empirical analysis rather than dogma.[7] However, Marxist theory went beyond any empirical analysis, for it was rooted in Hegelian rationalistic premises, and as such it often confounds where it should clarify, especially insofar as it attempted to provide a grand scheme of universal laws, which it maintained was applicable to all of history. As such, it claimed too much, and almost by definition was impervious to the concrete particulars of historical change.

Marxism vividly demonstrated how philosophical theories become engines of mystification, and how a reduction of history to universal dialectical concepts can distort reality. Moreover, infusing philosophical theories with salvational language and moral feeling impedes objective analysis. Marx was himself first and foremost a moral prophet. He was concerned with indicting the evils of exploitation. He did not simply seek to understand the capitalist mode of production, but to transform it. His goal was to alleviate the distressing conditions of the working class and to ameliorate its suffering. As such, his overarching system was basically moral poetry, designed to appeal to the intellect, but also intent on arousing compassion. In offering an overarching cosmic interpretation of human history, and in pointing to a solution to alienation and oppression, it claimed too much. The abstract idea of the dialectical process was thus virtually apotheosized. Class warfare would eventually be replaced by a classless society in which freedom, equality, justice, and harmony would prevail, but only

---

7. Sidney Hook, *Reason, Social Myths and Democracy* (1940) (Buffalo, N.Y.: Prometheus Books, 1991).

by means of a struggle in which everyone could participate. How tragic that Marx's many valuable insights were distorted by the Marxists and that a workers' society interested in reforming corruption and creating economic plenty ended up by establishing tyrannical rule and institutionalizing poverty.

Critics of this analysis will say that Stalinist-Leninist regimes were perversions of Marx and that socialism has never been really tried. There is some truth to these assertions. The Communist parties of the Soviet Union and elsewhere considered themselves to be the true representatives of the proletariat, in whose name they established dictatorships, but in so arguing they betrayed Marx.

Nevertheless, there is a communist myth similar to the myth of the invisible hand of the market, and the disciples of Marx were lured into believing that there are easy solutions for economic problems. The Marxist is concerned with equality, social welfare, and the communitarian good; and the laissez-faire disciples with individual liberty, self-interest, and free enterprise. Both function as theologies.

The problem with the Marxist theory is that it was too grandiose in what it promised. Given its sweeping range, its categories are not only difficult to verify, they are at times indefinable. To say that "contradictions" inhere in historical processes is to impose poetic metaphors on social events. Social and historical change is so complex that it resists any simple reductive generalizations. Many of Marx's predictions turned out to be wrong. Proletarian revolution occurred in backward, even feudal societies, such as Russia, China, and Vietnam, thus skipping the capitalist phase of development. Moreover, workers in capitalist societies were not ground down, but saw a steady improvement in working conditions and income. The economic substratum of society is not "ultimately" decisive in history, as Engels later claimed, attempting to modify the general causal theory; for religious, philosophical, and scientific ideas may likewise play decisive roles in determining the course of social change.[8] In some periods of history, racial,

---

8. Engels, in a letter to Joseph Bloch, said, "According to the materialistic conception of history, the *ultimately* determining element in history is the production and reproduction of real life. [It is not] . . . the only *determining* one" (September 21–22, 1880), see Lewis Feuer, op. cit.

ethnic, religious, and cultural factors may dominate economic considerations, as in the post–Soviet Union era, where there are intense national and ethnic rivalries. The state is not simply a reflection of the economic mode of production, but political issues themselves are often determining. Moreover, the expansion of scientific discovery and technology may not necessarily reflect the productive relationships of a society, but may be independent sparks of economic development. Ideas may thus play a larger role than material forces. All of these critical points have been made by skeptical inquirers.

What is of special interest to our analysis is the fact that Marxism became a substitute for religion and the moral inspiration for so many intellectuals. As heir to the Enlightenment, Marx believed in human progress, education, reason, and science. He thought that it was possible to liberate human beings from alienation so that they could lead more wholesome, free, and creative lives. The paradox of communist societies was that they ended up by providing a lower standard of living, with less creative freedom and cultural enrichment, than did bourgeois societies. All of this suggests that Marx's idealized interpretation of human nature as intrinsically altruistic and cooperative was basically flawed. Yet countless numbers of intellectuals were beguiled by his ideals. Men and women of expert intelligence in their own field were willing to abandon any pretense at objectivity when they strayed into ethical and ideological minefields. Many intellectuals were skeptical of religious claims. Many were highly competent in science and the arts (J. B. S. Haldane in biology, Picasso in painting and sculpture, Pablo Casals as a cellist), yet they were willing to swallow the Marxist line and were unable to see its Leninist and Stalinist deformation. They refused to admit that the revolution had been betrayed and that new and more terrible forms of repression had replaced the *anciens regimes*. Why was this so? Is it because skepticism generalized to the secular realm of ideology is not enough, and because there is a hunger for meaning deep within the human breast, a quest for a coherent theory that would order the scattered elements of the world and give a purpose in life? Was it the moral devotion of these intellectuals that enabled them to swallow as true, good, and beautiful that which was patent nonsense? Was it because, like others in history, they were prone to accept illusions and live by them?

Lest I be accused of being one-sided in my analysis, let me point out again that libertarianism can also function as a totalistic moral/ideological position for many individuals. Turned off by the excesses of Marxist/Bolshevist ideology, they move to the other extreme. Railing against the government as the source of all evil, they oppose any concern for the welfare of the disadvantaged and any effort to ameliorate the conditions of the poor. They argue with ferocious intensity that human beings are selfish, not altruistic, and that if the state would leave individuals alone we would all be better off.[9] But this again seems to illustrate how an abstract ideology (in this sense, based upon a psychology of human motivation and a generalized economic theory) can play a dominating role and can arouse passionate dedication. The dispute between the theoreticians of free enterprise and their enemies often concerns a battle of abstract categories. Dogmatic libertarianism is not a reliable guide in many situations, for example, where we may need to stimulate the economy in order to achieve economic growth but are precluded from doing so by emotional bias. Surely the lessons of experience are such that we recognize that we need both a vigorous market economy and some role for governmental action.

Postmodernist Nihilism

Another political ideology that seems to be gaining ground today is postmodernism. Disillusioned by the corrupting ideologies of the twentieth century, postmodernists abandon attempts to use reason or science to solve social problems. They are so turned off by the failed promises of the past that they surrender to despair and advise retreat. Unfortunately, this tends to lead to nihilism. One pernicious version of the postmodernist failure of nerve is Heidegger's odyssey with Nazism, ignored or denied for a long

---

9. See especially the writings of Ayn Rand.

period by his French disciples.[10] Heidegger rejected the world of science, technology, and mass culture; he abandoned humanism and its defense of human rights; and he expressed a loss of confidence in the power of modern society to solve social problems by democratic means. He wished to commune with Being, to get back to the primordial given. What this led to in concrete terms was Heidegger's flirtation with Nazism. Does the rejection of reason lead to mastery by the will? If so, whose? The totalitarians? Some postmodernists want to support liberalism, yet they can find no foundation for democracy in reason or experience. Is democracy simply a matter of taste and/or literary appeal? Has it no reliable justification? If this is what Richard Rorty's criticism of method entails, the implications would be unfortunate.

Skeptical Inquiry

At this point, let me return to the key challenge that I raised earlier in this book: Can skepticism help us to frame judgments of practice? My answer is in the affirmative. Skepticism need not be totally negative. It can be used as a tool of inquiry applicable to a wide range of practical concerns, including politics and economics. Thus a constructive skepticism can employ objective methods of inquiry and can draw upon the sciences to frame wise decisions. Matters are thus not hopelessly muddled beyond repair, in spite of the human tendency to illusion. Some *political and economic skepticism* serves as an antidote. It should be an essential ingredient of any educated mind. Without honest critiques of the dominant shibboleths of the age, there is always the danger that ideological and political nostrums will be swallowed, with disastrous consequences.

There is something banal about the nonsense masked as

---

10. See especially Luc Ferry and Alain Renaut, *Heidegger and Modernity* (Chicago: University of Chicago Press, 1990); Victor Farias, *Heidegger and Nazism,* ed. by Joseph Margolis and Tom Rockmore (Philadelphia: Temple University Press, 1987); see also Martin Heidegger, "Letter on Humanism," in *Basic Writings,* ed. by David F. Krell (New York: Harper and Row, 1977).

received doctrine that often dominates political discourse. Every society needs leaders with long-range visions, able to analyze social conditions and provide thoughtful policies. Yet at the same time there is the familiar lure of a Pied Piper, who tempts lemmings into following him as he marches into the sea. The beginning of public wisdom is the development of some intelligent mistrust of leaders and of skepticism about easy ideological solutions and quick fixes. This need not be overly negative or so destructive that it would be impossible for anyone to assume the mantle of leadership. There ought to be an end to excessively parochial party politics—the belief that Our Party has discovered Truth, Justice, and Piety, and that other parties are made of fools. No one is perfect. Statesmen ought to be able to admit that they have made mistakes. They need a touch of humility and a sense of their own fallibility. We need reflective men and women in positions of leadership who are willing to learn from experience and to modify programs in the light of criticism or altered circumstances, without being castigated as being contradictory or hypocritical. But to develop such leadership entails some capacity for reflective intelligence in the public at large and an educated approach to social problems. Skeptical inquiry cannot work unless there is an appreciation for how it works.

Let us turn our attention to what I think is the constructive use of skeptical inquiry on the level of political decision-making, but not without reminding the reader of the special pitfall of unexamined political abstractions perverting public discourse, and that it is necessary to see through the sacred cows of the day. I have mentioned only some that have played inordinate roles, particularly in recent history; but there are many others that we have not examined. There is always the danger that new and even more virulent ideologies will emerge, able to seize the imagination, become mass movements, and inundate human civilization with new forms of nonsense. The best therapy for all of this, I reiterate, is a sufficient dose of skepticism.

How can skeptical inquiry function in the political domain? First, the claims to political truths should be considered as *hypotheses.* Second, they are to be tested within the process of inquiry by appraising the evidence brought to bear in their support.

They are to be judged by their *consequences,* that is, how they work out in practice. Third, they should be related to other policies and rules of conduct that we have adopted and consider reasonable. Here, the criterion is *logical coherence.* Fourth, policies are to be evaluated on a *comparative scale,* weighed in balance with other alternatives. If and when such policies are judged as reliable, they then may become incorporated into the body of knowledge and may serve as guides to future conduct. We already possess a large fund of technological knowledge and applied expert opinion. In economic matters we draw upon the prescriptions of economists, financial consultants, auditors, and accountants. In political questions, we may consult political scientists, sociologists, and policy advisors. In other fields, educators, psychologists, psychiatrists, doctors, or social scientists may be called upon for advice. The point is there are teams of specialists who can assist us in making wise choices.

There is, however, some danger in believing that experts, philosopher-kings, technocrats, behavioral engineers, and bureaucratic planners can relieve us of the burden of deciding. This would be unfortunate, for entrusting the powers of decision-making to the authorities may lead to rule by elites. No one can claim infallible knowledge. In many fields the experts differ among themselves. We need to exercise some healthy skepticism of what the authorities declare to be true. The history of science illustrates the fact that scientific opinion fixed at one stage of inquiry can be easily transformed into dogmatic assertion in the next. The fact that the authorities may declare something to be true does not necessarily make it so. In principle, any claim to truth, even by the highest scientific authorities, must be open to challenge, and the grounds of their assertions must be independently corroborated. Open peer review by researchers in every field of inquiry is essential for the testing of knowledge.

We may generalize from this: In the last analysis, the best community is the open one, in which alternative hypotheses can be examined and the views of dissenters can receive a hearing. The democratic society is open to a wide range of viewpoints, and it allows for criticism of the decisions of political leaders and bureaucrats. *The justification for democracy is based on meth-*

odological grounds. It is presupposed by the method of inquiry itself. If no one class, party, or group can be said to have the Absolute Truth, then they cannot be entrusted with the power to decide the fate of everyone else. Power is thus widely shared by all of the citizens of the commonwealth. The underlying premise is that truth is difficult to achieve and that a free market of ideas will be most receptive to pluralistic claims to knowledge. Only with open dialogue may we draw upon alternative conceptions and perhaps better approximate the truth. In an open market of ideas, no group can demand immunity from criticism. This allows for the emergence of responsible leadership; and it also holds them accountable to the will of the electorate.

The democratic method of inquiry itself need not be justified by reference to metaphysical abstractions, nor is it deduced from first principles, themselves in need of further justification. Rather, it is tested experimentally. In the long run those societies that are open will tend to have less duplicity and cruelty and there is less likelihood that injustice will remain hidden. In opening the public square to debate, new discoveries and new ideas are likely to emerge.

Human Rights

The same considerations apply to the theory of human rights. These are not "natural," but *civil,* and they are vindicated by their consequences in society. Citizens who live in societies that do not respect civil rights and civil liberties enjoy far less freedom, have less opportunity for creative expression, and most likely have a lower standard of living. Human rights are tested not by where they are rooted—they are relative to human interests and needs and have a socio-cultural and historical context—but by what they lead to. They are justified by their practical results.

The human rights enumerated in the *United Nations Declaration of Human Rights,* now widely recognized throughout the world, are normative. They provide ethical principles and constructs that are part of the valuational base in terms of which we can formulate and test judgments of practice. The Declaration was designed to protect all persons equally. Human rights are essential to the emerging world community. Their recognition expresses an awareness of our obligations to a new global ethic applicable to all humans on the planet Earth. I will here simply enumerate them without further elaboration.[11]

I. *The right to life:* (1) the security and protection of one's person (freedom from fear), (2) defense from external aggression, (3) freedom from endangerment by the state.

II. *The right to personal liberty:* (1) freedom of movement and residence, (2) freedom from involuntary servitude or slavery, (3) freedom of thought and conscience, (4) freedom of speech and expression, (5) moral freedom, (6) the right to privacy.

III. *The right to health care:* (1) adequate medical treatment, (2) informed consent, (3) voluntary euthanasia, (4) reproductive freedom.

IV. *Freedom from want:* (1) the right to basic economic needs, (2) the right to work, (3) the right for the elderly to be cared for, (4) the right to leisure and relaxation.

V. *Economic rights:* (1) the right to own property, (2) the right to access public property, (3) the right to organize, (4) the right to protection from fraud.

VI. *Intellectual and cultural freedom:* (1) the right to free inquiry, (2) the right to quality education, (3) the right to cultural enrichment.

VII. *Moral equality:* (1) equal opportunity, (2) equal access, (3) no discrimination.

VIII. *Equal protection of the law:* (1) the right to a fair trial, (2) the right to judicial protection, (3) the right to humane treatment, (3) rule of law.

IX. *The right to democratic participation in government:* (1) the right to vote, (2) the legal right of opposition, (3) civil liber-

---

11. For elaboration, see: Paul Kurtz, *Forbidden Fruit* (Buffalo, N.Y.: Prometheus Books, 1988), Chapter 7.

ties, (4) the right of assembly and association, (5) separation of church and state.

X. *The right to marriage, family, and children:* (1) the right to marriage, (2) the right to divorce, (3) the right to bear children, (4) rights of motherhood and fatherhood, (5) parental rights; (6) rights of the child.

A human right is a claim made of, to, and before civilized society. It specifies that all persons should be afforded equality of consideration and that their liberties should not be violated. It also recommends that, where a society has sufficient economic resources, opportunities should be made available to all persons to satisfy their basic needs. Similarly, individuals should be afforded some measure of liberty to fulfill their personal values, so long as they do not harm others or deprive them of their rights.

The skeptic asks, "Why should we respect human rights?" I respond that those societies that violate such rights in the long run suffer more injustice, mendacity, cruelty, and hardship than those that do not. Those societies that respect human rights, on the contrary, are more likely to be peaceful, cooperative, and prosperous. Since most human beings share common needs and have a common desire to fulfill their diverse values, they need to live in harmony with their fellow human beings, and this entails respect for their rights. The respect for human rights is thus an essential precondition of any civilized moral community. The commitment to human rights, I submit, is not arbitrary or capricious. It may be justified on rational and experimental grounds.

The nihilist, however, demands an *ultimate* proof. "Can you demonstrate infallibly why I ought to accept human rights?" he asks. "Unless, I find such an ironclad proof, I will remain a complete skeptic." The doctrine of human rights cannot be proved in the normal acceptation of the term *proof,* at least not in a deductively necessary sense. Nonetheless, it is not unreasonable to accept human rights for reasons that I have specified above. Let me reiterate that human rights need not be based upon any ontological ground to be found persuasive. They do not inhere in persons per se as abstract properties. It would be difficult to justify that view on epistemological grounds. They are, I reiterate, *civil* rights and *civil* liberties because they involve transactions in civil society. The idea of a *right* as a *claim* entails the normative rule that we ought to respect it. A right is a prima-facie general rule, not an absolute commandment. Rights take on legal force when they are enacted into law and given a juridical basis, and when any violation of them is punished.

The catalogue of human rights has cognitive meaning. But we can also appeal to sentiment to defend them, and we can arouse sympathy for victims and disapproval of their inhumane treatment. Thus a doctrine of human rights is based on both belief and attitude. The list above is a product of long debate and struggle in human history, and new rights may be added in the future, if a case can be made on their behalf.

The open, democratic society that I have been defending allows for the maximization of freedom for individuals to make their own choices, consistent with the public good. The battle for human rights can no longer be dealt with on the level of the national state, but is truly international in scope and involves the entire world community. Indeed, many problems now emerging transcend the capacities of any one country to resolve, for they are truly planetary in scale. Here the relationship between national states and global needs is a central problem for the future of humankind. Since so many problems can only be resolved on the international level, we will undoubtedly need to guarantee the protection of the rights and liberties of individuals and groups throughout the world.

With this in mind, may I suggest a number of problems that will confront humankind in the future and will require the best methods of cooperative intelligence to solve.

1. The need to develop a new global ethic that recognizes that we are all members of the world community, transcending narrow ethnic, national, racial, or religious loyalties.

2. The need to ensure a peaceful world and to develop a system of world law in order to resolve military and political conflicts between national states.

3. The need to protect the environment, to limit excessive depletion of natural resources, and to restrict runaway population growth.

4. The need to stimulate and regulate technological and industrial development.

5. The need to encourage scientific research, economic development, and world trade.

6. The need to contribute to the development of the third world, to help solve the problems of poverty and inadequate health care.

7. The need to raise the levels of cultural enrichment, educational opportunity, and the quality of scientific information.

8. The need to provide opportunities for the expression of dissenting viewpoints in the face of intolerant and intransigent fundamentalist and ideological absolutisms.

9. The need to encourage a unified planetary effort to explore and develop space.

The solutions of these problems need to be resolved in a democratic framework, leaving room for both cooperative efforts and a basic respect for individual rights and liberties.

Conclusion

This discussion was meant to demonstrate that it is possible to frame reliable judgments of practice in both the ethical and political domains. We make such judgments all the time. Our discussion here presupposes some degree of sophistication and the application of critical intelligence by the public at large to the solution of social problems. Democratic methods will only function where there is an educated electorate, aware of its civic duties, responsible in its concern for the public good, and willing to exercise thoughtful deliberation. This level of educated public opinion has already been reached in many democracies of the world; so we are beginning not at the beginning, as it were, but in the midst of social development. Undoubtedly there is still a long way to go in order to raise the level of appreciation for reflective discourse in the public square. Given the sensationalized vulgarities of the mass media, it is often difficult to maintain standards of excellence; but the task is there, and it is particularly incumbent on our institutions of education to cultivate within the ordinary citizen the capacity for critical thinking.

The general implications of our discussion should take us one step further, for it suggests a new definition of political "liberalism"; namely, the liberal outlook is not committed to a specific ideological program or platform, but to "a method of inquiry." The values and policies of this agenda may vary from age to age. It should not be doctrinaire in its blind support of political parties or candidates. Its only consistent commitment should be to use the methods of intelligent discussion and rational debate, persuasion, negotiation, and compromise to deal with social problems as they emerge. Perhaps the terms *liberal* and *conservative* are no longer appropriate. This approach is *liberal* in that it would liberate us from blind dogma, prejudice, and passion, and it would enable intelligence to guide our policies and practices. It is *conservative* in that it is skeptical of new, untried proposals unless they have been tested in practice. Perhaps the best term to describe the new skepticism as applicable to society is *radical.* For attempting to consistently apply objective methods of inquiry to political and social problems would surely mark a radical new direction in human affairs.

Chapter 11

Eupraxophy

The Need to Integrate Knowledge

We are now brought full circle back to the original question of this book. If skepticism has a vital role to play in the development of reliable knowledge, and if it need not be totally negative, nor simply mitigated, what relevance does it have for human affairs? Can it leave room for the genuine commitment and strong convictions in ethics, politics, and life—or do any such attitudes betray the skeptical attitude itself? Does skeptical inquiry presuppose any first principles, and are these, like all other first principles, beyond proof? If so, does skeptical inquiry, if turned upon itself, entail an illegitimate leap of faith and a violation of its own program?

We face a unique crisis on the frontiers of knowledge today, and this is not necessarily due to the paucity of knowledge, but, on the contrary, to an embarrassment of riches; for scientific discoveries have grown so rapidly that it has become difficult to assimilate and interpret this vast body of knowledge. Concomitant with this is the extreme specialization that has developed. It is a truism to say that the advancement of scientific knowledge can best be achieved by a division of labor; that is, complex theoretical and technological problems can best be solved by the intensive concentration of efforts. Great progress has resulted, often by a relatively small number of workers in a field who follow the technical literature and are versed in its conceptual framework and the use of mathematical methods, and whose contributions are reviewed by their peers. This departmentalization of knowledge has had enormous success, yet at the same time specialists have so divided their subject matters that members of the same profession often are unable to communicate with one another as fields and subfields proliferate. The dilemma can be readily illustrated by reference to medicine, where general practitioners have declined in influence and where patients are referred to specialists for the diagnosis and treatment of most illnesses. The gap we face is that we do not always know how discoveries in one field relate to those in others. Nicholas Murray Butler, a former president of Columbia University, once defined an expert as "one who knows more and more about less and less." Clearly specialists within the same profession interact with their peers, and there is some interdisciplinary communication. But other scientists and the educated public at large are looking for generalizations that cut across specialities; they are seeking concepts, hypotheses, and theories of broader significance.

It was possible to provide such general interpretations on the frontiers of knowledge in earlier centuries. This often was the task of the philosopher, who had special analytic and interpretive skills. Aristotle summed up the main scientific, ethical, and political wisdom of his day, at least in broad outline; and he was able to synthesize this by means of his metaphysical categories. His doctrine of four causes, substance, form and matter, potentiality, and actuality, gave a comprehensive overview of how nature operated and how we experience and understand it. His idea of nature was organismic: species were fixed, and the universe was intelligible to the human mind. The Greek idea of nature was modified drastically by latter-day theologians, who viewed the universe as God's creation, fulfilling a plan in which Man played a central role. The Newtonian-Galilean world-view rejected teleology and overthrew Aristotle and the organismic universe. The new idea of nature was that it was materialistic, mechanistic, and deterministic. The great philosophers of the modern period, Spinoza, Hobbes, Descartes, Locke, Leibniz, and Kant, attempted to interpret nature in the light of the Newtonian scheme. In the nineteenth century a historical focus emerged, and this led to the sweeping theories of history of Hegel and Marx. This was also the century in which there was a great leap forward in biology, and in which Darwin's evolutionary hypothesis replaced the doctrine of fixed species. There were also important developments in the social and behavioral sciences, which attempted to understand and study human psychology and social behavior. The twentieth century has seen the expansion of quantum mechanics, the modification of Newtonian theories by relativity physics, and the dramatic advance in our knowledge on the cosmic scale in astronomy and on the micro-level in nuclear physics, chemistry, genetics, and biology. Moreover, the new technologies that have been created have enabled un-paralleled scientific advances: for example, computer science, space technology, and biogenetic engineering.

Today it is increasingly difficult to develop a comprehensive unified view of nature and of the human species. The philosophy of science has focused more on epistemological issues than on interpreting what we know. So the central questions are: What does science tell us about nature and life? Can we develop a larger cosmic *weltanshauung?* For any one mind to do so today would require an enormous capacity to understand conceptual and theoretical developments on the frontiers of knowledge. There are literally hundreds of thousands of scientific journals today, and they are expanding at an exponential rate. We would need a super-Aristotle to do so. Are there enough brain cells in any one mind to ingest and comprehend this massive amount of information?

But the need for such knowledge is as pressing as ever. Perhaps we do not need to store the megatrillion bits of information or even to sort or catalogue it; we need only to program and interpret it. What we need to develop today, as in the past, is some *sophia,* or wisdom. This means an ability to coordinate what we know, and/or to synthesize it. Now clearly there has to be an effort within the sciences to develop higher-level unifying theories, from which lower-level theories and hypotheses can be deduced. Efforts have been made to develop highly generalized theories in a number of fields: in physics, astronomy, psychology, biology, sociology, anthropology, and history. Such theories attempt to integrate all that is known in one particular area, and some creative scientists have attempted to do that. We see the bold insights of such endeavors, but also the possible snares: Hegelian, Marxist, and Toynbeean theories of history, generalized Freudian explanations of sexual behavior, Whitehead's *Process or Reality,* and so on. All of these were ambitious programs and all of them had pitfalls. Nonetheless, there is still a need for more comprehensive interpretations of what we know. These may serve for a time during an epoch when certain general paradigms dominate the scientific imagination, but these unifications may eventually give way as unexpected discoveries and unsettling new theories are introduced.

The postmodern intellectual world is in a state of disarray in comparison with previous periods, for we have not found a grand synthesis; and indeed we may never succeed in creating one. To place the burden of providing some integrated cosmic outlook on the philosopher today is inordinately difficult. The special problem with contemporary philosophy is that it has itself become highly specialized and fragmented into separate schools with their own gurus and literatures. Often great divides have been erected across which there is little communication. It was considered to be the task of metaphysicians classically to provide integrative systems of knowledge, but the classical metaphysical enterprise has been thrown into disrepute; for most metaphysicians attempted to spin out speculative theories of reality quite independent of the discoveries of the empirical sciences. They thought that it was possible to analyze the logical and ontological structures of nature without relating their conceptual schemes to perceptual experience. Many philosophical systems were purely formal and had no relationship to the real world, or to the concrete findings of the sciences. Many philosophers indeed were, or still are, anti-scientific, or at best nonscientific, drawing on formal logic, or literature, or the arts, quite independently of scientific inquiry. Existentialists, phenomenologists, postmodern deconstructionists and analytic philosophers have attempted to plumb the depths of reality or the relationship between language and the external world without considering essentially what science was discovering about it. Some philosophers, such as Heidegger, have disdained any contamination with science or technology, urging a return to the call of Being in a prelinguistic sense. Some have reverted to the literature of theology and mythology to fathom the nature of reality. Yet for any thinker to persistently ignore scientific interpretations of the world is difficult to comprehend today. For it is the methods of scientific inquiry that have been the most effective in developing reliable knowledge; and it is the concepts, hypotheses, and theories of the sciences that should be our starting point.

Nature is encountered by us as pluralistic. We discover what appears to be both order and disorder, chance and chaos. Hence we may never develop a reductive unified theory comprising all of the processes of nature. Corresponding to the variety and multiplicity that we find, however, are levels of description and explanation, and unifying theories in specific sciences. The quest for a comprehensive theory accounting for everything is faced with perhaps insuperable obstacles. Not only is it not possible for any one mind to absorb, let alone understand, the complex kaleidoscopic range of knowledge that we possess, but each of us is limited by the particular spatial-temporal slab in which we exist. We are each culture-bound, confined as it were by the intellectual, philosophical, and scientific paradigms that dominate our age. Yet in spite of the Herculean dimensions of the task and the complexity and finitude of a person's life, there is still some compelling urgency that we at least attempt to make some sense of our collective knowledge.

Any adequate interpretation of the body of knowledge cannot be focused only on our own present temporal-cultural framework, for we need some historical perspective that defines where we were in the past in comparison with where we are in the present. This requires some appreciation for the great literature of history to be knowledgeable about the struggles men and women underwent in seeking to explore and learn about the world. This would include some reckoning of their breakthroughs and discoveries as well as their failures and blind alleys. Alchemy, bloodletting, numerology, psychical research, phrenology, and astrology are testimonies to the failed pseudosciences of the past, fields in which countless generations of investigators were engaged, and in some cases, still are. Any effort to integrate knowledge must be made with the knowledge of the great conceptual systems of history, many or most of which have been replaced, and of the great civilizations that have had their day in the sun and have also disappeared.

But we need also to know of the great achievements that have remained and been incorporated into the body of tested knowledge today. In addition, we also need to have some sense of future prospects of the expanding frontiers of knowledge and the widening horizons of new ideals, goals, and ends to which we may aspire. These are all part of the human adventure in which we can collectively participate. But any world-view we work out will be *ours* at this particular nexus in history, and this will most likely give way in future generations that are faced with new challenges and opportunities.

No matter what the epoch, however, the demand of humans for meaning is perennial. And so we ask: What does it all mean and how does it fit together? What is my (or our) place in the scheme of things? What does this portend for me (or us)?

Unfortunately, some cultural lag is ever-present, for it takes time to digest and assimilate the knowledge that we already possess. It is a paradox that many of the integrative schemes that still dominate human belief hark back one, two, or three millennia. The explanatory tales and parables of God and spiritual forces, woven out of the human imagination by our nomadic-agricultural forebears, still sustain the bulk of humankind. They are the myths of consolation, spawned by the yearnings for the sacred and fed by the transcendental temptation.

The overwhelming fact of life is its finitude and fragility. It passes so quickly. We are each destined to be buried by the sands of time. In the desperate effort to cope with the contingencies and ambiguities intrinsic to the human condition, men and women are led to postulate hidden sources outside of nature. Life in any age is uncertain and indeterminate, fraught with tragedies; and so there is a deceptive quest for eternity, a search for moorings for our otherwise rudderless vessels in the uncharted seas of existence. That is apparently one explanation of why human beings cling to myths long since discredited, and why they are still fixated on their promises. What else do they have to make sense of what they perceive as an otherwise meaningless world? At the present moment, we have progressed rather far in what we know about the universe. We understand full well that eschatological divinity tales are mere illusions that have no foundation in fact. Those who wish comfort can seek out priests and prophets to make their passage through life more bearable. Those who wish truth can find no consolation in self-deception. Skepticism has shattered the idols of the temple.

But if God is dead, what is the human prospect? Must it remain forlorn in a bleak universe? Is is possible to develop an authentic alternative that has some rational support? But to whom shall we turn for guidance? Unfortunately, not to the scientific *specialist* who has divided up the world, investigates only his small portion, and does not know how it fits together. Shall we look to the philosopher who takes as his task cosmic *sophia?* Alas, the philosopher, in being committed to examining all sides of questions in the process, is often unable to make up his mind or resolve any of them. Philosophy from the earliest has been interested in analyzing meanings and unraveling mysteries; but the philosopher is often hesitant and indecisive, unable to solve quandaries, unwilling to stimulate motivation or action. Human beings want to know, not only for the intrinsic pleasure of knowing, but so that they may act. And it is the business of life that demands answers. We go to practical men and women to help us solve our concrete problems: doctors and lawyers, bakers and tailors, engineers and architects, business people and politicians.

But we need something more. We need *generalists,* who have a broader view of how the sciences interrelate. We need historians, who have an understanding of past human civilizations. We also need idealists, who have some sense of possible future worlds to create, men and women of inventive imagination. Surely we are mere mortals, not gods. Who among us can claim to encapsulate or plan the entire human prospect? We need to be skeptical of utopianists who offer unreliable totalistic visions of other worlds and strive to take us there. We need some ideals, but we also need to protect ourselves from the miscalculations and misadventures of visionaries.

The Eupraxophers

At this point, it seems to me, we need to make room for *eupraxophy,* a new field of knowledge and a craft.[1] *Eupraxophers* will strive to be generalists, able to understand, as best they can, what the sciences tell us about nature and life. Eupraxophers will thus study the sciences carefully—anthropology and paleontology, psychology and sociology, economics and politics, genetics and biology, physics and astronomy. They will attempt to work with other generalists in developing general systems theory, and in finding common concepts and theories that cut across fields and seem most reliable. They will attempt to incorporate the skills of the historian and the futurist at the same time. But they will also be skeptics, in that they will be critical of pretentious untested claims. They are able to analyze the meanings of terms and concepts and to examine the evidential ground for belief. They will attempt to be objective in their inquiries.

Eupraxophers will concentrate on two tasks: (1) They will seek *sophia,* or wisdom, a summing-up in a synoptic view of what the most reliable knowledge of the day tells us about nature and humankind. (2) They will also be concerned with *eupraxia,* that is, with *eu* (good) and *praxis* (conduct)—succinctly, good conduct. They will, in other words, attempt to draw the normative implications of *sophia* for living our practical life.

How will eupraxophers proceed? In the first sense, by applying the principle of *coduction.* If they cannot find a unified-field theory, incorporating all of the sciences, they can at least develop a factorial analysis. They can, in other words, seek to comprehend or explain nature by reference to pluralistic sets of causal hypotheses. There are levels of inquiry in which specific kinds of factual data are described and accounted for. These are drawn from the micro and macro levels, and apply to physical-chemical, biological, psychological, and socio-cultural systems of events. They refer to subatomic particles, atoms, molecules, cells, organs, organisms, persons, cultures, social institutions, and the global system. They are related to our planet,

---

1. I have outlined this concept in detail in my book *Eupraxophy: Living Without Religion* (Buffalo, N.Y.: Prometheus Books, 1990).

338

solar system, and galaxy, to other galaxies, and to the universe at large. I have introduced the term *coduction* to describe such an approach to understanding.[2] Clearly, the logic of coductive explanation would allow for both reductionistic and holistic theories. In the human domain they would allow for both physicalistic and intentional explanations of human and social behavior.

As a methodological program, coduction encourages the quest for general physicalist explanatory principles, but it would also allow for teleonomic explanations. For it must deal with the various levels of data under observation and the concepts that are introduced to interpret the complexities of higher-order systems. Coduction thus leaves a place for both bio-chemical explanations and psychological, behavioral, and socio-cultural explanations on the level of human behavior. We must always be prepared to exercise our skeptical criticisms about any such theories that are proposed. Selective skepticism within the sciences is essential to inquiry. Nonetheless we recognize that we have many well-tested hypotheses and theories, and that our cosmic outlook is best informed and constantly transformed by reference to this body of reliable knowledge. Here our *sophia* is not fixed but is a function of the historical-cultural epoch in which we live.

Eupraxophers will also have a deep interest in ethical and social questions, and will help us to frame reliable judgments of practice. Both individual and public choices can best be *act-duced* in the light of empirical knowledge. Our evaluations of good or bad, right or wrong, are most effectively formulated by reference to a valuational base. Included in the base are factual and technological hypotheses and theories about the world and ourselves. This includes causal knowledge, knowledge of means/ends, and predictions of the consequences of our choices. The valuation base also includes value-laden norms and ethical principles. This incorporates our own *de facto* prizings and appraisings, and our understanding of the normal needs of the human species, the common moral decencies, and the civic virtues that may prevail in our own socio-cultural historical context. What we will decide

---

2. For an extended discussion of coduction, see my *Decision and the Condition of Man* (Seattle: University of Washington Press, 1965), Chapter 5.

to do in any context of moral decision-making is open to ongoing criticism. All choices are tentative and hypothetical. Thus some degree of constructive ethical skepticism is intrinsic to our life as reflective members of the community. Nonetheless we can reach some measure of reliable ethical knowledge. Our *eupraxia*—the things we consider worthwhile—is related to our cosmic *sophia*— our understanding of the universe in which we live.

Are there a sufficient number of eupraxophers in our midst? Regrettably, they are all too few in number. Philosophers like John Dewey, Sidney Hook, and Bertrand Russell exemplified the eupraxophic life; they were interested not only in knowledge, but action. It was not simply the love of wisdom (*philo*) that they sought, but good ethical practice (*eupraxia*). They were skeptical of occult, theological, and transcendental theories. As free thinkers they drew upon the sciences to understand the world; they espoused humanistic values and defended the free society.

I submit that there is an identifiable need for the universities and colleges to develop a new profession, that of eupraxophy. In addition to training scientists or technocrats, economists or philosophers, we need men and women interested in the quest for wisdom and its application to the good life. Eupraxophers are concerned with questions concerning the meaning of life and the relevance of the sciences and the arts to the life of practical judgment. This is surely one of the tasks of liberal education. Students are exposed to a wide range of fields of human knowledge in the arts and sciences so that they can expand their horizons of appreciation and understanding. Unfortunately, the university curriculum today has been emasculated by the demands of the narrow specialty professions. Students have been given a smorgasboard of subjective electives. They are unable to interpret what they have learned, or reconcile it with their system of values. Moreover, few students really appreciate the methods of critical and skeptical inquiry or the nature of reliable knowledge. All too often, in the name of liberal arts education students graduate as scientific illiterates. Eupraxophy should be the mark of every educated person: the capacity for reflective judgment and skeptical inquiry, some understanding of the universe in which he or she lives; and some ability to formulate judgments of practice.

EUPRAXOPHY

Convictions

The final question that I wish to address is whether persons committed to skeptical inquiry in all areas of knowledge can live fully. Will they be sufficiently stimulated to undertake great tasks; or will skepticism corrode their judgment, undermine their zest for life, deaden their desire for exploration and discovery?

This is a crucial issue that is often raised, but its solution is *psychological* as much as it is theoretical. It deals with the question of human motivation and how to untap the vital potentialities for living exuberantly. The real test of eupraxophy is whether it can arouse conviction. Will it have sufficient motivational force so that people will consider their lives interesting and exciting, and will they readily embark upon robust Promethean adventures?

What is pivotal here is the recognition that, in stimulating great actions, we must go beyond purely cognitive thought. Human beings are not empty intellectual shells, but passionate centers of feeling, profoundly influenced by the intensity of their inner emotions and desires. Thought cannot and should not dominate everything. We have the capacity to be moved by aesthetic beauty and the arts, and to be inspired by ethical choice. This is testified to by the fact that humans are not only interested in ascertaining whether or not their beliefs are true, but in how to satisfy their passionate desires. A full life is infused with intensity and emotions. It is moved by love and affection, anger and pride, fear and hope, glory and despair. In both our private soliloquies and public expression, we need to interrelate our thoughts and feelings, our beliefs and attitudes. But although we need to savor the immediacies of the emotional life—the exciting thrills and the subtle delicacies—skeptical inquirers ask that personal beliefs not be deceptively influenced by feelings, and that beliefs be amenable to modification in the light of inquiry. There are constant temptations to sacrifice thought to other passionate interests. At some point we need to regain our cognitive composure. There should therefore be limits placed upon unrestrained temperament and, in the contest between true belief and deceptive passion, the former must eventually win out.

Plato observed that the "chariot of the soul" is pulled by three

341

horses: reason, ambition, and passion. The goal of the wise person is not to allow either passion or ambition to lunge out beyond the lead horse, reason, and to so entangle the chariot that it is overturned; but we need to have all three horses work together in unison. The chariot of the soul should be guided by reason if harmony is to be reached, but ambition and passion still have a place in the full life. For we still are irreducibly men and women of feeling. We fall deeply in love, are moved to laughter or aroused by victory. We need to taste and enjoy the hedonic pleasures of life. We need to be committed to helping others, to be involved in beloved causes. Sometimes our illusions may cloud our clarity of thought. Sometimes we may be overwhelmed by false prophets, grandiose schemes, or illusory projects. We need to be critical of mythic systems of fantasy and illusion and of unbounded goals that are destructive to ourselves and others.

We need a realistic appraisal of the human condition. This includes an appreciation for the positive reaches of life—and here some optimism is warranted. But there are also the sometimes tragic components of death, failure, disease, and suffering—and here some realistic pessimism is relevant. Secular humanists are impressed by the unbounded potentialities of the Promethean spirit and the opportunities for experiencing joyful living, yet we must not overlook the tears and sorrow that we sometimes experience. Eupraxophers need to offer some consolation to the bereaved, or else they will be outdistanced by the theological purveyors of empty promises of eternal life. The Old Testament admonishes us to remember: "Mine afflictions and my misery, the wormwood and the gall."[3] Or again, the tragedian reminds us: "Preach to the storm, and reason with despair. But tell not Misery's son that life is fair."[4]

Life must go on, responds the practical person, and we should try our best. No doubt we need a realistic appraisal of the human condition, but it needs always to be infused with some underlying optimism, or else the faint-hearted may be tempted to give up,

---

3. Lamentations 3:19.
4. From *Lines on Reading*, by the young English poet Henry Kirke White (1785–1806)."

exclaiming "What's the use?" Thus there is a basic principle of motivation that the skeptical humanist insists upon: that life is good, or can be good, and that living is better than dying. Indeed, it can be exciting, full of joy and zest. The empirical evidence that life can be intensely significant has been attested by the lives of countless men and women who have been skeptical, yet were passionately committed to the achievement of great ideals or to the robust fulfillment of joyful living. No doubt this is the first principle of the skeptical humanist: *Life itself needs no justification beyond itself.* The question, "*Why* life?" has no cognitive significance. Skeptical humanists and atheists need not be devoid of some form of natural piety, an appreciation of the wonder and magnificence of the cosmic scene—particularly as they stare into the heavens at night. "My atheism, like that of Spinoza," says the humanist philosopher George Santayana, "is true piety towards the universe and denies only gods fashioned by men in their own image, to be servants of their human interests."[5]

The decisive response to the nihilistic skeptic is that we encounter life head-on; and we find it good in the *living of it.* The basic problem of life is not *whether* to live, but *how* to live. The problem of whether to go on living may be raised in some existential situations, such as by persons suffering a painful terminal illness. Here voluntary euthanasia may be a meaningful option. Despair may also overtake individuals living in any overly oppressive society. Here revolt may be the only option. Still, the basic question we face is not whether to live, but *how to live,* and *how to live well.* The lust for life must precede everything else; if it is absent, there is little that can be said. Courage, motivation, affirmation, the intense desire to live is thus the first premise; but this is not imposed on life but is natural to it and at all stages—for the infant, the child, the adolescent, the mature adult, the aging person (providing that the person is not suffering some biochemically induced state of depression).

Skeptical inquiry is our second premise, but this grows out of the first. Life precedes reason, and reason can only minister to it as its servant. Skeptical critics will say, "Aha! another assumed

---

5. George Santayana, *Soliloquies in England* (1922).

principle! What is the justification for this?" To which I respond: *If* we wish to live, and to live well, *then* the methods of skeptical intelligence and the quest for reliable knowledge are the most effective instruments of our desires. Knowledge can only modify and transform our interests, but the lust for life itself must come first.

Knowledge is surely a good in itself, in that it can give us intrinsic pleasure; but more directly, it has high pragmatic value in helping us to define and explain who and what we are and what is happening in nature; and it best provides us with the instruments for resolving our problems. Knowledge can uncover the limiting conditions within the natural world; it can also discover creative new potentialities, and it can evaluate the consequences of our choices. The justification for knowing is found in the process of living, in helping us to cope with the obstacles that confront us. Practical reason is thus embedded in the very fabric of life. It defines what it means to be a civilized being.

We cannot demonstrate that the kind of skeptical inquiry that I have defended is ultimately provable to the nihilist. Yet it has become central to our lives. To abandon it is to slip back to brute biological existence; to expand its use in all areas of life is to advance the cause of civilized living. Beyond that, perhaps nothing more can or need be said.

Appendixes

Appendices

Appendix I

The Committee for the Scientific Investigation of Claims of the Paranormal

Having long been concerned about the widespread belief in paranormal phenomena, and with the questions discussed in the Introduction in mind, in 1976 I helped to found an organization of skeptical scientists and philosophers who were interested in examining paranormal and pseudo-scientific claims. This group is known as the Committee for the Scientific Investigation of Claims of the Paranormal (CSICOP). The purpose of CSICOP is threefold: (1) to investigate objectively the claims of the paranormal and to submit them to careful testing, (2) to publish and disseminate the results of these inquiries, and (3) to attempt to cultivate in the public at large an appreciation of the methods of scientific inquiry.

Science has become so specialized that it is often difficult to get authorities in the various fields to expend the time or develop the requisite expertise to examine such claims—of astrology, UFOlogy, parapsychology, and a whole range of anomalous events. Thus CSICOP (and its publication, the *Skeptical Inquirer*) came into being as an interdisciplinary team effort. Its task was to devote itself to investigating fields in which there were no readily recognized scientific authorities and to see if a demarcation line could be discovered between science and pseudoscience.

The announcement of the Committee's formation received an immediate positive reception from the scientific community—far beyond anything we had anticipated; for many scientists felt surrounded by a larger popular culture in which the level of pseudoscientific and paranormal belief was very high and at times made the scientific enterprise difficult to pursue. For example, astronomers encountered within their classes students who believed in the "Chariots of the Gods" hypothesis of Erich von Däniken, Velikovsky's *Worlds in Collision,* UFOlogy, and astrology. Psychologists were constantly asked whether people possessed "psychic powers" and whether ESP, precognition, or clairvoyance had been established by parapsychologists. Physicists were asked to evaluate the claims of psychokinesis (e.g., that the mind can bend metal) and levitation, which seemingly defy the laws of physics. Those who tended to believe in the immortality of the soul now had many reports from scientific researchers of "near-death experiences" to bolster their beliefs, and there was allegedly new evidence to support faith in reincarnation.

The immediate question that was brought to the fore was, How shall we deal with such claims? What should be our approach? Those who were at first associated with CSICOP were highly skeptical—they were aparanormalists and unbelievers—but if we were to be committed to the scientific agenda, we could not prejudge the truth or falsity of these claims but would have to investigate them dispassionately and impartially.

We had attracted to our fold some of the leading scientists and philosophers of the day, men and women of considerable stature, such as the behavioral psychologist B. F. Skinner, the astronomer Carl Sagan, the physicist Murray Gell-Mann, a Nobel Prize-winner, and Sidney Hook, Ernest Nagel, W. V. Quine, Antony Flew, and Brand Blanshard, all noted philosophers. In response to queries about whether we had prejudged the case, we said: (*a*) We would attempt to be open-minded, fair, and impartial in our inquiries. (*b*) We would analyze such claims to determine if they were internally consistent, coherent, and testable hypotheses and theories. (*c*) We would examine the evidence and/or the laboratory experiments that had been performed by proponents, or anecdotal accounts if that was all that was available. (*d*) We would judge the claims in part by their relationship to the established body of tested and scientific principles and theories. (*e*) We would not allow any preconceptions or prejudices to interfere with our examination of reports of anomalous phenomena—Fortean facts, they were called, after Charles Fort, who compiled an index of strange anomalies, such as reports of frogs raining from the sky. The main question was whether there were testable hypotheses that could be falsified (using Karl Popper's criterion). If there was sufficient evidence to overturn existing scientific theories, we would make the facts known. However, we said that extraordinary claims that flew in the face of confirmed scientific theories needed extraordinary evidence to confirm them. For example, if the laboratory evidence for precognition was of sufficient strength, we would have to radically alter our concepts of time and causation, but this evidence had to be reliable and strong. (*f*) Once we had such findings we would publish the results in order to balance out the cognitive side, i.e., we would provide accurate factual information and possible alternative causal explanations of the alleged phenomena.

We immediately became the center of controversy; believers maintained that we were closed-minded and dogmatic, that we had on a priori grounds already decided what was true and what was false, and that the research we did was merely a pretext to find evidence *against* the phenomena. Were we not self-proclaimed dogmatic unbelievers? they asked. Moreover, because some skeptics had exposed some paranormal claims to public ridicule, we were accused of being biased and unfair. Some critics of our efforts maintained that the only position for us to take was to present both sides of every issue, giving, for example, astrologers and psychics equal weight with their critics, and then allow the public to make up its own mind.* In no case, it was said, should we ever use pejorative language. The trenchant science writer and essayist Martin Gardner maintained that "one horse laugh may be worth a thousand syllogisms," and he constantly exposed excessive paranormal claims to ridicule. And the magician James Randi often placed psychics or psychic researchers in extremely compromising positions in order to demonstrate most effectively the gullibility of parapsychologists. But this was deemed by our critics to be in bad taste. How deal with a "breatharian"—someone who claims to be able to survive without eating or drinking—with a straight face or laughter?

But a deeper question was raised: If we are skeptics, what is skepticism and how should skeptics proceed? Is skepticism simply equivalent to *unbelief* and are skeptics simply naysayers, rejecting all such beliefs? What is the proper mode of skeptical inquiry? Are skeptics simply neutral? And more compelling, what should be the range of skeptical inquiry?

We decided to focus primarily on the *paranormal*. This term had been introduced by parapsychologists working in the field (the Greek prefix *para* means "beside, along side of, beyond, aside from") to denote that such studies were not dealt with, nor readily explainable, by the existing concepts of science. The Society for Psychical Research, founded

---

*Marcello Truzzi, an early supporter of this position, resigned from CSICOP, after having received a vote of no-confidence from the Executive Council, and founded his own group and journal to fulfill this aim. The lion's share of his attention has been devoted to defending paranormalists and attacking skeptics. He claims that he is virtually the only skeptic who is objective about paranormal claims.

in Great Britain in 1882, and its American counterpart, in Boston in 1885, focused on certain kinds of psychic phenomena. This included examining the evidence for survival, precognition, clairvoyance, and similar claims. J. B. Rhine, in the first half of the twentieth century, attempted to develop a new experimental approach to ESP and other "psi phenomena," as they were later labeled, using the techniques of laboratory science.

We also adopted the term *paranormal,* though it was by now more broadly applied to a wide range of studies over and beyond psychical research, and included astrology, UFOlogy, and other pseudosciences. We decided to restrict ourselves to those areas that enjoyed significant popularity among the public and in which we were beginning to develop some expertise. We resolved to focus primarily on examining the evidence for these paranormal claims, most of which were largely uncontested. Some philosophers and scientists have argued that psychic claims could virtually be ruled out on a priori grounds, because they violated the basic principles of physical science. For example, psychokinesis seemed to wreak havoc with our knowledge of material causation. Similarly for precognition, which seemingly implied backward causation and discarnate survival. "Did it make sense to say that a discarnate soul could witness its own funeral?" asked Antony Flew.* There is a school of analytic philosophy that maintains that many such puzzles are due to conceptual mistakes, that they can be resolved by analyzing the logic of the language, and that empirical issues need not be raised. I was always puzzled by this argument, for the linguistic-conceptual scheme of any one age is a function of the level of knowledge. Thus, although linguistic analysis is both necessary and useful as a propaedeutic to any inquiry, the basic issue appeared to me to be primarily empirical: Were the claims corroborated by objective empirical research? *If* the phenomena were discovered in fact to exist, how could they be explained—by postulating some hidden paranormal or occult cause or by seeking to discover as yet unknown natural causes? Physicist Murray Gell-Mann argued that the term *paranormal* almost by definition ruled out natural scientific causality, for scientific researchers could never abandon their quest for natural, hence "normal," causes.† Thus we decided not to exclude anomalous claims antecedent to inquiry, but to simply search for evidence for such claims. Were there genuine anomalies that did not fit into the

---

*Antony Flew, *A New Approach to Psychical Research* (London: Watts, 1953), and "Is There a Case for Disembodied Survival?" *Journal of the American Society for Psychical Research,* 1972, vol. 66, pp. 129-144.

†Annual CSICOP Conference at the University of Colorado, Boulder, 1986.

categories of the existing sciences? If so, what were they? If the evidence was reliable, and/or of sufficient weight, then no doubt these existing scientific theories would have to be modified or abandoned. This is the normal procedure used in the sciences and nothing could be harmed by it, for it was all part of the process of scientific inquiry.

There is no question that most of us were unbelievers, but still we were intrigued by the persistent reports of anomalies and were convinced that they had to be carefully examined. Thus we asked: What is the evidence for horoscopes? Do they work? If so, why? Are psychics able to help the police solve murders or locate lost persons? Can anyone foretell the future? Is there really evidence that UFOs are extraterrestrial in origin? Our conclusions were negative, for we could find no reliable evidence for these claims and could suggest natural explanations for them.

One question that kept emerging was the request that the Committee deal with religious issues. Why restrict our focus to paranormal claims? Our reply was that we would concentrate only on research topics that were amenable to empirical scientific scrutiny. For example, we were willing to deal with the Shroud of Turin. Was it the burial shroud of Jesus, as many proponents had proclaimed, or a forgery? Some scientists associated with the Shroud of Turin Research Project (STURP) claimed "scientific proof" that it was the burial shroud of Jesus. The explanation they offered for the image on the cloth was that it had been "scorched supernaturally" during the Resurrection. This topic could be investigated carefully, and so we organized a team of specialists to analyze microscopically small specimens of the Shroud to see whether blood or ochre pigment was present, investigated possible rubbing techniques to determine whether a duplicate shroud could be fabricated, and called for a rigorous protocol for carbon-14 dating, which was eventually carried out. Our working hypothesis was that the shroud most likely was counterfeit.* This was later supported by the carbon-14 dating permitted by the Vatican. Interestingly, in spite of this evidence some believers still think there is a paranormal mystery associated with the three-dimensional image of Jesus.

What about claims of the existence of God, the truth of the Bible or of the Koran, the claims of faith healing and of reincarnation? We decided—and this perhaps was an arbitrary decision—not to deal with these questions, for two reasons: First, we wished to confine ourselves to rigorous scientific tests, and many religious claims eluded such treat-

---

*Joe Nickell, *Inquest on the Shroud of Turin* (Buffalo, N.Y.: Prometheus Books, 1983).

ment and were held on the basis of faith and on extra-scientific grounds. Second, many people associated with the work of the Committee were themselves religious. They had a curiosity in examining the paranormal, but were offended by any effort to use CSICOP to criticize revered religious beliefs. In fact, many evangelical and fundamentalist Christians looked to us for ammunition against what they called "counterfeit spirituality." The New Age, as it was called, included many beliefs in the paranormal and so the theological critics were appreciative of our criticisms of astrology and psychic phenomena, but felt threatened by any skeptical examination of their own unexamined religious assumptions. It is clear that one did not need to be a humanist or an atheist to be skeptical of the paranormal, and as in other cases in science, it was possible to specialize in one field without dealing with others, just as one can examine and test economic theories without reference to other fields of inquiry.

I personally encountered a paradox here, in that I was extremely skeptical of cognate religious claims and had devoted much of my professional career to examining the belief in God and the immortality of the soul, both of which I found to be without adequate foundation. Thus I was deeply interested in the psychology of religious belief and *why* people accepted articles of faith. Nonetheless I thought it wise for CSICOP to concentrate primarily on the paranormal, since we were the only ones doing so, leaving out any consideration of religious questions.

One piece of evidence that soon emerged in our research was intriguing, namely, that there was a strong affinity and similarity between religion and the paranormal, and that many of the processes of belief and gullibility that we encountered in the one field—the paranormal— were virtually the same as in religion. The psychological phenomena were thus continuous and overlapped; and in both cases, we were dealing with a common experience: the psychology of deception and self-deception, and the willingness to accept beliefs that were without evidential foundations. I came to realize that the study of the paranormal was a test case. It could be examined independently, without offending religious sensitivities. As I have said, not all skeptics about the paranormal are skeptics about religion. But is it possible to be objective in one field and not in the other? Could a case be made for the application of skepticism to religion?

Appendix II

The Committee for the Scientific Examination of Religion

In order to deal with questions of religious truth and to redress the balance, in 1980 I was instrumental in founding the new journal *Free Inquiry* (published by the Council for Democratic and Secular Humanism). Our intention was to focus on examining religious claims—questions usually not discussed and left unanswered by the larger society. This led, shortly thereafter, to the formation of the Committee for the Scientific Examination of Religion (under the chairmanship of Professor Gerald Larue of the University of Southern California), which proposed to deal specifically with religious questions using the best tools of biblical criticism, historical analyses, and scientific research. These inquiries could be conducted quite independently of paranormal inquiries. Among the questions we examined were the following: Is the Bible the "revealed word" of God? If not, how and by whom was it written? What is the evidence for the claim that Jesus was born of a virgin and that he was resurrected after death? Does faith healing really work? What is the origin of a number of sects: Jehovah's Witnesses, Seventh-Day Adventists, Mormonism, Christian Science? Is the Bible contradictory in its moral commandments? What is the relationship between the Bible and politics, and so on? What about the Koran and other allegedly sacred books?

These issues aroused a storm of controversy, particularly at a time when the Bible had been injected into the political arena in the United States and was often used as a tool of political ideology. One key question that we dealt with was the relationship of the Bible to Darwin and science, whether or not "creationism" was a "scientific theory" equivalent to the theory of evolution, and whether or not it should be taught in the schools. It was clear that the tools of skeptical inquiry could be applied to the unexamined claims of classical religion, which more often than not were accepted without critical dissent, and which many people, including scholars and scientists, felt it in bad taste to criticize. However, any effort to apply skeptical analysis to revered religious beliefs immediately encounters a rash of protests from believers. And, historically, religious dissenters, atheists, and agnostics have been expelled from polite company or suppressed by religious establishments. It is thus not puzzling that there is a great reluctance in general society to criticize religious beliefs. This same timidity may be found among intellectuals, many of whom are nonbelievers but loath to expose their dissenting viewpoints in public. The greater part of humankind seems to crave positive belief about the universe and considers that belief in the supernatural and the immortality of the soul confers a kind of stability to their lives. For the Council for Democratic and Secular Humanism to contest truth claims throws them into a thicket of controversy that they would prefer to avoid. It is a surprise to discover that so many will advocate the use of critical intelligence and skeptical inquiry in general as the most effective instrument for extending human knowledge and well-being, except, that is, when it comes to religion, which continues to be held immune to any kind of skeptical scrutiny.

Index

355